Treasure Islands

The Fascinating World of Pirates, Buried Treasure and Fortune Hunters

Cameron Platt and John Wright

Fulcrum Publishing
Golden, Colorado

To Hillary Root

First published in 1992 by Michael O'Mara Books Limited,
9 Lion Yard, Tremadoc Road, London SW4 4NQ
Copyright © 1992 by Cameron Platt and John Wright

Copyright © 1995 Fulcrum Publishing
All Rights Reserved

Library of Congress Cataloging-in-Publication Data

Platt, Cameron.
    Treasure islands : the fascinating world of pirates, buried
treasure, and fortune hunters / Cameron Platt and John Wright.
        p.   cm.
    Includes bibliographical references and index.
    ISBN 1-55591-190-0
    1. Treasure-trove.   2. Pirates.   3. Islands.   I. Wright John.
    II. Title.
    G525.P527   1995
    364.1'64—dc20   94-34454
                                                                    CIP

Cover design by Karen Groves
Island maps and diagrams by Lisa Montague

Printed in the United States of America

0 9 8 7 6 5 4 3 2 1

Fulcrum Publishing
350 Indiana Street, Suite 350
Golden, Colorado 80401-5093
(800) 992-2908

⚓

Contents

Acknowledgments   iv

Introduction   v

Cocos Island   1

Oak Island   40

Agrihan Island   85

Lord Howe Island   95

Gardiners Island   100

Gasparilla Island   120

Galveston Island   128

Isles of Shoals   145

Mahé Island   157

Trindade Island   178

Balambangan Island   199

Notes   206

Bibliography   212

Index   215

⚓

Acknowledgments

The authors wish to acknowledge the singular contribution of Robert C. Ritchie, particularly, though not solely, for background on the final days of William Kidd, including his trial, incarceration in Newgate Prison and execution. For arguably the most complete study yet written of this enigmatic figure, we refer the reader to Ritchie's outstanding *Captain William Kidd and the War Against the Pirates* (Harvard University Press, 1986).

It is also the authors' desire especially to credit two excellent books on Oak Island, *The Big Day* by D'Arcy O'Connor and Rupert Furneaux's *The Money Pit Mystery*, each a compelling and highly readable account of one of the world's most astonishing treasure riddles.

Readers interested in the long-standing hunt for buried treasure on Cocos Island up to and including the various Forbes Expeditions would do well to consult Hancock and Weston's *The Lost Treasure of Cocos Island,* which both entertains and informs, and to which the authors owe a considerable debt.

To Dorcas Platt Wagenknecht who, with uncommon dedication and skill, found and translated *Die liegt Gold* and to the City Library of Osnabruck, which kindly provided a rare copy, our sincere gratitude.

Of all the help and support from around the world accorded the authors in the research and development of this book, the credit must begin at home with our publishers Michael and Lesley O'Mara and editors Catherine Taylor and Rosemary Pettit, as well as picture researchers Tracey Greenwood and Anne-Marie Ehrlich, whom we salute for their professionalism, *esprit* and above all, patience.

Finally, we wish special mention to be made of Mr. Casey Greene, the Rosenburg Library, (Galveston, Texas); the Historical Societies of New Hampshire, Maine and Massachusetts; the Public Archives of Nova Scotia; the *Halifax Herald-Chronicle*, the Halifax Regional Library; Mrs. V. Welcome, Deer Isle-Stonington Historical Society; Mr. Rene Morel, Central Information Service, Mahé, Seychelles; John and Mary Drysdale; Rosemary Drysdale; Gillian Flower; the Municipal Council of Chester, Novia Scotia; the Royal Geographical Society, London; the British Library; the National Maritime Museum, Greenwich, London; the New York Public Library; Billingshurst Library, West Sussex; Performance Publications; Mrs. Yvonne Ellis; Hilary Root and Vivienne Johns. And a personal thanks to Kent Carroll.

⚓

Introduction

Few of us would dispute the allure of the so-called desert isle. Nevertheless, psychologists—their analytical noses ever keen to the scent of our deeply buried desires—do not agree as to why this should be so.

Similarly, it is a rare individual that is immune to the siren call of buried treasure. Yet in a tame age, an age of numbered Swiss bank accounts and laundered cash, the notion of secreting a fortune beneath the sands of a tropical island—the keys to which reside in a crudely drawn map, imprecise bearings or even a riddle!—strike the modern sensibility as outlandish. However romantic, the practical wisdom of such an expedient may seem outrageous.

But take a step backward in history and consider the time of the great fleets when the wealth of distant civilizations gravitated inexorably toward the capitals of Europe. Secured in the holds of ships flying the standards of one or another royal house, treasure borne along before the four winds under armed escort was prey to determined men.

Buccaneers, brigands from every corner of Europe and the New World, mutinous Royal Navy tars, escaped slaves, as well as a number of good men gone bad, many were equivocal figures like Jean Lafitte and Captain William Kidd. Most, however, were simply out-and-out scoundrels with flamboyant names and vices to match.

Once plundered, it was hardly surprising that such riches often gravitated to one of the earth's myriad far-flung islands. Hidden in a cave or on the bottom of some shallow lagoon or beneath a rocky beach, there it might lie beyond the hands of other men, secure until better days. But in a world rife with hazard, where life was often cheap, such fond hopes frequently ended prematurely in a hanging by the yardarm. If pirates escaped such a death, they were often dashed by the vicissitudes of shipwreck, disease and treachery. So entered the treasure hunter.

Arguably a vocation dating to the era of Jason and the Argonauts, treasure hunting as an organized affair did not come into its own until the late nineteenth century. Once the pursuit of rough-and-tumble loners in the fading twilight of the pirate era, it was only later seized upon by the leisure class of Europe and America as a diverting pastime for the "gentleman-adventurer." Figuring among such company were Errol Flynn, Franklin D. Roosevelt and racing champion Sir Malcolm Campbell. Most recently dominated by state-of-the-art technology, the challenge of uncovering untold riches, sometimes on the flimsiest of evidence, continues to cast its spell over a new generation of treasure hunters.

Treasure Islands examines a broad range of islands, a handful of which remain, to the present day, under active exploration; others may only boast of a highly colorful, if dubious, past. The book covers diverse locations from distant Mahé in the Seychelles where John Cruise-Wilkins, following in his father's footsteps, struggles to unravel a £25,000 treasure riddle loosely based upon the Twelve Labors of Hercules, to the mysterious "Money Pit" of Oak Island, Canada, and to Gasparilla, one of Florida's barrier islands from which José Gaspar and Black Caesar conducted their depredations during the waning years of Gulf piracy.

Some islands, like Agrihan of the Marianas group, are names best known to a small fraternity of island connoisseurs. Others, such as Galveston and Cocos (the latter probably inspiring Robert Louis Stevenson's *Treasure Island),* will strike a more familiar chord in the reader. Not restricting themselves to the histories of treasure expeditions *per se,* the authors also look at a number of islands, including Gardiners and Shoals, whose respective protagonists, Kidd and "Blackbeard," have fascinated generations.

In all, an intriguing selection of the world's great treasure islands.

Cocos Island

The bearings 5°32'57"N., 86°59'17"W. mark no more on the pilot's chart than a precipitous volcanic speck barely ten miles square lying halfway between San Francisco and Santiago, Chile in the immensity of the Pacific Ocean. Located 333 nautical miles north of the equator and roughly as many to the southwest of Costa Rica, which claims it by treaty, Cocos Island has for three centuries been plotted with the keenest anticipation by three distinct classes of seafarer: buccaneers, whalers and, finally, treasure hunters. Isolated and doggedly obscure, it nonetheless has received three magnificent bounties from the first, answered the simple purposes of the second and largely confounded the last.

First charted, though imperfectly so, by Nicholas Desliens in 1541, Cocos long presented an enigma to navigators, thanks to faulty maps and imprecise instrumentation, no less than to its position on the boundary between the Southeast Trades and the Equatorial Doldrums. Vexing currents, capricious winds and calm all conspired to thwart approaching ships under sail and, indeed, it has often been said that a crew, having once succeeded in making landfall there, might find itself completely at sea during subsequent attempts. Visible, according to the *Central American Pilot* from up to sixty miles, during the nine months of winter rains it presents a cloud-shrouded target at best and numerous vessels are known to have passed it by at a fraction of that distance.

At times during the 1680s, Captain John Cook and his followers suffered similar difficulties. A pirate by trade, he was something of an iconoclast for that day. Having been wrested from their stronghold at Tortuga in the Caribbean by the British Navy and then scattered like so much jetsam before the devastation of a powerful earthquake that rocked Port Royal, Jamaica in 1692, many of his freebooting brethren sailed away for greener pastures in the Indian Ocean.

Not so Cook. Instead, accompanied by the famous privateering trio of Edward Davis, William Dampier and Lionel Wafer, he rounded the perilous Cape Horn in a captured thirty-six-gun Danish brig called the *Bacthelor's Delight* and contented himself with preying upon the Pacific coast of the Spanish Main. When Cook died of fever on the Galapagos Islands, his quartermaster Davis took command, joining forces with Captains Charles Swan and John Eaton of the *Cygnet* and the *Nicholas* respectively. Together they harried Spanish settlements from Baja California to Guayaquil, Ecuador between 1683 and the late 1690s, numbering, with the addition over the years of several more ships, perhaps 1000 brigands at the height of their depredations.

Mixing mayhem with a remarkable degree of temperance, given the nature of their calling, these rough-and-tumble outlaws prospered under Davis's generous and not unenlightened hand. Known for his leniency toward captives, particularly when they happened to be women, Davis took a serious and businesslike approach to privateering that stood him in good stead over a remarkably successful career that spanned two decades.

That having been said, the gentle Davis is credited, among other escapades, with having invested the oft-abused port of Guayaquil, Ecuador and, around 1685, with sacking the inland town of Leon, Nicaragua. After this last, which for all the hardship attendant upon it was a mission that reportedly fell far below remunerative standard, common cause among his associates began to deteriorate and Davis, escorted by Charles Swan in the *Cygnet,* hauled for the shelter of his headquarters at Cocos Island.

Davis dropped anchor at Chatham Bay, one of the island's two viable anchorages, both of which lie at its extreme northern end. Putting ashore in a dinghy, he and two trusted officers brought with them a number of chests. Towering above the lip of the Bay rose sheer palisades, honeycombed below with numerous surf-hollowed coves and rising as high as 600–700 feet. Before them spread a fan of boulder-strewn creeks. Slicing up through dense jungle these led to a high plateau "spiked," in the description of a nineteenth-century explorer, with a triple crown of volcanoes, the tallest, Cerro Iglesias, rising to almost 3000 feet.

It was in this volcano's shadow that Incan nobles had taken refuge during the dark days of the Spanish Conquest, or so goes island lore.

Exiled worshippers of a sun god sadly obliged to bow in his turn before the ever-present Cocos rains, the Incans languished here for generations. And from their lonely eyrie over a kingdom's purchase in gold they could scan the horizon for the dreaded sight of the white man's ships.

Cocos was uninhabited. Mute witnesses to the activities of Davis and his pirate chests can only have been red- and blue-footed boobies hobnobbing on the island's rocky shore or perhaps the terns, gulls and frigates wheeling above over the surf-capped waves. The cliffs of Chatham Bay had eroded over past ages creating a sandy beach ideal for the careening of the long-suffering *Batchelor* as well as the pleasant resort of her weary crew. Majestic

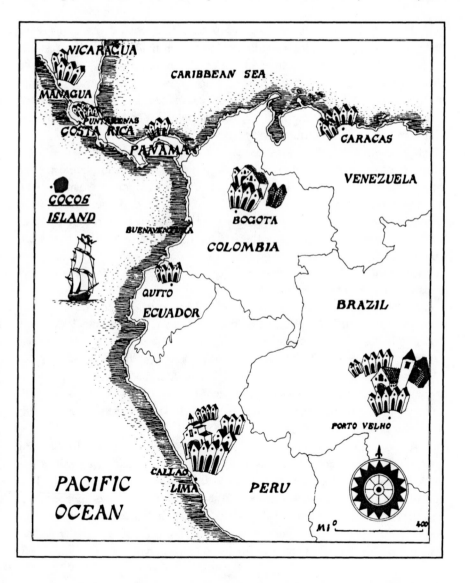

cascades of sweet water tumbling over the palisades were a delight to their eyes; cooling onshore breezes, touched with intermittent showers, refreshing to their souls. Lionel Wafer could not have been better pleased.

Here was a man who had marched with Sir Henry Morgan on the agonizing Darien Campaign in Panama. Wounded and taken prisoner by a fierce band of cannibals, he had barely managed to escape with his life after successfully "bleeding" the stricken wife of their chief. Trained as a "Doctor of Physick," whose timely ministrations to Davis's fleet earned him an extra share of all prizes taken, Wafer was not merely deft with a scalpel: in the manner of his companion-in-arms, William Dampier, he knew his way around a quill as well.

Lionel Wafer's colorful account of privateering aboard the *Batchelor's Delight* and other ships, itself made a splash when first published in London at the turn of the century. In it he takes a benign view of Cocos, oddly contradicted by hosts of treasure hunters who followed in his footsteps. Cursed in their eyes with a malignant climate madly fluctuating between extremes of torrid heat and torrential rains, many found the island "crawling with vermin and stinging ants" and, quite erroneously, "infested with snakes."

Not so much as a hint does he ever let drop concerning the real mission of the *Batchelor's Delight*. Nowhere in an ofttimes ecstatic narrative does the subject ever turn upon pieces of eight, silver bars or ingots of Spanish gold. Although on his gentleman's word Wafer now lacked the stomach for privateering, he had unquestionably so enriched himself through years of such industry that he might later retire at Spanish expense to a very comfortable old age. In the meantime he had sailed many a crooked mile to Cocos Island. Can it not have been that he landed here with Davis in order to bury treasure—rather than to praise it?

For his part, William Dampier was nowhere near as reticent. In fact, he was not above a little boasting. So great, he writes, was the weight of accumulated booty aboard the *Batchelor* as she gingerly wended her way toward Cocos that, on one occasion, he feared she might founder in a gale. Moreover, once riding safely at her Chatham Bay anchorage and the share-out begun, Dampier reports that her ship's master preferred to measure each man's portion by the flagon rather than *count* it, such being the sheer quantity involved. By the time he completed his office, every sailor was richer, he claims, to the tune of $20,000.

That done, Dampier and Swan of the *Cygnet* mustered a crew for the long haul to the Indian Ocean. Davis and Wafer, on the other hand, eventually sailed back around Cape Horn for Chesapeake Bay where each availed himself of the Royal amnesty for repentant privateers. Edward Davis purchased properties in Maryland or Virginia; Lionel Wafer settled down in Philadelphia to write his memoirs which were duly published in 1699. The *Batchelor's* former captain may not, withal, have had time to read them. Fast wearying of the sedentary life,

Davis outfitted a new vessel in 1702 and quietly stood away from America's shore. Some assert that he headed straightway for Cocos Island.

The second seafarer believed to have banked a fortune on Cocos Island was, by all accounts, cut from a very different cloth. "Benito of the Bloody Sword" is what one romantic chronicler dubbed him. Naturally, so colorful a name was bound to stick and so it has. Benito himself greatly preferred to be addressed as Don Pedro and affected a Portuguese lineage which may well have been spurious. A rollicking female pirate named Mary Welch, who claimed to have been his mistress, steadfastly maintained that he was, in fact, the renegade British naval officer Edward Bennet.

In any event, all are agreed that he was a particularly bloodthirsty villain and a great hit with the ladies. Thence no doubt sprang his most enduring sobriquet, Bonito, meaning "pretty" or "good-looking" in both Spanish and Portuguese. Thus, Benito Bonito.

It is said that his career as a pirate took off after he headed a mutiny aboard a Portuguese trading brig plying the African coast in 1816. Taking command, Benito later traded her for an English slaver, the *Lightning*, which he had captured in Caribbean waters and renamed in Spanish the *Relampagos*. The entire crew he dispatched with his infamous "bloody sword"—but for two officers, Messrs. Thompson and Chapelle, who would later claim to have been "converted" by that mortifying arm to the mere pretense of brigandage.

Aware of the impending collapse of Spain's New World empire, and tempted by the easy pickings there to be had, Benito, without further delay, steered a course for the Spanish Main. Seville's beleaguered representatives from Chile to Mexico were by now near the end of their tether as revolution spread across the realm like wildfire. High among a host of disconcerting priorities was the safe removal of what they feared might prove to be the last gold and silver from an Empire virtually hanging by a thread.

In 1819 Spain commissioned a new line of plate ships, sleeker and smaller than the old. Designed to carry half the load, these were introduced with the hope that they would stand an optimum chance of outrunning "Independents" and pirates alike. Benito, however, was undaunted. His tactics had always lent themselves to hit-and-run attacks on coastal settlements. Thus, when that same year he got wind of a consignment of Mexican specie to be moved from the capital's mint overland to Acapulco and its final destination of Spanish Manila, Benito was ready.

Lamentably for Spain, her timely seaboard innovations defied duplication on land where, naturally enough, beasts of burden were entrusted with conveyance of all manner of chattel, royal and otherwise. Lying in ambush in a rocky defile along the Acapulco road, Benito and his men silently waited upon the jingling bells of the mule train's lead, then swooped down on its military escort in a howling rush and made away with a fortune in silver dollars.

Back at Cocos, the share-out on the *Relampagos* went nowhere near as amicably as had that on the *Batchelor's Delight*. Not a man to suffer dissension gladly, Benito carefully buried his own fortune in two separate locations and then dealt with the offending parties in the manner to which he had long become accustomed. Shortly afterwards he was cornered near Buena Ventura, Mexico by the corvette *Espiegle*—and rather than be captured alive sent a bullet into his brain. His crew was reportedly hanged, all but for Thompson and Chapelle who, very much like two cats enjoying the best of nine lives, were spared the yardarm swing as, too, was Mary Welch.

Along with her, the two were sent to prison in Tasmania after successfully pleading clemency on the grounds they had been conscripted against their will. Chapelle may later have emigrated to San Francisco while Thompson reportedly started a new life in Samoa under the assumed name of MacComber.

The third and last great fortune buried at Cocos holds pride of place over the others and has remained first in the hearts of latter-day treasure seekers. A splendid jumble of the best marriage between Old World craftsmanship and the New World's largesse of gems and metals, it was by no means solely made up of the impersonal stuff of ingots, bars and freshly minted specie. Rather, the Treasure of Lima, as it came to be known, comprised much-esteemed objects, many of considerable veneration, belonging to the opulent Cathedral of Lima, along with crate upon crate of luxurious personal effects dear to its most noble patrons.

Robert Charroux in *Treasures of the World* pictured the hoard as a mouthwatering hodgepodge of "private capital, piastres, ducats, crowns, jewels, precious stones, the gold chandeliers of the Cathedral, the chandelier, ciboria and other objects of worship, gold and silver plate, books, archives and art treasures." Author Karl Baarslar preferred to speak of coffers packed with rubies, diamonds, sapphires, pearls, amethysts, opals and jewel-encrusted swords. All accounts seem to concur on the inclusion of one spectacular item, Our Lady of Lima, a life-size statue in solid gold of the Virgin Mary and Infant Jesus. Estimates of the treasure's total worth begin as low as $12,000,000 and simply skyrocket from there.

If much of the Spanish Main was caught up in a revolutionary ferment when Benito made off with the second Cocos fortune in 1819, by 1821 its political and economic capital Lima—City of Kings—was in a general uproar. Simón Bolívar bore down from the north, General San Martin from the east and the eccentric Lord Cochrane, Earl of Dundonald, ex-Admiral of the Royal Navy and now head of the Chilean fleet, himself lay offshore from the port of Callao at the head of a crippling blockade.

Caught in a classic pincer, Lima's high-born lost their nerve. At any moment, it seemed, the Great Unwashed—mestizo guerrilla fighters, Sierra Indians and coast Blacks—might descend en masse upon the once haughty Plaza de Armas. If little hope remained of evacuating the city's panic-stricken citizenry, clerics attached to the great Cathedral successfully argued the necessity of striving to safeguard the three centuries of treasure, both consecrated and otherwise, held within its walls. Thus supervised by a small army of exasperated padres, out into the harsh sunlight it was borne upon the backs of sweating peons before a crowd of startled onlookers.

An odder lot of fortune they could scarce have ever seen. Piled high onto wagons were crates and strongboxes and cedarwood coffers, bejeweled caskets, statues of the Holy Mother, skulls and sainted bones. By lantern light the work went on until most of the Cathedral's finest pieces were removed to the fort at Callao where, most promiscuously, they shared quarters with the likes of muskets, cannonballs and gunpowder casks. So close lay Cochrane to the Callao harbor that in his diaries he makes mention of having witnessed the entire operation through his spyglass. Somehow, the treasure would have to be removed by sea and under the Admiral's very nose. Regrettably, precious few vessels available for such a mission now remained at anchor. By far the most secure was the *Esmeralda* but, as a gun ship, she might at any moment be called upon in the defense of Lima.

That left the *Mary Dyer*. She was not a prepossessing brig; for that matter she was not even Spanish. Still, as she flew the Union Jack it was reckoned the *Mary Dyer* would stand a reasonable chance of successfully running Lord Cochrane's blockade. Equally important, her Scottish captain, William Thompson, enjoyed an unblemished reputation throughout Peru as an honest and capable trader. And so indeed he might well have remained, had not a singular fortune been thrust upon him and his flabbergasted crew by a bishop and a viceroy and a governor, beseeching them, all for the love of God!—mercifully to take it off their hands.

Thompson's instructions were straightforward enough: he was to cruise at a safe distance off the Peruvian coast and, as it were, test the waters. Should Lima fall to the "Independents" he was to make haste for the safe haven of Panama. However, should San Martin's and Cochrane's impending attack fail, the good captain might then be pleased to return to Callao forthwith. Whether blinded by his own cupidity or that of his crew, Thompson managed, of course, to do neither. Instead, his men overwhelmed Our Lady of Lima's meager escort, fed their bodies to the sharks and then tacked northward for Cocos Island.

Upon arrival a cargo which had reportedly taken Peruvian stevedores two days to stow aboard in Callao was now taken off on the double by the *Mary Dyer's* crew. Pulled ashore in eleven longboat loads, the Lima treasure was then hastily piled up on Chatham beach. Just where the bulk of it was hidden—whether beneath the sand or in some cave along Chatham Creek—is a question that has baffled treasure hunters.

Why Cocos Island in the first place? Worth bearing in mind is the fact that the highjacking of the *Mary Dyer* was clearly an improvised affair led not by seasoned pirates but rather by otherwise honest merchant seamen suddenly in the possession of a fabulous and very "hot" fortune. The instant Thompson's intentions proved renegade and the Spanish Admiralty had issued a hue-and-cry order against his craft, the *Mary Dyer* was a marked vessel which no port in the world might reasonably honor.

To tempt the Chilean Navy or the "Independents" with a run around Cape Horn would have been suicidal, and any thought of a 6000-mile crossing to the East Indies foolhardy at best. Besides the Galapagos Islands, which lay 650 miles west of Guayaquil and were much frequented by whaling ships, there was Plate Island where Drake, centuries before, had dumped overboard a cargo of unwanted silver. Here the disadvantage lay in its close proximity to the Ecuadorian port of Manta.

Cocos Island, on the other hand, was ideally situated. Lying some 300 miles southwest of Costa Rica, uninhabited, little visited and well beyond the normal shipping lanes, it boasted the added virtue of being extremely difficult to access. All Thompson had to do was locate it, cleverly secrete the enormous cache there and then somehow cover the *Mary Dyer's* tracks!

Some believe that, after departing Cocos Island, Thompson sailed to Panama where he presented a cock-and-bull story to Spanish authorities in a vain attempt to explain the startling absence of the Treasure of Lima in his ship's empty hold. A second theory is that the *Mary Dyer* was overtaken not far from Cocos by a Peruvian warship. A third has Thompson boldly sailing in close to the Central American coast and simply scuttling his craft.

The force of this last hypothesis is obvious: here was a man of new-found means and a deep dark secret who could ill afford to keep his *Mary Dyer* under present circumstances, yet might easily replace her at any opportune time. To that end, Thompson may have fired her at sea and come ashore with his crew posing as the victims of shipwreck.

Wherever they all ended up and whatever the alibi, it fell upon deaf ears. Under the sting of the lash, one of the *Mary Dyer's* sailors was moved to gratify his Spanish inquisitors with the truth behind the entire charade, and the jig was up. All hands were then summarily executed, with the exception of Thompson and his first mate, James Alexander Forbes, on condition they reveal the precise location of the eleven longboats of booty.

One version of the story holds that the two men took their escort on a wild goose chase to the Galapagos Islands, of which Cocos is a kind of geologic cousin. Knowing themselves to be doomed whether they produced the treasure or not, they jumped overboard. Paddling for dear life, Thompson reportedly succeeded in reaching a British whaler moored nearby while the hapless Forbes was devoured by sharks on route.

More popular by far is the belief that the prisoners, familiar as they were with the lay of Cocos Island, devised a plan on the journey out. Thus prepared on arrival, they were quick to spring their surprise. Drawing their disorientated captors far up Chatham Creek, Thompson and Forbes suddenly darted sideways into the dense undergrowth and scrambled for cover. A fortnight later the pair were still playing a nerve-racking game of cat-and-mouse with teams of infuriated foot soldiers when the hunt finally halted thanks to dwindling supplies. Over succeeding months at least two further search parties are thought to have been sent to Cocos. These also failed to flush out the fugitives who were eventually given up for dead.

Such a conclusion seems hardly illogical. Lacking both weapons and fire, the pair would truly have been put on their mettle to survive. That said, a man might dig a pit with the intent of trapping wild pig and kindle a flame by hand with two sticks. For one clever enough to catch them, fish abounded in Cocos' waters as did sea turtles which were obliging enough to bury their nutritious eggs in the island's warm sands. Sweet water was plentiful and wild oranges and limes—heaven-sent antidotes to the ravages of scurvy—ready to hand. Then, of course, a lucky castaway might savor the delights of Lionel Wafer's much beloved coconuts.

Even these last, however, may finally have palled on the men. According to the story, if they had been on Cocos Island a week they had been there six months by the time the first friendly ship arrived. She was the British whaler *Captain,* come to Cocos for fresh water, and Thompson and Forbes were greatly relieved to find that this time around their claims as shipwrecks received a considerably more kindly hearing. Indeed, their ravaged features and tattered rags must alone have spoken volumes.

Of the two, Forbes was by far the worse for wear. Judging the man perilously close to death, the *Captain's* skipper felt obliged to put him ashore at Puntarenas on the journey back where he was believed to have died in the hospital some weeks later. Thompson, however, was sufficiently strong to make the haul back to the West Indies and from there, finally, to his home in Newfoundland.

Without a ship, or for that matter, a penny with which to bless himself, William Thompson never succeeded in raising the kind of capital required for an expedition back to Cocos Island. A halfhearted brigand at best, perhaps he preferred to sit upon a fortune he knew would at least remain uniquely *his* if only he left it well alone. Then, too, the captain of the notorious *Mary Dyer* may have deemed himself lucky enough to have escaped from Cocos Island with the most inestimable of treasures—his life.

In 1844 the laconic and reclusive Scot was befriended by a fellow sailor with whom he was finally willing to share the secret of Our Lady of Lima. John Keating was his name and he possessed all the burning passion for adventure by now long past rekindling in the older man. Much reduced in health no less than in estate, Thompson would breathe his last in Keating's tumbledown house in St. Johns later that year or early in 1845. Having been made reasonably comfortable during his declining months by the kindly attentions of his host, Thompson bit by bit unburdened himself, much to Keating's delight, of a tale he had held close to his chest for over twenty years.

Illiterate but by no means simple, Keating was avid for such intelligence. Even as Thompson's grip on life weakened and his story came alive, the younger man traded on the information in a desperate search for financing. At this he succeeded, quite possibly with Thompson's blessings, though up till the very end without the treasure's precise location.

For his efforts Keating gained, in the *Edgecombe,* a seaworthy Bristol brig and, in her Newfoundland owner, a respected merchant for a partner who was mercifully short on conditions. In fact, the only one outstanding was that the gentleman's close friend Boag, just to keep the venture honest, should be entrusted with the vessel's charge. Keating readily acquiesced since he was sorely in want of a captain.

That he hardly needed *another* goes without saying. Still, that is what the Fates had in store, for when the *Edgecombe* finally arrived at the port of St. Johns her skipper, surnamed Gault, staunchly declined to relinquish command. He may have been part owner of the vessel because there was absolutely no hope, as the saga is related, of shaking him. In addition, the surprising destination of the *Edgecombe* may well have aroused his suspicions. Be that as it may, the warring factions eventually arrived at a tenuous *modus vivendi* whereby Gault was entitled to continue on as captain, a circumstance which later made for considerable tension aboard ship.

In the meantime, Keating was content to push ahead with preparations for the expedition and to await the death throes of his house guest, no doubt praying that Thompson might finally divulge the treasure's exact location. Such in fact he did receive—and none too soon—from the Captain's dying lips. After burying his unfortunate patron, he set off with Boag, treasure map in hand, and the much resented Gault around Cape Horn in the spring of 1846.

The voyage proved a nightmare. Gault managed to make himself especially hateful to Keating and Boag throughout with querulous demands for information which the two steadfastly ignored. Such an acrimonious climate surrounding the venture's leadership so poisoned the air that it was a nearly mutinous crew that eased the *Edgecombe* into Chatham Bay in early summer.

For all that, Keating and Boag were in luck. They had taken a dying old sailor at his word and now would follow to their great good fortune his instructions to the letter. Putting ashore alone, they had between them a crudely drawn treasure map and the following set of details:

Turn your back on the sea then make your way toward the
mountain that is in the north of the island. On the mountain
slope you will see a brook to the west. Cross this and go
twenty more paces due west. Then take twenty more paces
toward the center of the island until the sea is completely
hidden behind the mountain. At the place where the ground
suddenly falls away you will see a white mark on the rock.
This is where the cave is. It has a well hidden entrance covered by a stone slab and the tunnel entrance leads sideways
into a chamber.[1]

Marvelous to relate, Keating and Boag managed, though with some difficulty, to find Thompson's white mark on their very first attempt. Clearing
away a tangle of undergrowth nearby, they further discovered a tight-fitting
stone expertly set into the mouth of what appeared to be a natural cave.
Prying it loose with a crowbar one of the men had smuggled off the *Edgecombe,*
they entered the tunnel. Keating led on all fours, feeling his way along the
narrow walls until they opened into a pitch black chamber. Straightening up
he lit a tallow candle and then almost immediately dropped back on his
knees. Spread out before his eyes were crates and chests and coffers. This
was surely Thompson's true-to-life fortune ... the infamous cargo of the *Mary
Dyer* ... Our Lady of Lima!

The ecstatic pair might, with the sublimest pleasure, have tarried there all
afternoon, greedy as they doubtless were to plumb the mysteries of each and
every sealed delight before them. Despite a positive embarrassment of riches,
however, they would somehow have to face Gault and pass themselves off as
the mere indigent seafarers they had been all their lives until only a few
moments before. Excited as they were almost to a frenzy, the men quickly
realized that carrying off such a charade would require dramatic skills far
beyond their ken. The glint of gold in their eyes would betray them. Besides,
if they were to interest a more compatible crew in a subsequent expedition it
would be necessary to carry back samples with them from *this* trip and they
were certain to be searched upon returning to the ship.

It was Boag who determined to reveal a small handful of coins to the
Edgecombe's crew, the better to judge its reaction to the sight of gold and silver.
Not surprisingly, the men were galvanized by the sight and immediately fell to
making threatening noises over where the rest of it lay and how much each of
them would be paid and what would likely happen if they weren't.

Keating and Boag were aghast. Suddenly the prospect of perishing alone
in the Cocos jungle seemed far preferable to risking their necks at the mercy
of this beastly rabble. Promising to lead the whole sorry lot of them on the
morrow to the cave, the two instead slipped overboard later that night with a

few basic necessities, a gambit suspiciously similar to that employed twenty years earlier by the team of Thompson and Forbes. At any rate, after a hair-raising swim through shark-infested waters they apparently landed safely on the beach and immediately set off at a killing pace up Chatham Creek toward the wild and unexplored interior.

So well had the pair advanced by dawn that they could barely make out the curses of the *Edgecombe's* crew which had poured ashore at the first sign of their disappearance. What lends this particular episode the spice dear to most treasure seekers' hearts is that, by the time Gault had finally called off the search in disgust and sailed away, only one of the two men emerged from the jungle alive. Keating was that man.

Picked up by a passing vessel he explained to her captain that Boag had drowned some weeks earlier. On his return to Newfoundland, an attempt to prosecute Keating on a charge of murder foundered for lack of evidence. Still, many investigators are convinced that he sealed Boag up in Thompson's cave and left him to starve.

Keating is believed to have made at least one, and possibly two, further trips to Cocos Island. Residents of St. Johns reported that, after returning from a first long sea voyage, he purchased a farm and several commercial properties and, not long after a second, his own private schooner. It is in her that Keating was shipwrecked near Codroy village in 1868 where he chanced to be aided by a humble quartermaster, Nicholas Fitzgerald. In gratitude, Keating turned over to Fitzgerald various documents relating to the location of the Cocos cave.

Their intimacy notwithstanding, neither man appears to have taken the other into his fullest confidence. For his part Fitzgerald never acted directly upon the information and even admitted in a letter to a friend that, although Keating had invited him on a future expedition to Cocos, he had demurred. "I thought I would be running grave risk of my life to go single-handed with him. This disappearance of Boag was unsatifactorily explained to me by him."

Whether Keating had ever killed a man, he seems to have been entirely capable of hoodwinking several. Not only did he bequeath contradictory information to his bosom friend in 1882, his young widow was made the beneficiary of rambling and near-incoherent documents pertaining to the Cocos Island fortune as was a third party, Thomas Hackett. To further confuse the matter, Keating's son-in-law, Richard Young, claimed to possess vital details of the same, told to him by his dying relative. Young refused to make common cause with the widow and failed to raise sufficient capital for the grand recovery mission. Thomas Hackett died before managing to organize *his*. That left the field wide open to brother Fred of Vancouver who, in turn, inherited from his deceased sibling an envelope full of Keating's maps and charts.

If Keating had no particular motive for deceiving the faithful Fitzgerald, such was not necessarily so in the case of his second wife. Tittle-tattle around

St. Johns had it that the young woman had fallen madly in love with Keating after catching sight of him one evening through his kitchen window counting out a stack of gold doubloons. She herself came to doubt the sincerity of her husband's legacy and so schemed to join forces with Fred Hackett whom she suspected of possessing information superior to her own.

In 1897 the two outfitted the *Aurora* and set out on a fruitless voyage to Cocos Island which, if lacking in high drama, did provide an element of farce. Such were their mutual suspicions that each was reduced to breaking into the other's cabin and rifling it for clues which they stubbornly declined to pool.

Hardly surprisingly, their professional association foundered well before they ever put in at Chatham Bay. Once there, solo efforts bore only bitter fruit and after only ten days the widow Keating was heading home convinced that, from the grave, her dearly departed husband John was now laughing up his sleeve at her. Almost too terrible to contemplate was the possibility that he had actually turned over all the true information to that dreadful man, Nicholas Fitzgerald.

Meantime, the quartermaster had sailed for Australia where, a world removed from Codroy village, history chanced to repeat itself. Not unlike Keating before him, Fitzgerald fell victim to shipwreck. Rescued at sea by a fellow mariner, Commodore Curzon-Howe, he was moved to honor the gallant intervention of his benefactor with the bestowal of a most unusual gift.

However rugged the topography of Cocos Island and impenetrable its jungle, cutting through the riot of fact and fiction sprung up around its elusive millions has generally proved as daunting to fortune hunters as the pick-and-shovel work that surely followed. Vital documents pass from hand to shipwrecked hand; clues proliferate like the very fishes of the sea. Names, dates, dying words and shifting landmarks together form a kind of palimpsest, with one revelation laid over another and another until, at best, a bewildering composite picture dimly emerges.

Clouding it further, as regards the Treasure of Lima, is the animal cunning of John Keating. He could hardly have feared the ghost of poor Boag, but perhaps he was aware that another man—believed dead—was familiar with the Cocos cave. Whatever his reasons, investigators suspect that, on his second trip to Cocos, Keating moved portions of the treasure with the aid of several mysterious strangers to a new location on the southern end of the island.

Registered under the number 18,755 at the Nautical and Travellers' Club in Sydney are the following instructions passed down from Keating to Fitzgerald and finally to Curzon-Howe. These tend to support just such a thesis:

> Disembark in the Bay of Hope between two islets in water
> five fathoms deep. Walk 350 paces along the course of the

stream then turn north north-east for 850 yards. Stake, setting sun, stake, draws the silhouette of an eagle with wings
spread. At the extremity of sun and shadow: cave marked
with a cross. Here lies the treasure.[2]

Along with these cryptic directions Fitzgerald possessed a series of disjointed
logs dictated by the illiterate Keating and transcribed by some unknown hand:

At two cables' lengths south of the last watering-place, on
three points. The cave is the one which is to be found under
the second point. Christie, Ned and Anton have tried but
none of the three has returned. Ned on his fourth dive found
the entrance at twelve fathoms but did not emerge from his
fifth dive. There are no octopuses but there are sharks. A
path must be opened up to the cave from the west. I believe
there has been a fall of rock at the entrance.[3]

In stark contrast to such nebulous clues concerning the actual site of the
Treasure of Lima, Fitzgerald was pleased to provide Curzon-Howe with a
minutely detailed inventory of its priceless contents:

We have buried at the depth of four feet in the red earth:
1 chest: altar trimmings of cloth of gold, with baldachins,
monstrances, chalices, comprising 1,244 stones.
1 chest: 2 gold reliquaries weighing 120 pounds, with 624
topazes, carnelians and emeralds, 12 diamonds.
1 chest: 3 reliquaries of cast metal weighing 160 pounds,
with 860 rubies and various stones, 19 diamonds.
28 feet to the northeast at a depth of eight feet in the yellow
sand: 7 chests: with 22 chandeliers in gold and silver weighing 250 pounds, and 164 rubies a foot.
12 arm spans west, at a depth of ten feet in the red earth: the
seven-foot Virgin of gold, with the Child Jesus and her crown
and pectoral of 780 pounds, rolled in her gold chasuble on
which are 1,684 jewels. Three of these are 4-inch emeralds
on the pectoral and six are 6-inch topazes on the crown. The
seven crosses are of diamonds.
1 chest: 4,000 doubloons of Spain marked 8. 5,000 crowns of
Mexico, 124 swords, 64 dirks, 120 shoulder belts, 28
rondaches.
1 chest: 8 caskets of cedar wood and silver, with 3,840 cut
stones, rings, patens and 4,265 uncut stones.

What Curzon-Howe chose to make of all this is unknown as he simply passed the entire jumble along for the edification of his son. It is certainly nothing if not bewildering. "Red earth" gives way to "yellow sand" and caves both submarine and subterranean figure prominently. The syntax of the documents is such that they appear to have been garbled in transmission.

As to the measurements themselves, two cables' lengths are roughly 400 yards and the "last watering-place"—Wafer Bay, according to later researchers. Ned diving "twelve fathom" or seventy-two feet would simply be a man pushing world records. Treasure-hunter Pierre Mangel, for one, later chose to interpret such arcane details in the light of code words rather than in their literal sense; twelve fathoms would then mean twelve "swimming strokes."

Such extrapolations did their small part in helping to tidy up an otherwise (and perhaps intentionally) cluttered trail of clues. But would they finally lead fortune hunters any closer to Our Lady of Lima?

For all the attention focused on her over the years and, conversely, the lack of interest in Edward Davis's hoard, that of the pirate Benito cannot be said to have been totally forgotten in the shuffle. One curious common denominator running through the otherwise Byzantine saga of Cocos Island relates to the work ethic of its sundry connoisseurs. Treasure seekers over the past 100 years, come from far and wide at considerable expense and no small risk, more often than not conducted their expeditions in a manner that might best be described as "short and bitter sweet."

Not so August Gissler. An imposing German adventurer standing well over six feet tall with steely eyes, a noble brow and a billowing black beard that fell almost to his waist, Gissler remained dogged to the bitter end. Convinced his destiny was to discover the whereabouts of Benito's silver, Gissler spent seventeen years eking out a precarious existence on Cocos Island. He suffered the intrusion of interloper as well as the duplicity of bureaucrats and wound up for his pains with a single gold doubloon.

Had he been a madman or simply a fool Gissler's contribution to the Cocos story would have earned him no more than a footnote at best. As he was intelligent, competent and well-educated—if touched with a certain eccentricity—no recounting of the island's history is complete without him and no man was better conversant with it than August Gissler. Moreover, the clues which led him to devote a quarter of his life to the Cocos treasure were among the best of a very odd lot indeed.

Gissler, as he enters the picture, was a passenger bound for Hawaii on the *High-flyer* which departed Southampton, England in the year 1880. Stopping en route in the Azores, she happened to pick up a crowd of Portuguese laborers emigrating to the South Pacific. During the long crossing Gissler made the acquaintance of one of their numerous company who had an intriguing shipboard tale to tell. His name was Manoel Cabral and he would utterly transform Gissler's life with the story of an old seafaring grandfather, long since dead, and an island of which the well-traveled German had never even heard.

According to Cabral, his relative had served under the infamous Don Pedro, known also as Benito Bonito. Starting from rude beginnings in the Azores they had wound up secreting a fortune in silver, *"stolen from Spanish priests,"* on an obscure Pacific island called "Las Palmas."

Benito had anchored his vessel—the *Relampagos* if Manoel rightly recollected—in Wafer Bay not far distant from a conical rock that looked to the eyes of his grandfather "something like a farmer's haystack." Having remarked on a splendid waterfall that fell some 300 feet into dense jungle, Benito sent a half-dozen hand-picked men, commanded by Cabral senior, to reconnoiter sections of the creek that appeared to lead up to it.

Nearby stood a small grove of coconut palms, 600 feet to the southwest of the creek's mouth. Twenty feet behind these trees, Benito buried the first load of silver. A second load he buried a few days later somewhere beyond the same grove, four feet deep at the foot of a hill beneath a large boulder. Upon it Cabral's grandfather swore that he witnessed Benito carve the letters D.P.I. followed by the numeral 600p. Circumstances afterwards caused the two to part company in Costa Rica from where Cabral eventually shipped home alone to the Azores.

Gissler later recalled that, while interesting, Manoel's tale made only a slight impression upon him at the time. He recorded the particulars in his diary and then put them out of his mind for the next eight years which he happily spent as a colonist in the Hawaiian Islands.

Having been pleased to take a wife, Gissler now counted among his kin a man named Bartells. Bartells had a father-in-law notorious throughout the islands as a salty old reprobate with a checkered, though ill-defined, past. Well known for his indisposition to speak much about it, "Old Mac," as he was called, took a liking to Gissler and once, while in his cups, drew him aside. Might he perchance care for a look at a genuine treasure map? The island's name read "Las Palmas" on the crude map and its coordinates were 5° 32'57"N., 86° 59.17"W. Fascinating, too, was the fact that "Old Mac" was well acquainted with the story of Thompson and Chapelle, although he refused to comment further upon them and likewise declined the opportunity of explaining just how he had come by the map in question.

The old man (and he would indeed have been hoary with age by the late 1880s) insisted that his memory played tricks on him but that, as Gissler could plainly judge from the map, Benito's treasure was buried not far from a creek which emptied into Wafer Bay. Moreover, he was certain it lay "eight feet deep under a high bluff." Unclear is whether or not Gissler ever knew enough of Mary Welch's story to make the connection between the pseudonymous MacComber of the *Relampagos*, who was said to have settled in Samoa, and "Old Mac."

In any event, by this time Bartells himself was interested and he and Gissler wound up making the trip together to Puntarenas, Costa Rica the following year, 1889. Bartells's son accompanied them as well but fell ill in Puntarenas while awaiting passage to Cocos Island; it was eventually decided that he and his father would do better to return home. Gissler, then, would have to carry on alone.

As had many a voyager before him, Gissler found himself ill served by the elements on his first attempt to reach Cocos. Having handsomely paid the captain of a Swedish vessel to sail 300 miles out of his way and drop him there, Gissler instead suffered a hapless trajectory taking him all the way to Santiago, Chile—the ship's erstwhile destination—after she was becalmed and then blown completely off course on her approach to the island.

Undaunted, Gissler finally succeeded in landing in a private vessel with her captain and five crew members to whom he had pledged a share of Benito's silver in exchange for his passage. After an exhausting seven days of combing Wafer Bay, though the spirit of Gissler's associates was willing enough, the flesh proved weak. Dangerously short on provisions and unwilling to live off the land, the Swede and his men deemed it politic to depart while they still had enough food for the run to the mainland. Back they would come, promised the captain, with better implements and a well-stocked larder.

Six solitary months later Gissler was not mourning their absence half as much as he mourned a mortifying gap in his own education. Otherwise well rounded in that respect he remained, nonetheless, woefully ignorant of the fundamentals of navigation. Such an oversight now appeared to Gissler a matter of great concern for he was baffled by a crucial set of indications entrusted to his care by "Old Mac": "After we buried the treasure we planted a coconut tree on top and took bearings by compass which showed the location to be north east by east half east to east mountain, north ten east to west mountain."[4]

Having so often turned them over in his mind, they came to embody to the lonely castaway a kind of sacred mantra imbued with mystery and an ineffable charm:

North East by East to East Mountain
North Ten East to West Mountain

Gissler was certain that with a little study he might determine from which point the bearings had been taken in the first place and thus solve for good and all the riddle of Benito's silver. After a half year's regimen of the obligatory wild pig, fish and coconuts, he was at last taken off Cocos Island determined to improve his mind with practice on the sextant and to improve his digestion by bringing back with him seeds for a vegetable garden. Upon his return in 1894 he had accomplished that and a good deal more.

By now a citizen in good standing in Costa Rica, its President had further bestowed upon Gissler the title of "First Governor of Cocos Island." Better still, he was granted a concession to half the island as well as exclusive treasure rights to two thirds of everything he discovered. In return, the "Governor" pledged to colonize Cocos and to develop whatever small potential the island held as an agricultural region.

True to his word, Gissler lured six families of immigrant farmers to her patently unenticing shores and even managed to persuade his wife to join him. These various domestic arrangements accomplished to satisfaction and the new community's fledgling attempts at husbandry bearing early fruit, he felt he could now in good conscience devote himself to the real business at hand.

Unfortunately, Gissler was a man doomed to constant interruption. During his long tenure as Governor, treasure parties came and treasure parties went as through a revolving door. Where Cocos Island was concerned, it seemed that there was no such thing as bad publicity. Indeed, failure was in a sense its own reward, since one expedition's lack of good fortune could only mean hope—that sprang eternal—for the next. Nowhere was this more true than in the case of John Keating whose mischief loosed an endless line of furies on the beleaguered Governor.

Left throughout 1875 to a peace that doubtless brought him solace though negligible material reward—beyond the discovery of a mysterious boulder scrawled with an arrow and the letter 'K' beside it—Gissler was treated the following year to a particularly disturbing visitor.

Putting ashore in a Costa Rican supply boat, the stranger greeted Gissler with a handshake and an official document granting him digging rights on Cocos Island for an indefinite period. He was an American named Haffner and, much to the Governor's chagrin, made free with such privilege over the next nine months. Mortifying indeed for Gissler was the realization that his hard-won suzerainty over Cocos Island might be sundered at will by venal bureaucrats on the mainland. Having brought this intolerable plague to his door Haffner, naturally enough, became anathema. Little could Gissler have imagined, though, that the insufferable upstart would soon lead him to a confrontation with invading British marines!

Haffner finally departed peaceably enough aboard the *Aurora* which had returned to Cocos in 1897 with a chartered party of Canadian treasure hunters. During the voyage back to Vancouver a crew member named Jim Dempster was taken deathly ill and it was Haffner who mounted a doomed effort to save him. In the course of their friendship Haffner startled Dempster with the revelation that he had discovered a great cache of gold. At odds with Gissler and chary of the Canadians, Haffner had thought it wise to keep his explosive secret under wraps. Might Dempster, he now wished to know, be interested in helping out with an introduction to sailing circles in Vancouver as they would shortly be in need of a trustworthy captain and seaworthy craft?

Dempster breathed his last aboard the *Aurora* but not before handing Haffner a letter addressed to one Captain John Claus Voss. The two met up at the Queen's Hotel in Vancouver and Voss, who later made a name for himself by circumnavigating the globe in a dugout canoe, was intrigued with Haffner's story. On condition he secure a 100-ton vessel, Haffner promised Voss a third of the Cocos gold. Pleased with the generous terms of the proposal, Captain Voss set about complying with his end of the bargain.

George Haffner kept his options open. Knocking about the dockside taverns, he had finally succeeded in ingratiating himself with an officer of HMS *Imperious* and was one evening invited aboard for dinner. Primed for the occasion, Haffner regaled his host, Admiral Henry St. Leger Bury Palliser, with a riveting account of buried treasure on the island of Cocos. Palliser was himself familiar with its history and wonderfully susceptible to the lure of fortune. Beyond that, no more independent maverick sailed in the entire Pacific Fleet. Seventy-two hours later the free-spirited Admiral departed Esquimalt Harbor, escorted by the cruiser *Champion,* with an American vagabond at his side on the bridge and a sealed treasure map of uncertain provenance locked below in his wardroom.

There was, of course, no longer any good reason to include the unfortunate Voss and his pitiful 100-ton craft. Here in the *Imperious* was everything the wealthiest expeditionary could possibly ask for in the way of tools and provisions. Best of all were the 300 strapping young "blue shirts" eager to dig, tunnel or dynamite their way to fame, if not fortune, under their Admiral's command.

Still, for all that was going his way, there was a curse now lying in wait over Haffner's answered prayer. Through a conversation he happened to overhear among officers en route, Haffner learned to his horror that any treasure located on Cocos would automatically devolve to the British Government who would serve as caretaker until such time as Costa Rica, or even Peru for that matter, might prove a just claim upon it. Thus, Haffner declined fully to cooperate with Palliser on the finer details of his treasure's location and apparently removed himself from Cocos shortly after the *Imperious* anchored. He headed for Acapulco where he was killed but not before he had despatched a letter to his ex-partner Voss, urging him to find another vessel and sail straightway for Mexico.

To Palliser, Haffner's defection hardly seemed to matter. Unfettered by bothersome and arcane detail and, it may be said, lacking Haffner's government permit, the Admiral made up with a vengeance for these slight shortcoming by his instinct and main force. As high explosives concussed the otherwise tranquil Cocos air, Palliser's 300 sailors and marines ran roughshod over the island and its outraged settlers, digging up Gissler's vegetable garden in their zeal for treasure and placing his scandalized wife under virtual house arrest.

Gissler himself was away on the mainland at the time of the incident and returned to Cocos only to find the island in an uproar and Palliser long gone. Furious, he lodged a heated protest with the Costa Rican government which, in turn, protested bitterly about the "invasion" to the British Foreign Office. Palliser was called on the carpet upon his return to England and British officers were put on notice that, henceforth, Cocos Island was strictly off limits.

Gissler, though perhaps mollified, had not begun to see the last of Palliser. Unrepentant, and with his formidable appetite for treasure hunting now thoroughly whetted, he retired five years later from Her Majesty's Service and made a beeline back for Chatham Bay. Bringing the entire episode full circle was the later appearance of Voss, the Johnny-come-lately who discovered no riches on Cocos and doubtless created nothing like the sensation of Admiral Palliser. He is remembered as the man first to be treated to a sardonic greeting by Gissler—forever to become the Governor's trademark—"After the treasure, of course?"

Palliser's highly embarrassing excursion into fortune hunting at British taxpayers' expense made for muckraking newspaper copy which soon caught the attention of Nicholas Fitzgerald. Sensing an opportunity he now began a running correspondence with the Admiral which led to further headaches for August Gissler. Over a period of months between 1897 and 1898, during which time Palliser checked on Fitzgerald's credentials—such as they were—and Fitzgerald for his part received reassuring noises from the ex-Admiral as to his honest intentions, the two struck a bargain; Fitzgerald would reveal his information (as he had earlier to Curzon-Howe) in return for a 5 percent share of any treasure Palliser might discover.

An oft-quoted letter dated May 23, 1898, from Fitzgerald to Palliser concerning Keating's fabulous cave, reads in part as follows:

> The cave, if found without the door being damaged or blown up will surprise all who see it, on account of the ingenious contrivance and workmanship, possibly done by Peruvian workers in stone, whose skill was noted. In Keating's words, the cave is between twelve and fifteen feet square, with sufficient standing room. The entrance to it is closed by a stone made to move "round" in such a peculiar manner that it sets into the rock when you turn it, leaving a passage through which one man can crawl into the cave at a time, and when the stone is turned back into its place, the human eye cannot detect it; it fits like a paper on a wall. Keating told me that the first time he went to the island he had no trouble in finding the cave; but the second time, there had been a disturbance or eruption which changed the features of the place, but he found it all the same.

Palliser, however, did not. Having teamed up with Hervey de Montmorency, he formed a consortium with a half-dozen other principals and outfitted a tramp steamer in Mexico which they called the Lytton. The now publicity-shy ex-Admiral chugged into Chatham Bay, August 9, 1903, under the *nom de guerre* "Captain Shrapnel." On this trip the devious Palliser had hedged his bets. Rather than relying solely upon Fitzgerald's information, which was looking by now more than a little shopworn, he turned to two other sources.

The first was the testimony of one Bob Flowers who had featured in several expeditions to Cocos during the 1870s. On his last, he claimed to have lost his footing while reconnoitering a section of Chatham Creek and to have then tumbled down a steep embankment into a hollow. Momentarily stunned, he quickly apprehended that his downward progress had been painfully broken by a wall of stones. When he had finally succeeded in gathering his wits about him, Flowers spied a crevice in the wall near ground level. Putting his eye to it, he was dumbfounded by the sight of gold ingots stacked six feet high within.

Lacking a proper set of tools with which to pry the rocks free, Flowers headed back to his ship but not before taking a rough set of bearings. Once aboard, he divulged his secret to a friend and the following day they searched for the embankment. To their mutual distress Flowers was quite unable—thanks, perhaps, to the bump he had taken on the head—to deal artfully with his own bearings and, try as he might, never managed to retrace his steps to the hollow.

Palliser's second lead was flimsier still. Attributed to a Swedish sailor, Lars Peter Lund, it was an unauthenticated section of a logbook alleged to have belonged to the shadowy Chapelle who claimed to have smuggled it off the *Relampagos.* Within were details describing the site of Benito's hoard.

Only an enemy like Gissler would ever have wished such clues on Palliser. But then the Admiral was the closest thing so far to a rival as regards sheer tenacity. Nothing and no one seemed capable of putting him off the trail. This time it led back and forth between Wafer and Chatham Creeks. Montmorency and "Shrapnel" found neither caves nor stone walls in either locale, though they did come upon a suspicious-looking bluff. Unfortunately, it had collapsed in an avalanche of tree trunks, boulders and tons of earth so that if a cave had been dug into it, as the ever sanguine Palliser believed, it was now probably beyond the power of mortal men to reach. The two in question gave up, exhausted, on August 23.

Back they came the following year, this time in different vessels and on opposite sides of a dispute that once again made a big splash in the English papers. The presence of Lord Fitzwilliam, one of England's wealthiest peers, added a new dimension to the story. He and Palliser cruised into Chatham Bay with 100 eager hands on the luxury yacht *Veronica* and almost immediately began blasting. Neither man happened to have a permit to do so; this lack of official assent did nothing to repair relations with the Costa Rican officials as soon as they received word of it.

Over the years, even as the specter of pirate treasure waned with each decamping expedition, the Costa Rican Government waxed increasingly proprietary whenever matters turned upon their now famous and popular Isla de los Cocos. Stamps were eventually issued bearing its likeness, gunboats routinely patrolled its shores and limited but exclusive concessions upon its treasure rights were granted with a regularity that was enough to set poor Gissler's teeth on edge. Cocos, after all, had by now become nothing short of a national treasure. Whether the millions of Davis or Benito or Thompson would ever be unearthed, seemed somehow beside the point. Cocos was on the map!

Fitzwilliam and the indefatigable Palliser wasted no time on random clues. Instead, they made straight for the avalanched cliff face which they reckoned to be their best bet. His Lordship, though a mortal man, possessed among his admirable stores more than sufficient dynamite to blow to blazes the welter of tree trunks and boulders obstructing the presumed cave's mouth.

In the course of their exertions, Montmorency apparently turned up in the *Rosmarine* and took to duplicating their efforts from a spot nearby. Here versions wildly differ but that which made its way into print had the competing parties locked in a desperate grab for treasure. Desperation ended in mayhem. The truth seems to be, unhappily for all concerned, that a premature blast of dynamite took the life of one man and injured several others, Fitzwilliam among them. Having been treated to a taste of his own mortality in the form of a chunk of flying debris which landed upon his head and all but killed him, Fitzwilliam found that his interest in the cave, and indeed Cocos Island in general, suddenly flagged. Had it *not,* Fleet Street papers might have made hay with a juicy sequel to the story for hardly was the *Veronica* gone from Chatham Bay when a launch of Costa Rican soldiers hove to with guns drawn.

This performance was to be Fitzwilliam's and Palliser's swan song on Cocos Island though Hervey de Montmorency stayed on with his partner Harold Gray from the *Rosmarine*. Gissler had taken a liking to them both and proposed that they investigate a theory he had long harbored concerning the silver of the *Relampagos*. He believed that after her crew had anchored under a headland between Wafer and Chatham Bays, near the "haystack" rock of Cabral's grandfather, the pirates had winched Benito's silver to a plateau above and there buried it. In support of Gissler's notion the discovery of an eyebolt, rusty with age, set into the bluff just below the top was presumed, with some justification, to have once secured a tackle. Gissler and Montmorency concluded that, were they to dig a trench seven feet deep across the plateau, they would surely hit upon any large cache of hidden treasure. It evidently was *not* there and Montmorency and Gray soon sailed off empty-handed, leaving Gissler very much to fend for himself.

The Governor's colony had long since drifted off and taken with them his high hopes of developing tobacco and ginseng as cash crops. His credibility with the Costa Rican Government was nil and his treasure-hunting star woefully dimmed. Fated to have spent seventeen years of his life on a tropical island, he ended it in the jungle of New York City at the height of the Great Depression, improvident but for a single gold doubloon dated 1788.

With the exception of American William Beebe's 1925 Oceanographic Expedition, Britons in the main continued to dominate Cocos Island exploration. In 1924 Scottish racing-car driver, Captain (later Sir) Malcolm Campbell, holder of various world speed records in boats as well as automobiles, met up by chance with an old friend, K. Lee Guinness, on the island of Madeira. Campbell was an irrepressible optimist with a love of adventure and all things technical; Guinness possessed wealth, a handsome yacht called the *Adventuress,* and plenty of free time. Herein, at least by the standards of treasure hunting, were the personalities and ingredients ideally suited to a marriage made in heaven.

The Salvage Islands lay temptingly close to Madeira and the two first debated whether to cut their teeth on a legendary cache reportedly buried there in the early nineteenth century. No sooner had they begun to investigate the story, however, when local gossip reached them of an unidentified team having recently departed from the Salvage Islands after making a major find. Better, reckoned the pair, to return to England, regroup and take up where Palliser and Fitzwilliam had left off on Cocos. Campbell had heard talk of a recent spate of dynamiting there and convinced himself that the easiest way to determine what lay beneath the ton of avalanched rock and soil was either with the aid of technology or through what may be considered its polar opposite—mysticism.

The first option might at least be tested on English soil or, indeed, *in* it, for the device seized upon by Sir Malcolm was an early prototype of the modern metal detector. Whatever success this particular model might have had with a superior conductor such as gold or silver, Campbell never ascertained. Failing to live up in the slightest to its name with pieces of scrap iron he had buried in pits dug at random about his paddock, Campbell turned his back on empiricism and instead put the question of buried treasure to a medium. Might it perchance rest in Keating's Cave up Chatham Creek, he wondered? "No," whispered the medium. "The treasure lies up high, perhaps 1000 feet above sea level."

Though impressed, for here was a truly novel and untested approach to a hoard which so far had eluded everyone, Guinness and Campbell sailed from Southampton in 1926 with a copy of Nicholas Fitzgerald's much debased instructions, passed on to them by the kindness of Curzon-Howe's son.

Quite apart from discovering a fortune on Cocos, Campbell professed to be much interested in solving the mystery of what had befallen Captain Boag.

Had the unfortunate man been accidentally drowned, as Keating claimed? Or had Keating indeed walled him up, his pockets stuffed with a part of the *Mary Dyer's* treasure? Campbell was also taken with the legend that certain Incan nobles had eluded capture by the Spanish Conquistadors and had somehow found their way to Cocos Island where, for generations, they had been hiding around the 1900-foot Mount Iglesias. Here, Campbell agreed, was the perfect place in which to store their gold and an ideal lookout for any visitors. Campbell's sympathies for such an improbable tale were, no doubt, emboldened by the whispered words of the medium, "high up."

After landing on Cocos Island, Campbell and his men spent a couple of harrowing nights camped upon the beach at Chatham Bay. "The land crabs," Campbell later informed the readers of the London *Sunday Express*, October 6, 1929, "are brutes as big as one's two fists. They have been known," he emphasized, "to eat a wounded man alive." Elsewhere in the article Campbell claims to have found, in the rugged center of the island, the ruins of an Inca Sun Temple.

The first order of business, for the crew of the *Adventuress*, was to investigate details of the Fitzgerald file. One was advised to pace off a certain distance up Chatham Creek until "this brought one to a great rock in the top of which was a hole big enough to take a man's thumb." A crowbar fitted into the opening would move the rock and reveal an entrance to the treasure cave. Wrote Campbell:

> We searched at once for the creek and found it, a rippling little stream. I could scarcely contain my excitement when I proceeded to high water mark at the bottom of the creek and, with compass in hand, stepped off forty paces. Having done this with some difficulty, I stopped and turned north but the only bare rock I could see was some little distance out at sea, a huge table-top still partly covered by the sea.
>
> We worked our way inland but could find no rock or boulder that might apply to our clue. I could not keep my eyes off the huge bare rock out at sea and decided to investigate it, two other large rocks lay in a direct line nearer the beach and I investigated both these too. On none of them could I find a hole or see any crack where an opening could possibly be hidden.

Campbell and his men searched several different locations around the island including Observation Hill, a tall conical rise that dominates Chatham Bay and behind which was said to lie a cave filled with gold and silver.

Effecting a landing at Observation Hill—its steep sides sprayed with a constant wash of swells—Campbell found difficult, dangerous and ultimately unrewarding. Returning there a few days later, he did discover the ruins of an old stone house and a barely discernible path which, surprisingly enough, led to the edge of a cliff.

Another hill nearby seemed more promising, although the author declined to illuminate his readership as to why this was so. At any rate, Campbell and his men climbed it and then worked their way down toward the camp. Here, he reported,

> in the dense undergrowth behind the camp we found what I am still convinced is the real site of the buried treasure—a nearly dried-up stream whose course had been diverted by a landslide into that of the first stream we saw on the first day. Great boulders lay about in gigantic profusion as though they had either been blasted out of the hillside or brought down by a landslip. I took all sorts of bearings from this creek and spent three days investigating rocks and boulders which seemed to fit in with the clue. The men were convinced that somewhere under one particular group of rocks lay the treasure ... We found one huge rock exactly on the spot given by the compass bearing and when we had scraped it clean of moss and fern, earth and tree roots, we discovered a great crack running around three sides of it.

Lacking the services of a medium, Campbell and his men simply blew away the entire top of the rock. Having successfully done so and the air now filtered clear of dust and powder, the anxious crew moved in close for a look. Fierce was the tropical sun above them and only for a few minutes did the blast give them a reprieve from the torment of swarming insects which constantly bedeviled them. Not a sign of the door did they find.

Campbell at least was able to turn his mere seventeen days on Cocos into a semblance of gold with a best-seller titled *My Greatest Adventure*. Despite his unsatisfactory experimentation with electrical conduction he set a standard of sorts for subsequent expeditions. In future they would be more lavish, more technologically inspired, indeed, more expensive, the high costs often being shared among large numbers of stockholding partners.

Malcolm Campbell's fame as a sportsman and the popularity of his book about Cocos Island lent it a notoriety that attracted increasing numbers of treasure hunters as did, in a curious way, the general collapse of the world economy. During the Great Depression, probably more expeditions were mounted in search of the Cocos riches than at any other time. These were difficult years in which to make an honest dollar and the lure of quick profits from buried gold exerted a powerful claim upon the imagination and the avarice of men.

Captain Tony Mangel caught the Cocos "bug" in 1926 in Sydney after investigating Keating's now famous letters in the Nautical and Travellers' Club. The instructions, we may recall, advised the following:

> Disembark in the Bay of Hope between two islets in water five fathoms deep. Walk 350 paces along the course of the stream then turn north northeast for 850 yards. Stake, setting sun, stake, draws the silhouette of an eagle with wings spread. At the extremity of sun and shadow: cave marked with a cross. Here lies the treasure.

This sole clue had fascinated and baffled previous expeditions, some of whose members *had* observed that, with the setting sun in perigee with Mount Iglesias, the island's highest volcano, a shadow roughly resembling an eagle's head was thrown across the Bay of Hope.

En route from Sydney in 1927 Mangel stopped off at Cocos just long enough to observe this very phenomenon and returned two years later in his yacht *Perhaps I.* In the meantime he had worked over certain bearings included in Fitzgerald's documents and had developed an entirely novel theory as to the whereabouts of the Treasure of Lima. He first surmised that the treasure had been hidden in September but that the notes had been taken down in winter. Second, he concluded that the indications were inaccurate and "this," he told his closest friends, "is where the secret lay." Mangel later reported:

> They were false because we were now in the twentieth century and therefore working with the sextant and other accurate instruments which took into account the declination of the compass. Thompson, on the other hand, had hidden his treasure in 1820 and had worked out the spot with an octant when he had come back to fetch some of the treasure sometime between 1820 and 1823. His watch, however, was only relatively accurate and his compass pointed to a well-determined magnetic north. Thompson's calculations would have to be made all over again, repeating the same mistakes and using data from the nautical tables of the years between 1802 and 1823. Corrected in this way, the point I obtained in 1929 was the following: five degrees thirty minutes seventeen seconds latitude north and eighty-seven degrees zero minutes forty seconds longitude west. Within a hundred yards of that spot lay the treasure.[5]

Thus, Mangel believed the Treasure of Lima had been hidden north-north-east of Muele Island in the Bay of Hope and, in fact, he came upon a cave at just that location only accessible for a few hours at low tide. Inside, lacking proper lighting, he managed to dig down approximately a yard until his spade struck against something hard, possibly, he thought, a layer of protective stones.

Now Mangel was working against time and particularly the action of the rising tide which washed sand down into his pit as fast as he could remove it. Absorbed in his work, Mangel suddenly realized his dinghy had lodged under a protruding rock in the cave as the water rose and, frantically struggling against time and tide, he barely escaped drowning. The alarming incident apparently made such an impression upon him that he never again returned to the cave.

Mangel's new data seems to have found its way into the hands of a shadowy Belgian adventurer named Petrus A. Bergmans who is credited in most accounts of the Cocos story with a bona fide discovery. Scouting the Bay of Hope in 1931 not far from the site of Mangel's cave, Bergmans allegedly uncovered a two-foot gold Madonna which he reportedly sold in New York City.

"Clues have been the downfall of generations of treasure hunters," Commodore Frank Worsley sagely informed readers of the March 1934 issue of the *London Illustrated News*. "Clues do not enter into our program."

The distinguished captain of the *Endurance* during Ernest Shackleton's acclaimed Antarctic campaign of 1914–16, Worsley was referring to an ambitious enterprise, registered as Treasure Recovery Ltd., which had been floated on the London Stock Exchange in 1932. TRL's abortive expedition to Cocos Island a year later received the loan of a luxury steam yacht, the *Queen of Scots,* belonging to Anthony Drexel of the Philadelphia banking family, and was headed by a smooth-talking roué named Captain Charles Augustus Arthur. A former aide-de-camp to Sir Hari Singh, the fabulously wealthy Maharaja of Kashmir, Arthur had been implicated in the notorious "Mr. A" trial of the 1920s.[6] On TRL's maiden voyage he managed to get the entire crew of the *Queen of Scots* arrested by furious Costa Rican authorities after planting the Union Jack at Wafer Bay and claiming Cocos Island in the name of the British Crown.

This time, TRL's director, a figure named Alers-Hankey, touted his venture as a technical watershed and attracted better than £10,000 in risk capital, exploiting in the process Worsley's good name. Investors were cheered to learn that TRL would utilize all the latest treasure hunting gadgetry including "portable ratiometers" equipped with "rapier-electrodes" in tracking down the elusive Cocos Island fortune and would thereby seize the higher scientific ground in what was pledged to prove *the* progressive model for all future expeditions.

All the more ironic, then, that its disciples should slide from so lofty a plane and precipitately abandon their noble ideals for the likes of a string in a bottle. Such, however, proved Treasure Recovery's grotesque fate.

Unbeknownst to either Commodore Worsley or the stockholders, the avatar of this inglorious descent was an equivocal Belgian felon named Petrus A. Bergmans.

A few weeks before TRL's flagship, *Veracity*, was due to set sail for Cocos Island, George Lane happened to pay a visit to the syndicate's London offices. A stoker in the British Navy recently returned from duty in Colombia, Lane had read Worsley's piece in the *Illustrated News* and by the purest chance had with him information concerning treasure buried on Cocos. The only real problem was that the better part of it was locked away with a prisoner in Antwerp jail.

The two of them, explained Lane, had met on the *Caribea* of the Hamburg-American Line and, during the voyage, Bergmans had told him a very convincing story of discovering a treasure of gold, silver and church ornaments and jewels while a castaway on Cocos Island in September 1929. Lane, for his part, was there to represent his friend and only knew the fortune lay safely in a "large cave near a certain creek."

Not all TRL directors were charmed by Lane's tale. Captain Arthur, however, was impressed and so seemed his partner Alers-Hankey who, in a breathless "progress report" hastily mailed out to TRL stockholders, opened with the portentous words: "The company is now in possession of certain clues ... "

Captain Polkinghorne, a veteran of Arthur's previous expedition, was despatched to Antwerp for the purpose of interviewing Bergmans. Himself familiar with the island, Polkinghorne came away convinced that, at the very least, so too was the young Belgian engineer. Among other things, Bergmans was able to describe in detail the tumbledown remains of Gissler's settlement which he claimed to have occupied during his enforced sojourn.

The gist of Bergmans's account was that he had departed San Pedro, California in late July 1929 on the *Westward* under Captain H. Peterson, with a "party from the movie colony." Caught in a hurricane off the Nicaraguan coast, the *Westward* "foundered with all hands" on September 25—all but himself and her Captain. Adrift in a lifeboat, the pair bobbed on towering seas for three days until making landfall at Cocos Island.

One morning while out foraging, Bergmans trod upon a spot where the undergrowth suddenly gave way beneath him. Thereupon he discovered an opening leading to a natural cave forty paces long by fifteen wide.

> I saw stacks of gold and silver, bars and coins piled loosely
> on the floor, large quantities of golden ornaments such as
> are used in churches, numbers of gold statues resembling
> those found in Roman Catholic churches, large chests full of
> jewellery and precious stones, two large unopened chests,
> and the skull and bones of a man. In company with Peterson,
> I later removed about half a sackful of the treasure and

secreted it in two secluded spots on the island. We then
sealed and covered up the entrance to the cave.[7]

For Petrus Bergmans, good fortune surely came in threes. First he was snatched
from a watery grave; next he blundered upon one of the world's most sought-after
treasures and finally, on October 16, a "derelict ship's boat" providentially washed
ashore at the island. In her, he and Peterson put to sea (or so Bergmans claimed) on
November 30 and were rewarded for their pains on December 11 when "sighted
and picked up by the German steamer *Nachwezeld.*" Bergmans stated that he and
Peterson sold a quantity of jewelry they took off Cocos Island for $56,000 to an
"underworld firm" in New York City known as the Strauss Brothers. Peterson then
returned to his home in Portland, Oregon where he died in 1932.

Bergmans promised to lead TRL to the cave for a 10 percent cut of the treasure
and, in the nature of an advance, asked only that the syndicate make the payment of
a small bond to the Antwerp authorities towards his freedom. Upon conferring with
his superiors, Polkinghorne formally agreed to these conditions and, within a matter
of days, the newly liberated Belgian found himself strolling through a London spring.

To their credit neither Commodore Worsley nor the *Veracity's* crew knew anything of the bizarre arrangement with Bergmans whose very existence was kept
secret from all but the most inner circle of TRL. Pursuant to orders, Bergmans arrived
independently at Puntarenas in late March, posing as a mining engineer. The tight-
lipped Belgian carried off his charade brilliantly, flashing bogus credentials for a non-
existent mine with the kind of sangfroid that might have given his duplicitous han-
dlers pause.

Led by Alers-Hankey, they had meanwhile been hatching a plot to remove Captain Arthur from the expedition. *Veracity* reached Barbados on
April 4 and was in Panama City by early May when Arthur received word
through the British Legation that the Costa Rican Government wanted no
part of him. In any event, when the *Veracity* docked at Puntarenas on June 6,
1934, she did so without her flamboyant captain.

Petrus Bergmans (his vital role in the mission now spelled out for the first time
to Worsley and the crew) was now pleased to take over Arthur's cabin on the short
run to Cocos Island. At 3:50 P.M. on Sunday, June 10, Worsley telegraphed President
Jimenez of their safe arrival. An Associated Press stringer quickly latched on to the
story and by the very next day the good news was out: the *Veracity* had arrived!

For all the breathtaking speed of modern communications, treasure hunting on
Cocos Island would yet prove a dilatory business. Despite the prodding of Commodore Worsley and his mining consultant, Richard Studdert, Bergmans seemed of a
mind to temporize. While the two professionals went about their own business, days
passed during which the Belgian simply loafed and muttered to himself and took
only the most dilatory of bearings. Utterly lost as he was to some maddening strain of
island funk, rational minds could not reach him.

Finally, over breakfast one morning, Bergmans came clean. "I've got it, Mr. Studdert," he exclaimed. "You remember how I told you in London that when I first found the treasure in 1929 I took away a small part of the main treasure and cached it on the beach where I could lay my hands on it quickly at some future date? Well, I recall now that in order to be sure of the spot I buried a beer bottle under a nearby palm tree on the beach right here in Wafer Bay. In the bottle I put a long piece of string. All I have to do is put one end of the string against the tree, run the string out in a certain direction and, right at the other end of it, we'll find my cache!"[8]

Much to their relief, Worsley and Studdert, under Bergmans's direction, indeed uncovered a bottle of Gambrinus Beer in eighteen inches of sand. Putting the two men through their slightly foolish paces, Bergmans worked over the precise route to the twine's end more than a few times until at last he seemed thoroughly satisfied with the business. Over a spot he then marked in the wet sand with an "X," Bergmans instructed the men to once again dig.

Dig they did, that day and into the next and a good deal deeper than Bergmans can ever have managed as a castaway with his bare hands! When it was all over and nothing had been unearthed, no one appeared more crestfallen than Bergmans himself who retired sulking to his hammock. Finally driven out by hunger, he thereafter nursed a paralyzed arm which hung limply from his side and may have helped to deter Worsley's infuriated crew from throttling him to within an inch of his life. Worsley and his men conjectured that Bergmans had probably secretly hidden the bottle only the night before. Moreover, it was later confirmed that Gambrinus had not even begun to brew their popular beverage until 1932.

Deprived of clues, Treasure Recovery now fell back on its erstwhile stock-in-trade. Studiously bent over the dials of their highly touted ratiometers and potentiometers, Worsley's team combed beaches and creeks alike for weeks to no purpose. Growing more disheartened by the day, the Englishman began to slide into a tropical lassitude all recognized as fatal to their mission. By mid-July, with little to show for their efforts, Worsley and Studdert could see that the men had had enough and the expedition duly received the go-ahead to weigh anchor and head for home.

TRL ended its days in the ignominy of an English bankruptcy court where it finally came to light that 90 per cent of their working capital had somehow been expended in "administrative costs" at the London headquarters. Captain Arthur died in 1939.

Word that young James Alexander Forbes had ended his short life at Puntarenas, Costa Rica in 1821 would have come as a revelation to his wife, the former Anita Maria Galindo of Santa Cruz, California, no less than to their twelve children.

It may be recalled that a James Forbes had served as physician and first mate on the *Mary Dyer* under fellow Scotsman, William Thompson, and that the two had absconded with eleven longboat loads of Peruvian treasure which they buried on Cocos Island. Captured by the authorities, they were spared the hangman's noose on condition they revealed the whereabouts of the *Mary Dyer's* cargo. Hoodwinking their escorts, the pair escaped into the Cocos jungle and were rescued months later by a passing whaler. Thompson and Forbes afterwards parted company at Puntarenas where the latter allegedly died.

In fact, evidence unearthed by Hancock and Weston suggests that the canny Scotsman sailed very much alive through the Golden Gate to the fledgling port of Yerba Buena (later San Francisco) in 1822. Here Forbes is believed to have found an ideal land in which to begin a new life.

Well before the days of the early Conestoga wagon trains, the Gold Rush and statehood, California was a freewheeling land where a man's past counted for less than his pioneering spirit. Forbes reputedly enjoyed both, along with native shrewdness. He was thought to have spent two years in California taking the lie of the new land and then sailed quietly away.

Three years later Forbes was back for good, gentleman suitor to Señorita de Galindo whose family were the proprietors of a hacienda encompassing most of present-day Santa Clara. Believed to hold a medical degree from a Scottish university, Forbes never practiced in California and shunned the title "Doctor." Instead, he devoted himself to horticulture, real estate, industry and sundry good works. Well-heeled in his own right, Forbes let it be known that, during his three years' absence, he had visited family in Scotland, tidied up his affairs and made a small fortune in gold somewhere "down south."

The very embodiment of rectitude, James Forbes acted as British vice-consul in Santa Clara and through generous donations of property and capital helped found the University of Santa Clara. A partner in the prosperous New Almaden Mines, Forbes was plaintiff in an 1863 Supreme Court property case, ultimately found in his favor after the intercession of President Abraham Lincoln.[9]

This most respectable of men died in the bosom of his family and left behind him a sizeable estate. He may also have died in the bosom of the Lord for it was said that, throughout the whole of a blameless life, Forbes's only marked deviation from habit was that, near its end, he found religion. A good deal more startling, unbeknownst to all but his lawyer and a notary, Forbes bequeathed to his eldest son a treasure map.

James Alexander Forbes II was, by all accounts, a man thoroughly occupied with a wide range of business concerns. He had neither the inclination nor the need for such a treasure map and thus did nothing with it. His first-born, James Alexander Forbes III, nevertheless seems to have had better reason to do so. He was more adventurous than his father and less wealthy because, by this time, the Forbes estate had been divided up among so many heirs. Striking out on his own he did well for himself in the southern California citrus business until the Great Depression all but wiped him out.

In 1937 Forbes III was ready to take a gamble on the Treasure of Lima and cast about for a partner wealthy and enterprising enough to join him. In Douglas Narron, a prominent Corona, California insurance broker, he found such a man. After carefully assessing Forbes's family documents on Cocos Island, he pronounced them authentic. "No father," reasoned Narron, "would knowingly send his son on a fool's errand."

Narron in turn brought another partner aboard—George Bosley of Balboa Island—and the two then spent months in a frustrating search for the ideal vessel, suffering in the process the ridicule of countless skippers who were often rudely ill prepared to swallow the story of a $60,000,000 treasure. One who did had, by chance, taken an interest in accounts of expeditions to Cocos Island over the years. Hugh M. (Cappie) Davenport was known as a crusty, irascible old salt with a reputation for petulance. Still, he was a yachtsman of proven ability; he owned a fine sixty-foot craft and, best of all, was primed to set her sail for Cocos in late 1939. Just as they were ready to set sail the sixty-seven-year-old Forbes dropped dead.

The irony of carrying forward the mission was that "outsiders" were now called upon to persuade "Jimmy" Forbes IV that the behest of his great-grand-father—following a faded treasure map to a stretch of sand on an obscure Pacific island—was that of a reasonable man. This Narron, Bosley and Davenport succeeded in doing and, on November 23, 1939, the *Spindrift* made port at Puntarenas.

The Forbes Expedition, oddly enough, was granted digging rights on Cocos Island until such time as its "entire surface [had] been turned over with a shovel." Unfortunately, this extraordinary largesse availed the team but little on its first attempt which lasted barely ten days. The clash of egos was to blame as were the differing interpretations of great-grandfather's directions. For his part, "Cappie" felt that Forbes was going about the business all wrong and simply refused to budge from his cabin.

On Christmas Day, 1939 the party arrived back at Puntarenas in anything but a festive mood. Davenport believed he not only knew the site of the treasure but that, as owner of the *Spindrift,* he had first claim upon it. Forbes, supported by Narron, espoused the view that the owner of the map took precedence. Costa Rican authorities made a pretense of carefully weighing the issues and then, since it was most probably money that finally talked, found in favor of Jimmy Forbes.

The second Forbes Expedition to Cocos was a truly California-style extravaganza. A grand curiosity when she docked at Puntarenas on March 5,

1940, the *Stranger* was, in the words of Hancock and Weston, "a beautiful double-ender of fifteen knots, fitted with every modern convenience, and worth even in those days around half a million dollars." Two hundred and fifty tons of luxury yacht belonging to millionaire Fred Lewis, she boasted a crew of fifteen as well as a beautiful young wife, an archeologist, a painter-publicity man-photographer, Lewis, Jimmy Forbes and an elderly gentleman guest known simply as "The Seaman." Among the equipment aboard figured the very latest in metal detectors and, most central to the mission, power-lifting winches.

Construction of the Chatham Bay camp took much of the first two days and was greatly facilitated by ten young Costa Rican soldiers sent along by their government as "chaperones" to the expedition. When they were through, Jimmy had eight roomy tents set up and a portable kitchen with an adjoining fourteen by twenty screened mess hall. The food was said to have been excellent. On the third day, when it came to the actual task of excavating, there was no dissension. All agreed, after a thorough study of the bearings handed down by James Forbes I, that the *Mary Dyer's* sumptuous cargo most likely lay fifty feet to the south of the previous year's dig. On hand to verify their assumption was the newest generation of gold-divining tools. Dubbed the "Doodle-bug," it promptly brought forth reassuring noises almost directly over the area in question.

According to Forbes's sworn statement, it was he rather than Thompson who had been responsible for the taking of the Treasure of Lima in the first place and it was he, also, who had been responsible for its burial in the last. To that end the *Mary Dyer's* first mate made a careful survey of the Chatham Bay beach and found to his satisfaction that, beneath its sand, ran a rocky shelf capable of supporting great weight. Picking out a section below high-water mark Forbes set his crew to digging. When the men had completed the task some days later, they laid the Treasure of Lima in the trench, covered it with two feet of stones and rubble, plus several layers of rag mattress, and finally dropped a great stone slab over the top. As a final touch, Forbes chiseled the outline of an anchor into its rough face, took careful bearings of the site and then made good his escape.

Now 120 years later his great-grandson, behind the controls of the "Doodlebug," thrilled to the expectations of homing-in on the dream of a lifetime. Here, naturally enough, the story becomes confusing once again. Later, one member of the crew recalled what happened next:

> There was nothing else to do but dig—so we dug. The going was pretty tough on account of the many huge boulders and some water which seeped in. A boom, with a hand winch was erected and handled the boulder situation very well.

> After working for about two days we uncovered a boulder
> with an arrow and a large "K" inscribed on one side and a
> pair of boots on the other. Everyone was convinced that this
> was the mark left by John Keating, but we were unable to
> derive any benefit from the find.
>
> We continued on with the hole to the extent of about sixty
> feet long, twenty feet wide and sixteen feet deep. At the same
> time, having more manpower than we really needed, we picked
> out several likely spots in the same locality and had some of
> our men dig there. There were no results of course.[10]

Indeed? Had not August Gissler supposedly come upon a similar "K"
inscription with an arrow alongside it years before? What could such a find
mean, lying many feet beneath sand and rock under the tide at Chatham Bay?
Further, where was great-grandfather's anchor?

Finally, why did this second Forbes expedition capitulate so readily?
The crew member concluded:

> I will say that there was a very systematic, honest effort made
> to uncover something. We found the rock filled with some
> kind of ore which caused the Doodle-bug to function at that
> particular spot. After ten days of continual digging without
> any encouraging signs, everyone became quite disheartened
> and from then on it was just a question of staying longer or
> going home ...

Home they went after little better than a fortnight, but did they necessarily go empty-handed? Curiously, Jimmy Forbes returned on a third, fourth and
fifth expedition and some suspect that he might have mounted as many as
three more. Why? Was he simply the greatest glutton for punishment since
Gissler? Or had he truly uncovered the Treasure of Lima and, unwilling to split
it with the Costa Ricans, taken it off Cocos piecemeal?

For the record, Jimmy Forbes took away with him, for all his pains, nothing more than a broken section of gold chain and, by the late fifties, he and
his associates had reportedly invested over $100,000 to that meager end.

Arguably the best organized expedition ever to land at Cocos Island was
mounted in 1966 by rank amateurs. Its leader, Jacques Boucaud, came upon a
magazine article written by an ex-RAF pilot living in Canada whose expedition had spent what Boucaud reckoned was a paltry ten days at Wafer Bay. At
once fired by the treasure story and perplexed that so costly a mission had, in
the end, devoted so little time to uncovering a fortune of such magnitude, in

the autumn of 1964 he entered upon a thorough investigation of Cocos Island's history. Assisted by three young Parisian students, he mined the archives of *Le Monde* and a host of reputable French magazines, in addition to combing the Bibliothèque Nationale and the Musée Maritime.

To his astonishment, Boucaud soon discovered that much-publicized expeditions like the one conducted by the Canadians—in the main "rich dilettantes from America and Great Britain"—were less the exception than the rule. Securing detailed maps of the island, over the next two years Boucaud, his friends Charles, Rene and Jean-Pierre painstakingly secured all necessary equipment within the scope of their limited budget and familiarized themselves with the island by means of detailed maps which they marked with the sites of all the recorded expeditions which had preceded them.

Furthermore, Boucard divided his maps into thirds: one for Benito, one for "other pirates," and the last for the Treasure of Lima. So as to circumvent the vexatious Costa Rican authorities, the Frenchmen determined to bypass Puntarenas entirely, conduct their mission on Cocos in secret and depart unseen.

In September 1966 the men headed north from the Colombian port of Buenaventura and the cautious Boucaud has since kept his counsel as to the logistics of his subsequent landing at Wafer Bay. However he accomplished it, the mission's impedimenta—put together against a projected three-month sojourn—clearly covered most contingencies. Among the items carried were:

> a six-hundred-watt generator for the drill, a chain-saw, petrol, several kilos of explosives, a transistor radio, two short rifles with silencers, four walkie-talkies, cameras, pharmaceuticals, a tent, hammocks, diving tanks, a small dinghy, underwater pistols, Vietnam War-issue anti-dog spray, canned goods and four U.S.-made metal detectors.[11]

Despite all their research, the French team found themselves quite unprepared for the daunting scope of Cocos Island which is ten square miles of mist-shrouded virgin forest. To make matters worse, heavy rains immediately forced them to seek shelter for the first forty-eight hours in two abandoned huts near Wafer Bay which, after a thorough fumigation with DDT, afforded them a reasonably comfortable *pied-à-terre* in which to rest and take stock.

As soon as the weather cleared, the team took turns mounting an observation post above the Bay while the others reconnoitered. Jean-Pierre was the first to discover a thirty-yard-long cave inland beside a waterfall originally described in the narrative of Manoel Cabral. With the aim of secrecy, the team struggled to clear the cave of debris and transfer their gear, along with a pair of work tables, benches and a bookcase from the Wafer Bay huts—a job that required the better part of two days. Now feeling considerably more secure, no sooner had they set about a systematic survey of the various island sites on their agenda than Charles reported by walkie-talkie from Wafer Bay that a Costa Rican patrol boat was fast approaching, accompanied overhead by a single engine plane.

After lying low through the fourth day, Boucaud resumed operations and, late in the day, was reached again by Charles, this time from the eastern end of the island. Six hundred yards from Cabo Atrevida in the face of a 780-foot hill, Charles had come upon a fissure. Thoroughly overgrown with dense vegetation the crack, some 5 feet high, had only come to his attention thanks to the fact that he happened to have spied a number of wild cats issuing from it. After clearing away the undergrowth with his machete, Charles tossed a stone into the opening which "widened from bottom to top." To his amazement, the fall of the stone echoed back as if it had landed in a large "vault."

Boucaud instructed him to wait while he called in the others by walkie-talkie and retrieved torches from their "home" cave. Then together they all squeezed inside. Working their way into the cavern's recesses, the first thing they came upon was a skeleton seated on the floor with its back to the wall. The first thought that raced through Boucaud's mind was that here must be the remains of Keating's partner Boag. On closer examination, however, they made out a second skeleton curled up on its right side on the floor with a gaping hole in its skull. The seated figure still clasped the handle of an axe and stuck between its ribs was a knife. Clearly, the two individuals had murdered one another!

Carefully removing them to the sunshine outside Charles, who had recently been a medical student, studied the remains, after cutting away with scissors the tattered remnants of their clothing. In the course of his detailed examination he discovered that one wore a gold ring on its right hand, engraved with the initials AR and the date 15.3.41. The other sported a leather belt with a silver buckle and had by its side a leather knife-sheath carved with the initials GM. Drawing forth the knife from between the ribs of AR, Charles noted that it fitted perfectly into GM's sheath. To judge from the healthy state of their teeth, neither man appeared to have been more than thirty years old at the time of his death.

Meanwhile, deeper within the cave the explorers discovered a sort of museum of nineteenth-century artifacts including pickaxes, crowbars, a pewter oil-lamp hanging from a hook, several collapsed barrels, ceramic vessels in a basket, a large ceramic water jug wrapped with woven hemp, thick ropes with wooden blocks, two large piles of moldering jute sacks, a pair of bush-knives, a rusted flintlock, an open tool box and two wooden boxes, one stacked above the other.[12]

Each box measured roughly 20 inches wide by 28 inches high by a yard long, had metal handles and metal ornamentation. Burnt into the lid of the top box were, again, the initials GM. Inside were two yellowing shirts which came apart in their hands; a Holy Bible printed in Boston in the year 1840 and a leather-bound third volume of Captain George Vancouver's *A Voyage of Discovery to the North Pacific Ocean and around the Globe* (London, 1798) whose frontispiece bore the inked-in legend: "Property of Gerald Macintosh." And down towards the bottom, beneath rolls of tobacco, a revolver and a leather-bound box containing a quadrant, Boucaud and his men uncovered 1000 Spanish gold coins and fifteen long, thin, half-pound gold bars.

Remarkably, the second chest held an equal quantity of coins and gold. Along with it the young Frenchman discovered a ball of yarn, a wind-up toy and a faded newspaper "personal" signed by Thomas W. Gardiner of Chaptico, St. Mary's County, Maryland, dated July 28 of an indistinct year. It gave the description of a runaway mulatto slave, named William, accompanied by an offer of $50 reward for his return.

> In the corner near the fire we found pieces of a larger wooden crate which had been partially burned. In the tool box lay a board which contained nail holes and which was possibly fashioned from a wooden chest. Carved into it was an obviously unfinished inscription which bore the words, "The Bird IS."[13]

Such was the highlight of Boucaud's expedition, cut short by two weeks because of the onset of heavy rains. Who were these two men and what might have been the provenance of their small fortune? While the two appear to have been contemporaries of John Keating, whether they were about to bury their own treasure or had, in fact, just finished uncovering portions of another, is a mystery likely to remain so forever.

The British actress Moira Lister may have rued the day she ever laid eyes on a pirate map of Cocos Island. She was eleven at the time yet vividly recalls its contours and that it had belonged to her uncle, a priest, who, in turn, had received it from a dying sailor after administering him the Last Rites. Later on, recalls Miss Lister, the map was lost.

In 1987 in Monte Carlo she met the descendant of Admiral Cochrane, Victor Frederick Cochrane Hervey, Marquess of Bristol, who had followed his own ill-starred trail to Cocos Island some thirty-five years before. The elderly Marquess, not without a hint of his bygone wickedness and charm, wove a pretty tale for Lister. He had, he promised her, located the probable site of the Treasure of Lima on Chatham Beach. There was a photograph of him standing there pointing towards the spot to prove it![14]

Shortly before his death that same year Bristol bestowed upon her a map.

Casting about for the ideal man to lead her own expedition, Moira Lister found a highly decorated, Scripture-quoting, retired Army Colonel. Veteran of the Vietnam War, he impressed her with a noble pledge to invest his share of the fortune, if discovered, in a mission to free POWs. Lamentably, she admitted, the Colonel's love of Scripture proved less than perfect for, no sooner had he taken from her trusting hand a copy of Bristol's map and a $100,000 advance, than he disappeared into thin air.

Determined to carry on at all costs, Lister raised fresh capital, mustered a new team and eighteen hard months later arrived at Puntarenas with a new leader, an Englishman named Nicholas Head. Her tough luck continuing, and now suspecting that a curse hung over Cocos Island, she was laid low with a case of shingles and obliged to remain cooped up in a dingy hotel room while the rest of her team sailed on ahead.

Consolation of sorts came quickly from Head who made some interesting discoveries. Concentrating on Benito's silver, a treasure largely overlooked by previous expeditions, he had observed four palm trees planted, for some mysterious reason, precisely fifteen feet apart. Nearby, Head also chanced upon a moss-covered boulder with an arrow and what appeared to be a map scratched in its face. Head carried with him a copy of a document alleged to have been the sworn testimony of one of Benito's *Relampagos* crew the night before he was hanged. It read in part:

> She [*Relampagos*] was moored between two conical rocks which lay off the northeast of the island. The yards and light spars were set on deck and the vessel's sides covered in kelp to prevent any vessel from seeing her. A portion of the crew was sent to cut a look-out place and another portion to make the excavation on the point where the brig lay moored. A derrick was rigged and one hundred and seventy-five tons of silver dollars dumped into the excavation. The surface was covered with debris and young trees planted on top. This was called Pacific Deposit Number Two.

Head reckoned that 142 men had winched the silver up to the top of the bluff in half-hundredweight sacks and tipped it into a great ditch on the very point once worked over by Gissler and Montomorency. Now armed with Lister's $44,000 magnetometer, and receiving positive readings, the men dug two feet below the seven-foot depth reached by Gissler. Despite all the encouraging signs, however, the expedition found nothing.

Moira Lister had by now sufficiently recovered and was on the island, hopeful, if not entirely confident, that Bristol had not sent her on a wild-goose chase. To her considerable distress though, where Commodore Worsley's ratiometer, and the "Doodle-bug" of Jimmy Forbes had all seemingly failed, so too did the latest in state-of-the-art magnetometers along that rocky shelf at Chatham Bay. If the "mysterious crosses" and "laconic directions" sniffed at by Worsley back in 1934 had let down generations of treasure seekers, then so too had her magnetometer.

In the end "Fortune's slaves" might have done no worse than by simply turning to the frontispiece of Robert Louis Stevenson's *Treasure Island*. There one discovers a remarkably familiar map struck by the hand of Jim Hawkins. On this map, the treasure lies halfway between Skeleton Island on the south shore and Spyglass Shoulder to the west and roughly corresponds to John Keating's directions for a hoard he may well have moved to the south of Cocos Island in the 1840s. Hawkins and Long John Silver in the pirate classic are directed thus: "Tall trees, Spy-glass Shoulder, bearing a point to the N. of N.N.E. Skeleton Island E.S.E. and by E. Ten feet."

Wrote Stevenson:

> As we passed the two-pointed hill we could see the black mouth of Ben Gunn's cave ... A gentle slope ran up from the beach to the entrance to the cave ... It was a large airy place with a little spring and a pool of clear water, overhung with ferns. The floor was sand. Before a big fire lay Captain Smollett; and in a far corner, only duskily flickered over by the blaze, I beheld great heaps of coin and quadrilaterals built of bars of gold. That was Flint's treasure we had come so far to seek and that had cost already the lives of seventeen men from the Hispaniola. How many it had cost in the amassing, what blood and sorrow, what good ships scuttled on the deep, what brave men walking the plank blindfold, what shot of cannon, what shame and lies and cruelty, perhaps no man alive could tell ...

Much the same sentiments might well be expressed over the countless attempts to uncover Our Lady of Lima during the past 150 years. If anyone along the way has made off with her, they are not saying. For those who have tried and failed, perhaps Stevenson's final lines of *Treasure Island* strike a responsive chord.

> The bar silver and the arms still lie, for all that I know, where Flint buried them; and certainly they shall lie there for me. Oxen and wain-ropes would not bring me back again to that accursed island; and the worst dreams ever I have are when I hear the surf booming about its coasts, or start upright in bed, with the sharp voice of Captain Flint still ringing in my ears: "Pieces of eight! Pieces of eight!"

Oak Island

Every age is fed on illusions, lest
men should renounce life early and
the human race come to an end.
—Joseph Conrad
Victory

The mystery of the Oak Island "Money Pit," as it came to be known, first attracted the attention of a sixteen-year-old farm boy from Chester, Nova Scotia, in 1795. Two centuries, a half dozen lives and millions of dollars later, when, why and by *whom* this diabolically ingenious engineering feat was accomplished remains unanswered.

The youngster could hardly have picked a grander morning for a row on Mahone Bay. It was soon to be the summer solstice and Daniel McGinnis had risen with an early sun and fairly breezed through the day's chores. His parents, who had migrated in 1782 from New England, owned a 200-acre farm in rugged Lunenburg County and neither of them suffered idle hands lightly. The day's outing to Oak Island was an unusual treat for the boy; just *how* unusual was born out in subsequent years by the burgeoning moonscape of derelict shafts and sunken pits which scarred the island's easternmost shore.

Pulling for the island in his dinghy that morning in 1795, McGinnis could make out across several miles of calm Bay water the distinctive umbrellalike tops of the lush red oaks crowning Smuggler's Cove. Of the more than 350 islands dotting Mahone Bay, Oak alone was thought to foster such giants.

Previously known by other names, including Gloucester and Smith Island, developers in 1785 simply referred to it by the number "28." Surveyed at about the time Daniel's family settled, agents later divided the island into thirty-two lots of four acres each. Few had been sold to date and the island remained uninhabited. Reportedly, more than a few of the McGinnis' neighbors believed Oak haunted, a notion which doubtless prejudiced the developers' early hopes of selling land on the island.

The womenfolk around Mahone Bay objected to rearing children there after repeated sightings during the late eighteenth century of "strange burning lights." One popular legend even held that a pair of Chester fishermen had once dared to sail to Oak Island of an evening in order to investigate the phenomenon—and never returned. Perhaps nothing more than tall tales designed to frighten small children. Daniel for his part thrilled to such stories, particularly as it was common knowledge that a pirate colony *had* existed between 1632 and 1710 but a few miles south at Le Havre. Indeed, Mahone Bay was thought to have taken its name from the French word *mahonne,* meaning a swift and shallow-drafted Mediterranean sailing craft once greatly favored by pirates.

For a sixteen-year-old country boy growing up at the "civilized" turn of a century, all this was good value and hardly to be feared. Nevertheless, as he drew one last time on the oars and then glided through the clear, still waters of Smuggler's Cove at Oak Island, Daniel decided then and there to honor his mother's command and return home before dark.

Taking care now for the bottom of his dinghy as he hauled her up onto the pebbly beach, Daniel scanned the hill before him. It looked to be some thirty feet high and etched into its gentle slope was a barely discernible trail. This he followed to the top and from there gazed across the three-quarter-mile island which appeared separated at its midsection by a low swamp. On its western fringe stood a copse of young oaks dotted with numerous stumps. What immediately caught young McGinnis's eye was a lone towering oak whose lowest limb had apparently been sawn off some four feet from the trunk. Fifteen feet beneath it spread a saucer-shaped depression blanketed by red clover.

Moving in for a closer look and then walking round the depression, McGinnis reckoned that it must measure a dozen feet or more in diameter and that the fork of the great oak's lopped-off limb extended out over its very center. Odder still, the limb appeared *scored* as though it had once borne the friction of a heavy rope or cable.

On his way back to Chester later that day, Daniel decided to put in at the Vaughan place on the mainland not far north of Oak's landward shore. His friend Anthony, whose parents hailed from Rhode Island, was smart and fearless though barely thirteen. Anthony's uncle Daniel had owned a couple of lots on Oak Island before selling them off a few years back and the youngster had, on occasion, accompanied him there. Perhaps Anthony would know something about the curious old tree.

Cutting short his visit after learning nothing new on the subject, McGinnis rowed the three-and-a-half miles back to town where he meant to consult a second friend, John Smith. Born in 1775, Smith was therefore considerably older and had formed part of a group of American Tories known as the "United Empire Loyalists" who were evacuated to Nova Scotia after the defeat of the British in the American War of Independence. Already five years a married man, Daniel reckoned that if anybody would know what to make of his strange discovery it was almost certain to be his mentor, John Smith. If you were to have asked the boy himself, though, Daniel would have told you "pirates": the sawnoff limb, the rope burns and the broad depression—the whole thing had the look about it of Captain Kidd and buried treasure!

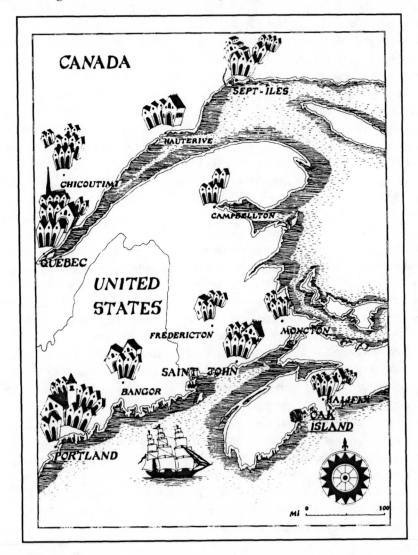

To McGinnis's delight, Smith was charmed by the notion of a possible treasure buried at Oak Island, although he balked at his friend's reference to the infamous privateer. After all, despite the fact that William Kidd, as everyone knew, had been arrested in 1699 in Smith's home town of Boston, he was not thought to have sailed as far north as Nova Scotia.

In any event, Smith readily agreed that the matter of the red oak bore needed looking into. On the morrow, then, chores or no chores, they would meet up. Young Vaughan might come too, if he wished. And Daniel would do well to spirit a shovel and pickax out of his father's barn just in case, before his rendezvous with Smith at the Chester boat landing.

The following morning it happened to be low tide when the three moored at the island. Stepping out of his boat, Smith immediately remarked on a glint of metal in the sheet-smooth water of Smuggler's Cove. Wading off-shore, he was surprised to see that it was a rusty eyebolt fixed to a partly submerged boulder. The trail that led them up the slope of the low hill was also peculiar. Granted, it had once been the custom of New England immigrant farmers to drive small herds of cattle across the 200-yard wide channel separating Oak from the mainland, the better to fatten them during the summer months. As Smith well knew, this method saved them the bother and expense of fencing. What then was a path—and quite a wide one at that—doing on the *seaward* end of the island?

Descending the hill slightly to where he could make out the swamp and everything before it, Smith found the great gnarled oak just as young Daniel had described it, sawn-off limb and all. Beneath it lay a saucerlike depression where the ground had visibly subsided. Peculiar, too, was the look of the surrounding copse for, despite the fact that all the old trees had evidently been cleared away and judging from the girth of the rotting stumps they had been hearty specimens indeed—no sign whatsoever of any construction remained. Briefly puzzled, Smith soon persuaded himself that these singular oaks had likely been felled by lumber cutters and sold years before to the shipyards at St. Johns.

By now the two younger boys, eager to get on with the business, had begun digging in the center of the depression and Smith saw no reason not to join them. As his spade bit cleanly through the carpet of red clover, he figured that if anything *was* buried thereabouts, they were certain to find it soon enough. In fact, John Smith would breathe his last more than sixty summers hence within sight of the very spot on which he now mused—without ever unraveling the secret of the clover-topped depression.

Although it was not printed until 1864 the story as told by McGinnis, Smith and Vaughan is well documented. In 1849 Smith gave the facts to Robert Creelman who was involved in an extensive dig that year on Oak Island.

Smith lived on the island almost continuously until his death in 1857. His daughter was employed by Judge Mather Des Brisay who, in 1870, published his *History of Lunenburg County* in which he recorded the story of the discovery and the subsequent excavations.

On June 25, 1795, Smith purchased Lot 18, the area surrounding the site of the discovery, and, by 1825, he had in addition acquired lots 16, 17, 19 and 20, comprising the twenty-four acres which make up the island's entire eastern end.

McGinnis, like Smith, settled on the island. Thanks no doubt to the extent of his mentor's holdings, the spot where young McGinnis first landed became known, little by little, as "Smith's Cove."[1]

Back in 1795 the boys found the labors in the center of the depression unaccountably easy. Far from encountering resistance, their picks and spades fairly licked through the earth. Then equally surprisingly, they suddenly met with solid rock at a depth of four feet. This eventually proved to be a complete layer of flagstones covering the entire area of the depression, only later identified as matching similar stone from the environs of the Gold River two miles distant on the mainland.

Once the diggers had cleared away the first obstruction to the rim of the depression and worked their way down a few feet further, it became apparent that they were excavating a clearly defined circular shaft. The earth was anything but compact as though the shaft had been dug and then later filled in. In fact, its hard blue clay walls bore numerous pick marks.

Six feet below the level of the flagstones, Smith and his astonished companions next met with a wooden tier. Oak logs, presumably fashioned from the old timber of the surrounding copse, had been securely set into the walls of the shaft. Smith figured the work had been done a good many years earlier since the uppermost sides of the logs were plainly rotten.

The treasure hunters now paused in their labors to reflect. Dislodging these formidable timbers would certainly require a great deal of effort. Besides, the young men of Chester could only guess as to whose land they were trespassing on. Better, it seemed, to cover their tracks, return home—keeping their counsel one and all—and wait upon a discreet investigation by the eldest among them. Referring to the Registry of Deeds at Bridgewater, Nova Scotia, Smith soon learned that Lot 18, that which encompassed the gnarled oak, belonged to one Casper Wollenhaupt. As it turned out, the Chester merchant just happened to be looking for a buyer and since, of the three, Smith alone could meet Wollenhaupt's asking price of £7.10, it was he who obtained the preference on June 25, 1795.

Beneath the oak tier which Smith had managed to chip out and pry loose as soon as he secured the title to Lot 18, the ground had settled a full two feet. Once again, Smith and his two partners found the digging remarkably easy. At the twenty-foot level a second platform of timbers presented itself, as did a third ten feet below. Now thirty feet down, the young men realized that, without technical assistance and increased manpower, the task before them was a daunting one. After all, who knew how far these regular intervals of devilishly well-set platforms continued?

Marking the depth they had reached with sticks, they then filled in the pit and attempted to enlist support. Such, however, proved difficult, as there were precious few farmers or fisherman in the area willing to waste their time fooling about with a hole in the ground. Eking out a living in Lunenburg County in the year 1795 was hard enough. Moreover, folks were suspicious. A number of Chester's strapping young farmers admitted that the thought of spending the night on Oak Island gave them pause. So it was that, notwithstanding the intriguing aspects of the discovery, Oak Island's pioneering dig now languished for fully nine years.

In the winter of 1804 Simeon Lynds of Onslow, Colchester County, Nova Scotia visited Chester on business. A relative of the Vaughans, it was arranged that he would be their guest at the family farm near Oak Island. Let in on Anthony's secret, Lynds decided to assess the matter for himself. He was about thirty years old and tolerably well-heeled, as were many of his acquaintances. Convinced, after reconnoitering the land around Smith's Cove, that his enthusiastic relative was quite possibly on to something worthwhile, he took leave of his hosts with a firm promise to return in early summer with money and equipment.

As good as his word, Lynds docked at Chester the following June with a boatload of tools and provisions sufficient for the needs of a full crew of workmen. The Onslow Syndicate, so-called, was backed by a consortium from Pictou, Colchester and Halifax counties that included a surveyor named Robert Archibald, his nephew, Captain David Archibald, and Sheriff Thomas Harris. Smith, Vaughan and McGinnis figured as full partners.

During the intervening years their pit had collapsed and, according to an article in *The Colonist* of 1804, "formed the shape of a sugar loaf resting on its apex." Onslow's first concern, then, was the removal of thirty feet of mud. This troublesome task accomplished, its workers came upon the sticks left behind by Smith and Co. in 1795. Ten feet below, Onslow struck another wooden platform, this one sealed with putty. A second oak platform was found at fifty feet, and a third at sixty was covered with an unidentified brown fibrous material. Only later was it confirmed to be coir, the tough fiber of the coconut palm, tons of which would one day be discovered beneath the beach at Smith's Cove. The nearest coco palm grew some 1500 miles from Oak Island and the fact that sixteenth to eighteenth-century shippers widely employed coconut fiber as "dunnage" may have meant little to Onslow's rural laborers.

A man named James McNutt, who worked the pit in the 1860s, stated that at about fifty feet Lynds's crew also uncovered a "tier of smooth stones from the beach with figures and letters cut on them," though his account is otherwise uncorroborated. Nevertheless, it is a fact that, at regular intervals of precisely ten feet, the Onslow Syndicate encountered oak tiers down to ninety feet, at which level the workmen made a singular discovery. Here, resting upon the customary wooden platform, lay a flat stone, reportedly inscribed on its bottom side with a double row of arcane symbols; "freestone," in the later words of McNutt, "and different from any on that coast."

Judge Mather Des Brisay described the oddity as being:

> about two feet long and one wide, with a number of rudely cut letters and figures upon it. They [Onslow] were in hopes this inscription would throw some valuable light on their search, but unfortunately they could not decipher it, as it was too badly cut, or did not appear to be in their own vernacular.[2]

Apparently the relic, whose alleged inscription only briefly troubled the frenzied workmen of Onslow, graced John Smith's fireplace at his Oak Island cottage for many years until finally being removed to Halifax by Mr. A. O. Creighton, treasurer of a later consortium, the Oak Island Eldorado Company (also known as the Halifax Company). Creighton was a partner of A. H. Creighton Bookbinders of 64 Upper Walter Street in whose window the stone was for some years prominently displayed, presumably as bait for would-be investors. James Leichti, a language professor at Dalhousie College, Halifax, deciphered the stone's inscription in 1864 to read: "ten feet below two million pounds are buried."

Unaccountably, the mysterious stone was eventually tossed out. One witness who recalled gazing at it in wonder as a young man at the turn of the nineteenth century was Harry W. Marshall. An employee of the original firm, he described it in 1935 in this manner:

> The stone was about two feet long, fifteen inches wide and ten inches thick, and weighed about 175 pounds. It had two smooth surfaces, with rough sides and traces of cement attached to them. Tradition said it had been part of two fireplaces. The corners were not squared but somewhat rounded. The block resembled dark Swedish granite, or fine grained porphyry, very hard, and with an olive tinge, and did not resemble any local Nova Scotia stone.
>
> While in Creighton's possession someone had cut his initials "J.M." on one corner, but apart from this there was

no evidence of any inscription either cut or painted on the stone. It had completely faded out. We used the stone for a beating stone and weight.

When the business was closed in 1919, Thomas Forhan, since deceased, asked for the stone, the history of which seems to have been generally known. When we left the premises in 1919 the stone was left behind, but Forhan does not seem to have taken it. A search of Forhan's business premises and residence two years ago [1933] disclosed no stone.[3]

Over the years, British and American cipher experts have drawn differing conclusions from the inscription. There is little question that the reading "ten feet below two million pounds are buried" is an accurate rendering of the alleged text. Doubts, however, as to the provenance of the inscription have been most recently raised by a computer technician at IBM's Crypto Competency Center in Manassas, Virginia, who considers the letter-for-cipher code so simplistic as to be highly suspect.

At any rate, the 1804 incident of the stone—inscribed or otherwise—set a disconcerting precedent. Convinced that the treasure always lay "just around the next corner," this and future Oak Island consortia, incontinent in their quest for fortune, often as not ran roughshod over crucial evidence, not unlike so many children in a candy store. Maintaining desultory records at the best of times, succeeding work crews managed to blight the trail to the Oak Island mystery in precisely the manner no doubt foreseen by its sardonic innovator.

What began as a single vertical shaft sometime prior to 1795 wound up as a welter of collapsed deathtraps, one barely discernible from the other, until the original itself became lost in the shuffle. Lamentably for the Onslow Syndicate, the incubus of the Oak Island mystery might be argued to date from the summer of 1804 when its workers, ninety feet below ground, injudiciously hoisted away the famous relic from what would come to be referred to, with eminently good cause, as the "Money Pit."

Wasting but little time on the stone which, after all, could only presage better things to come, the Onslow workers proceeded to tear away the oak platform beneath it just as they had done, without untoward incident, throughout the previous levels. This time, however, the shaft commenced slowly, but inexorably, to flood until the beleaguered crew found themselves hauling up "one tub of water for every two of earth."

Anticipating yet another platform at around ninety-eight feet an unidentified Onslow hand, on a late autumn afternoon in 1804, probed with his crowbar two feet down into the mud. Flushed with excitement, he shouted up to his companions that he had struck something across the full width of the shaft but that, this time, it hadn't the feel of an oak tier about it. When eagerly probed by other excavators, "some," according to *The Colonist*, "supposed it was wood, while others called it a chest."

Whatever it was—and the notion of its being a chest made an infinitely more gratifying option to the exhausted men—the thrilling discovery would have to wait until the following morning, on account of the impending darkness.

At the first light of dawn, however, Onslow's dazed workmen stared down into a pit now filled with sixty feet of turbid water! To make matters worse, subsequent bailing by bucket proved futile. After hours of grinding toil the water level, maddeningly enough, stood precisely at the same level, thirty-five feet from the surface. Finally, as if to put a fitting end to Onslow's operation that year, its newly acquired pump promptly exploded when it was set to work at ninety feet.

During the spring of 1805, Simeon Lynds decided to sink a shaft parallel to the original, fourteen feet to the southeast. Reaching a depth of 110 feet, he then had his crew angle a tunnel in towards the spot where the probe had made contact the previous autumn at the ninety-eight foot level of the Money Pit. Suddenly, the men inside the shaft were treated to a flood of swift-rushing water that sent them scrambling for their lives. A mirthless Lynds discovered the following day that the water level of his new shaft rested at precisely thirty-three feet down from where he stood.

The fiasco of Lynds's parallel shaft rang the death knell for his laborious, though short-lived, venture. It seemed that some fiendishly clever individual had certainly beaten him! Drawing Onslow's team to within an ace of what appeared to be an enormous chest or chests, his men had somehow tripped a booby trap that simply exploded in their faces. By a miracle, the flooding cost no lives but clearly some seal had been broken and it was now anybody's guess as to how to siphon off the flooded pits. That very question would remain moot for the next forty-five years.

By the time the second consortium was formed, Daniel McGinnis was dead and Vaughan and Smith getting on in years. Still, the two long-standing Oak Island residents maintained their resolute faith in the treasure, the search for which had already consumed most of their lives. Naturally enough, John Smith was only too eager to give his permission for the opening of a series of new shafts on his property in 1849.

The Truro Company was made up mostly of investors from the Nova Scotia town of Truro. It included Jotham McCully, John Gammell, Robert Creelman, a mining engineer named James Pitblado, another Lynds, this one Dr. Daniel B., unrelated to his namesake from Onslow. Sheriff Harris's faith had obviously survived the vicissitudes of the previous venture for he signed on with a modest investment in this one as well.

Before the bottom quite literally "dropped out" on Truro it would manage, in only two years' time, to sink four new shafts, drill straight through what appeared to be a stack of treasure chests and uncover an artificial beach at Smith's Cove.

Upon arriving at Oak Island in late spring 1849, Truro set immediately to work re-excavating the original pit which had once again collapsed. Within twelve days its laborers had reached a depth of eighty-six feet when they, too, were forced to the surface by flooding water. Bailing again proved fruitless and the new operation's digging ceased until later in the summer.

By that time a pod auger—a rather primitive 1 1/2-inch drill employed in those days in coal prospecting—had been ordered and, in the meantime, a platform was erected just above the pit's waterline at thirty-three feet. Once installed, drillers failed with their first two holes to bring up anything with their new auger but small stones and mud. The next three attempts, however, provided a breakthrough. Jotham McCully, writing to a friend in 1862, describes what transpired:

> The platform (of 1804) was struck at 98 feet just as the old diggers had found it when sounding with the iron bar. After going through the platform, which was five inches thick, and proved to be spruce, the auger dropped twelve inches and then went through four inches of oak; then it went through twenty-two inches of metal in pieces; but the auger failed to bring up anything in the nature of treasure, except three links resembling the links of an ancient watch chain. It then went through eight inches of oak, which was thought to be the bottom of the first box and the top of the next; then twenty-two inches of metal, the same as before; then four inches of oak and six inches of spruce; then into clay seven feet without striking anything.
>
> In boring the second hole, the platform was struck, as before, at ninety-eight feet. Passing through this, the auger fell about eighteen inches and came in contact with the side of a chest. The flat chisel revolving close to the side of the chest gave it a jerky and irregular motion. On withdrawing the auger, several splinters of oak such as might come from the side of an oak stave, a piece of a hoop made of birch and a small quantity of brown fibrous substance closely resembling the husk of a coconut were brought up. The distance between the upper and lower platforms was found to be six feet.[4]

Here for the first time was evidence, if circumstantial, pointing to the possible existence of two chests, one atop the other, and a third to the side, resting in the Money Pit at a depth of ninety-eight feet. Interestingly enough, a crucial portion of this physical evidence seems to have been concealed.

Pitblado, the man behind the drill, was reportedly seen washing a sample he had removed from the auger and, after scrutinizing it carefully, sticking it in his pocket. When Gammell demanded that he turn over the specimen at once, Pitblado refused point-blank promising, nevertheless, to present it to a future meeting of Truro's directors. Instead, the mining engineer apparently submitted it for detailed analysis to Charles Dickson Archibald of the Acadian Iron Works of Londonderry, Nova Scotia, after which the two unsuccessfully endeavored to purchase Lot 18 from the aging John Smith. Pitblado soon after dropped out of sight.

Emboldened by the successes of the previous summer, Truro was back in the spring of 1850 ready to sink its first shaft. This, the third at Lot 18, was placed ten feet to the northwest of the Money Pit and excavated to a depth of 109 feet through hard red clay. Its purpose was twofold: with it McCully and his associates aimed either to tunnel in toward what they hoped were treasure chests at the bottom of the Money Pit or, that failing, at the very least to draw off the water flooding it. Unluckily, this third shaft quickly filled with water and once again the workmen were forced to the surface. A possibly apocryphal version of the story is that one of their number happened to swallow a mouthful of water on his way up and noticed to his distaste that it savored of brine.

Be that as it may, after a full half century the cat was finally out of the bag. The water in the Money Pit was definitely *salty,* as was that in the parallel shafts, and after a belated round of sleuthing it was found to rise and fall with the Mahone Bay tide! The Mastermind had evidently engineered some manner of flood tunnel leading from Smith's Cove and sure enough, on closer inspection, it became obvious that, as the tide ebbed, fanlike rivulets of water trickled down across the beach or rather "gulched," in the colorful idiom of one of Truro's eyewitnesses, "like a sponge being squeezed."

Truro's full attention was now riveted upon the shoreline where it soon became equally apparent that numerous large boulders had once been removed over an area its workmen eventually surveyed for 145 feet. A quick bit of shoveling further revealed that three feet below the surface lay a two-inch-thick layer of brownish fiber in an excellent state of preservation, identical to that discovered by the Onslow Syndicate on one of the Money Pit's platforms. Below this layer workers next discovered a *second,* four or five inches thick, fashioned of rotting eel grass and lying beneath a surface of well-fitted beach stones. The eel grass showed itself to be absolutely free of sand and debris which had been ingeniously trapped by the web of fibrous mesh above.

Now that they had uncovered a "giant sponge," McCully, Creelman and Lynds were treated to the sight of a "super drain." The better to proceed with their singular investigation, Truro's engineers next erected a cofferdam around a portion of the exposed workings. That done, excavators went on to uncover a remarkable network of five troughs or "box-drains," so called, fanning out from what was presumed to be a central point, much like the fingers of a hand. The edges of the drains lay roughly eight inches apart and their bottoms were lined with flat stones. These, as explained in the January 2, 1864 *Colonist* article, "had been prepared with a hammer, and were mechanically laid in such a way that the drain could not collapse."

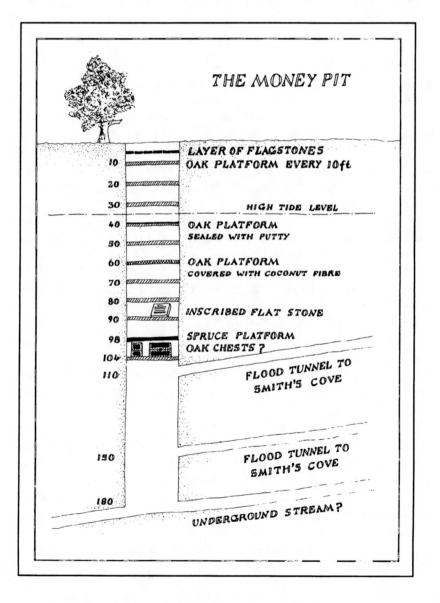

THE MONEY PIT

LAYER OF FLAGSTONES
OAK PLATFORM EVERY 10ft

HIGH TIDE LEVEL

OAK PLATFORM
SEALED WITH PUTTY

OAK PLATFORM
COVERED WITH COCONUT FIBRE

INSCRIBED FLAT STONE

SPRUCE PLATFORM
OAK CHESTS ?

FLOOD TUNNEL TO SMITH'S COVE

FLOOD TUNNEL TO SMITH'S COVE

UNDERGROUND STREAM ?

The higher sections of it were reportedly strengthened by a series of tiers over which lay eel grass and, on top of that, "blue sand." Finally, covering the whole, was gravel from the Smith's Cove beach.

> Having laid bare the large drain [continues the Colonist article] for a short distance into the bank, they found it had been so well made and protected that no earth had sifted through the arch to obstruct water passing through it.
>
> They then attempted to follow the inward direction of the drain, in search of a perpendicular shaft, but on account of the surrounding soil being so soft, and so much saturated with water, it was given up as impracticable.

Having succeeded in exposing the brilliant clockwork interior of Oak's manifestly artificial beach, disaster struck the Truro Company. Unusually high tides, exacerbated by a summer squall, sent waves crashing against the walls of its imperfectly engineered cofferdam and the whole affair ended up by melting away like a child's sandcastle.

It was now left to McCully and Co. to agonize over how best to proceed. The 150 feet of stone-and-clay cofferdam were ruined and had cost Truro a month in the construction. They might replace it with an improved model or attempt to tap into the flood tunnel itself further inland. Their investigating work having been interrupted by the high tides, Truro's men had not yet succeeded in isolating the point at which the five box-drains converged onto a central "main." Still, McCully remained confident of being able to estimate the flood tunnel's probable route to the Money Pit and then intercept it along the way. To that end he made the mistake of turning his back on the cove in favor of concentrating his efforts on sinking an exploratory shaft 140 feet inland on a line between the "sponge" and the Money Pit, 500 feet west.

How McCully happened to arrive at the particular site for his shaft— whether by dowsing or by some manner of hit-and-miss inspiration all his own—is unclear. Suffice it to report that, praying hard for a shaft blessed by precedent with a baptism of Mahone Bay water, McCully instead came up the first time dry as a bone!

Twelve feet to the south a second shaft was sunk which met with obstruction thirty-three feet below ground. An immense boulder lay directly in the vertical path of the diggers and no sooner had it been pried loose than a veritable torrent of sea water flooded in upon them. Attempts to staunch the flow by driving down timbers proved unavailing. Nevertheless, McCully and his men derived solace from the fact that they had apparently succeeded in their efforts to tap into the floodline.

After carefully assessing the situation, Truro's engineers embarked late that summer upon their most ambitious shaft to date—a 118-footer sunk just slightly to the south of the Money Pit. Reaching the desired depth without so much as wetting their feet, excavators then began work on an eighteen-foot tunnel, measuring three feet high by four feet wide, squarely up under the center of the Money Pit. Not unlike a rat worrying cheese from a trap, McCully hoped to confound the Mastermind by stealing in upon his elusive treasure and, in a manner of speaking, taking it off unmolested through a side door.

Having burrowed *up* from their own shaft nearly twenty feet to within striking distance of the ninety-eight foot platform, Truro's workmen left work late one autumn afternoon in 1850 with a sense of relief. Congratulating one another on a job well done and anticipating over supper that evening the *coup de grâce* they fully intended to deliver at dawn tomorrow, suddenly all present stiffened in reaction to an ominous rumble and crash emanating from the work site.

Choking down their supper, out of the mess hall they tumbled. By the dim arc of lantern light it was plain to see that both the Money Pit and the southern shaft were a mud-filled shambles. Thousands of board feet of cribbing inside the Money Pit had taken down with it a wealth of valuable pumping equipment and the new shaft and the tunnel were speedily filling with water.

As morning dawned, crestfallen workers realized the full extent of the disaster: the supposed treasure chests at the ninety-eight foot platform had, it was thought, dropped through an open space in the Pit and down, at the very least, a further thirty feet before lodging there! Just as the Money Pit once again reposed, brimful of mud and brine and the costly detritus of yet another derelict venture, Truro's coffers stood empty. The moral backbone of its work crew broken, and new financial backing at a premium, the ill-fated company itself soon collapsed under the weight of failure.

Truro's success with the pod auger and its qualified discovery of the flood tunnel, not to mention its laying bare of the intricate drainage system—the "giant sponge"—at Smith's Cove, all came at a price, the cost of which might best be measured in the havoc Truro left behind in its wake for future treasure hunters. A brilliant trap set God only knew when and by whom had now been fully sprung in the year 1850 and whatever it had served to protect lay further beyond reach than ever before. "Treasure," according to the well-known superstition, indeed seemed to "run away from the seeker."

The "Mastermind" of Oak Island had gone to extraordinary lengths to safeguard something which, it could only be assumed, was of immense value. In effect, the sardonic genius had conjured a sort of maelstrom triggered to overwhelm wise men and fools alike; the logistics of his mischief could only inspire admiration, not unmixed with envy, in the finest of late nineteenth-century engineers.

In addition to sinking a shaft thirteen feet in diameter to a depth of perhaps 150 feet or more, interspersed every ten feet with "hydraulic seals" of oak and caulking, he had apparently devised a subterranean flood tunnel running 500 feet from the sea and engineered to strike exactly at the Money Pit, connected to, and served by, an enormous fanlike system of drains 145 feet long and protected against silting by tons of coconut fiber and eel grass. To do so he would have been required to erect a cofferdam stretching across the length of Smith's Cove until the entire operation was completed (a task much later estimated to have necessitated 100,000 man hours), at which time it was obviously destroyed. Only aerial photographs betray a hint of the full extent of his handiwork in the faint remains of this Smith's Cove cofferdam.

Here, then, lay a positively masterful treasure pit, built to withstand the ravages of time and the ingenuity of modern man, coupled with a fool-proof booby trap to end all booby traps.

The Oak Island Eldorado Company (also known as the Halifax Co.), incorporated in 1866 and liquidated a year later, hardly lived up to its glittering name. In a prospectus aimed at the businessmen of Halifax, a limited offering of 200 shares at $20 apiece were tendered under the assurance that the "operation must succeed and will lead to the development of the hidden treasure, so long sought for." H. G. Hill served as the company president, A. O. Creighton of A. H. Creighton Bookbinders, treasurer and it was at this time that Smith's inscribed stone was put on display in Halifax, doubtless for the edification of prospective shareholders.

The "operation" in question was an ambitious new cofferdam 374 feet long and twelve feet high to be constructed at a cost of $6,200, 120 feet below highwater mark at Smith's Cove. Unerringly, Mahone Bay tides despatched this engineering marvel in the cradle and Eldorado reluctantly fell to the time-honored drudgery of clearing out the Money Pit.

Thanks to the efficiency of steam-powered pumps, its laborers made short work of the job, progressing rapidly to a depth of 108 feet, ten feet below the level of the sundered "treasure platform." A workman from Stillarton, Nova Scotia, named Robinson, was standing at that depth when he "felt the earth give under his feet a little." Water now rushing in from the eastern wall, he just had time enough, before scrambling to the surface, to drive his pick down into the wet clay. Once safely up, Robinson swore by all the heavens that his pick had sliced through the ground like so much butter and that he had been able freely to swing it about for an instant within what he reckoned was a chasm yawning directly beneath his feet.

Eldorado now resorted to boring. Rigging a platform at ninety feet, a 1 1/2-inch drill was set into a three-inch pipe and, on November 26, 1866, sent downwards. At between 106 and 108 feet it first struck spruce wood and below that, to roughly 125 feet, simply mud and clay. At 126 feet water began to burble up through the tube carrying with it charcoal, oak chips and coconut fiber. Eight feet below, the auger brought up more chips and fiber, then at 134 feet seemed to run alongside a plank. Here the flow of water ceased and then, quite as suddenly, recommenced. A reddish-brown material appeared between 155 and 158 feet, beyond which, down to 163 feet, nothing significant was encountered.

Hampered by the troublesome seepage, Hill fell in line behind precedent, determining to intercept the flood tunnel and stem the Mahone Bay tide come hell or high water. To the chagrin of future treasure seekers, Hill's admirable resolve led him to burrow a veritable rabbit warren of labyrinthine tunnels along the supposed floodline, a half-hearted survey of which was imprecisely recorded. Some of Eldorado's efforts were later confused with the original work and the only common denominator among them—their signature as it were—was that all its lateral tunnels seem to have been dug from a central shaft 110 feet deep and roughly 175 feet from the Mastermind's apparent floodline. Still, Eldorado's "swan-shot" approach may have paid dividends.

Here is foreman S. C. Fraser writing thirty years later to A. S. Lowden of the Oak Island Treasure Association:

> The Halifax Company's work was at a base of 110 feet, excepting two circling tunnels which were on a higher level. As we entered the old place of the treasure (by a tunnel) we cut off the mouth of the pirate tunnel." As we opened it the water hurled around the rocks about twice the size of a man's head, with many smaller and drove the men back for protection. We could not go into the shaft again for about nine hours. Then the pumps conquered and we went down and cleared it out. The water tunnel was found near the top of our tunnel. I brought Mr. Hill, the engineer, down and he put his arm into the hole of the tunnel, up to his shoulder. Nothing could have been more particular than our search on the old place of treasure. There was no mistake about our search of the old place.[6]

In another letter dated June 19, 1895 in which Fraser describes the "pirate tunnel," he assures his correspondent that Eldorado certainly encountered "round stones, such as are found abundantly on the beach and fields around the island." Other sources more specifically recorded that the tunnel measured 2 1/4 feet wide by four feet high and that it ran at a downgrade from Smith's Cove of 22.5°. That this tunnel was in fact the true "pirate" floodline seemed to have been established beyond a reasonable doubt when clay dumped along Smith's Cove on a rising tide at the presumed entrance to the tunnel was observed to cloud the water some thirty minutes later in the Money Pit.

Just as water is known to reach its own level, that of the Eldorado Company seems to have been precisely 110 feet. By now at the end of its investment capital, Eldorado in 1867 discontinued operations and, ostensibly out of concern for the safety of those to follow, filled in the top thirty feet above their drilling platform in the Money Pit before abandoning Oak Island altogether.

At the equivocal denouement of this early chapter in the often confusing saga of the Money Pit, a number of writers, Harris and Furneaux among them, record as a kind of epitaph on the Eldorado Company—and an ominous foreshadow of things to come—a statement made in a letter by one of the firm's employees and uncle of a future patriarch of Oak Island, Isaac Blair. Writing thirty years later to his nephew, Frederick, he cautions: "I saw enough to convince me that there was treasure buried there and enough to convince me that they will never get it."

Mrs. Sophia Sellers, one of two daughters of Anthony Graves,[7] was urging her team of oxen across a stretch of ground 350 feet east of the Money Pit in 1878 when the earth suddenly gave way beneath her. The depression measured approximately eight feet in diameter by twelve feet in depth and would come to be known as the "Cave-in Pit."

Sophia's father had observed at the time that the unusual occurrence took place directly on the line of the "pirate tunnel" leading from Smith's Cove but, as the island was enjoying a temporary hiatus from the depredations of treasure hunters—one that would last a full quarter century—the curious subsidence aroused little notice. Less heralded still was the discovery of a bo'sun's whistle near the shoreline in 1885. Said to be of peculiar design and ancient origin, another similar whistle, this one shaped like a violin, was uncovered in the same area in 1901.

The Oak Island Treasure Company was chartered at Kittery, Maine in 1893 under the stewardship of a prosperous insurance agent, Frederick Leander Blair. Born at Thomson Station, Nova Scotia, but now working from offices in Liberty Square, Boston, Blair was a diligent researcher and proved himself Oak Island's first orderly chronicler. By the age of twenty-five he had interviewed many of the principals involved in earlier treasure recovery missions on the island, including the descendants of McGinnis, Smith and Vaughan. A highly talented salesman, Blair attracted close to $60,000 in working capital of $5 shares, half of which he intended to set aside for a three-year lease of the Money Pit lot.

Aside from the dubious claim that a young man had recently discovered a copper coin dated "1317" (later versions amended the date to a more probable "1713") his company's prospectus was straightforward enough:

> It is perfectly evident that the great mistake thus far has
> been in attempting to "bail out" the ocean through the various
> pits. The present company intends to use the best modern
> appliances for cutting off the flow of water through the tunnel

at some point near the shore, before attempting to pump out the water. I believe, from investigations already made, that such an attempt will be completely successful, and if it is, there can be no trouble in pumping out the Money Pit as dry as when the treasure was first placed there.

Blair's stockholders included old names like Creelman, S.C. Fraser, the tenacious McCully and Robinson of the free-wheeling pickax, along with hundreds of new ones from Nova Scotia, New Hampshire and Massachusetts. Through fair times and foul, Blair would buy up most of their stock certificates and remain involved in the activities on Oak Island until his death in 1951. Fred Blair was instrumental in bringing some order out of the chaos of haphazard records left behind pell-mell by his marauding forbears and a certain debt is owed to him for his timely contribution to the otherwise Byzantine history of Oak Island's many digs.

Preferring to intercept a floodline rather than bail out an ocean, Blair concentrated his initial efforts in the summer of 1894 on the spot of ground that had so precipitately given way beneath Sophia Sellers and her oxen. Stopped with boulders in 1878, Blair's team cleared these away and soon arrived at the conclusion that they were working in a circular "man-made" shaft evidently sunk by the builders of the Money Pit. He could only guess at its likely function.

Some reckoned it had served as an airshaft for the experienced miners of the 500-foot-long tunnel as well as a convenient means of removing to the surface the hundreds of tons of displaced earth excavated during its construction. Others were of the opinion that it led to a valve where sea water, entering on the tide from Smith's Cove, might be shut off when the time came to retrieve the Money Pit's treasure. Finally, there were those (years later) who felt that "if it wasn't an airshaft, it may have been designed as an access point to one or more subterranean treasure locations."[8] Responsibility for the subsidence was laid at the door of the Eldorado Company, notorious for having allegedly sunk a welter of unrecorded "branch tunnels" in the vicinity.

Whatever the true intent of this fascinating new discovery, and wherever it may have led, the trail ended cold at a depth of fifty-five feet. Sea water gushing in from the east absolutely defied bailing and the Cave-in Pit project was abandoned forthwith.

If one is to credit a June 1894 article in the *Halifax Herald-Chronicle*, crowds of tourists were now regularly boating over to Oak Island for a firsthand look at the Money Pit, most of the half-dozen nearby houses being booked by the curious. Throughout 1895 and 1896, little actual work was to be seen, however, as the Oak Island Treasure Company had fallen to internecine bickering. Disagreements between the Nova Scotia faction and that of Massachusetts finally led to a shake-up in the consortium's top leadership, not fully resolved until the spring of 1897. Contrary to the terms of its original prospectus, the new directors voted to favor precedent by renewing excavations in what they mistakenly believed to be the Money Pit. Only at the 110-foot level did Blair's dazed minions fully apprehend the fact that they were digging within cribbing erected by Eldorado thirty years before!

Moving over ten feet to the southeast on June 9, 1897, at a depth of 111 feet in a shaft now correctly identified as the true Money Pit, a transverse tunnel was struck. Measuring 2 1/2 feet wide and lined with stones, gravel and sand, it delivered a rush of water that sent Blair's crew to the surface like a shot. The company's steam pump having earlier broken down, and the water pressure at the inlet such that no amount of desperate plugging would ever abate it, Blair and his confounded associates cast about for an alternative course of action. Since they were now certain to have uncovered the "mouth" of the elusive floodline, why not, they reckoned, go straight to the source?

Fifty feet above high-water mark at Smith's Cove and perpendicular to the supposed floodline, five borings, each five inches in diameter, were made to depths of 95, 90, 80, 90 and again 95 feet. Then the call went out for dynamite. Detonations set off in the first, second, fourth and fifth level, each "primed" with water, sent geysers spewing 100 feet in the air, though without gainful result. Only in the third attempt had the boring struck rock and when a 160-pound charge of explosive was detonated *there,* a curious thing happened. Workmen at the Cave-in Pit and the Money Pit reported that the water within "fumed" and "boiled."

Clearly, Blair had now established a positive link between the two pits and the outlet at Smith's Cove. Certain that his men had successfully intercepted the pirate floodline and effectively blocked it, steam pumps were sent into action bailing out the Money Pit, this time, it was thought, for good and all.

Nevertheless, Blair was in for an unpleasant surprise. Regardless of the dynamiting, the water level of the Money Pit stood at thirty-three feet and it was all the pumps could do, running around the clock, to bring it down to ninety feet. Determined at the very least to prove the existence of a treasure chamber of some sort within the Money Pit first and then worry about how to get at it *later,* Blair had a platform rigged at the ninety-foot level and prepared to bore. It was now getting well on in the year 1896 and, for the Oak Island Treasure Company, time and money were beginning to run out.

In brief, what the Treasure Company succeeded in bringing to light was evidence of "puddled clay" to roughly 122 feet in the Money Pit; wood and iron at 126 feet; "soft stone" a trifle below 151 feet; wood at 153 feet; "soft stone" again at 160 feet; and at 171 feet an impenetrable iron plate.

This information translated into a hopeful picture of a sealed, watertight treasure chamber thirteen feet wide and seven or eight feet deep, constructed of wood, iron and what would later be identified as a crude yet effective type of cement, 150 feet below ground. The well-regarded industrial chemist, A. Boake Roberts of London, had analyzed samples of the "soft stone" brought up in Putnam's auger and guardedly averred that "we are of the opinion that it is cement which has been worked by hand." The "puddled clay" was later tentatively identified as a primitive variety of putty.

One startling discovery made as a result of the Treasure Company's five borings came at a depth of 126 feet, the drill apparently entered a *second flood tunnel* gushing at the rate of 400 gallons a minute. This finding, after a century's worth of nuisance from the original "pirate floodline," at once daunted Blair's men and exhilarated them. After all, given the Herculean effort necessarily expended by the builder of the Money Pit in the 500-foot-long tunnel from Smith's Cove, to have excavated a *second* most certainly implied that he was safeguarding a treasure trove beyond anyone's wildest dreams!

No less exciting was another curiosity brought up from inside the alleged treasure chamber itself. For Frederick Blair, good things were now coming in proverbially small packages; small enough, in fact, to slip past the eagle eye of T. Perley Putnam who had been picking oak chips from his auger, lately drilled to a depth of 153 feet. Only later, on September 6, 1897, did Dr. Andrew E. Porter single it out among samples he was empowered to investigate before two score witnesses at the Amherst, Nova Scotia Court House.

Although Dr. Porter first identified the minute specimen as just another scrap of wood, on closer examination he galvanized his audience by pronouncing it to be a "compact ball of fiber about the size of a grain of rice." Covered with a bit of "fuzz or short hair on the surface," once untwisted and spread out flat under a strong magnifying glass, Dr. Porter further attested that the fragment was, in truth, *parchment* (a judgment later independently confirmed by experts in Boston) on which, in India ink, were penned—evidently as "part of some word" the letters "vi," "ui," or "wi." This hallowed grain of evidence, more telling to Blair than anything else previously exhumed from the Money Pit, survives today in the possession of the Triton Company at its museum on Oak Island.

Misfortune soon struck the Oak Island Treasure Company. On March 26, 1897 a laborer named Kaiser, riding a hoist up one of the shafts with a cask of water, tumbled to his death when the horse-drawn winch slipped a gear. This was the second recorded death during treasure hunting operations on Oak Island, the first having occurred in 1861 when a man was mortally scalded when a boiler blew up in his face. Although several others were injured in that mishap, the death of Kaiser had broader ramifications.

The spirit of Captain Kidd, it was quickly reported, had paid a visit to one of Kaiser's mates the evening prior to the fatal accident, warning him that doom awaited all who proceeded with the treasure search. Superstition soon got the better of common sense and hardly was poor Kaiser laid to rest than the entire crew went on a wildcat strike. Shaking off the incubus of William Kidd ended up costing Blair and his directors a full month.

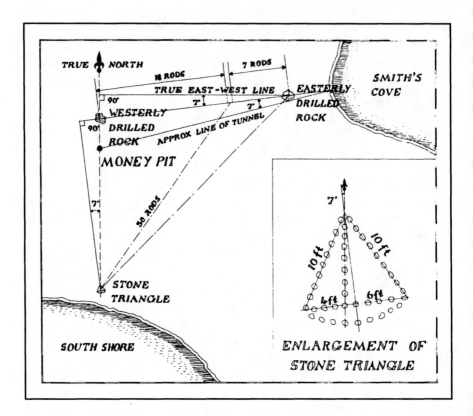

On the strength of this last spate of drilling, "insiders," among them Blair and William Chappell, convinced of having located a treasure vault likely filled with gold bars, jewelry and, quite possibly, "priceless historical documents," bought out the firm. Late in 1897, before bad weather turned them away, the much inspired workmen of the Oak Island Treasure Company sank two new shafts forty-five feet and seventy-five feet south of the Money Pit. The results, however, were discouraging. Blair's first shaft struck water at seventy feet and his second did likewise at 160 feet. Vigorous pumping got them nowhere and work was abandoned for the season.

In spring, one of the company engineers had a brainstorm. With a view towards plugging the flood outlet at Smith's Cove, red dye was dumped into the Money Pit. After pumping in water above the pit's thirty-three-foot tide level, Blair's men expected the easily identifiable backwash to work its way out on the Smith's Cove shoreline, revealing the outlet's exact location. To their considerable surprise, however, the red dye instead turned up in *three separate places at South Shore Cove!*

In the course of his investigation into this new phenomenon the Treasure Company's Operations Manager, Captain John W. Welling, made what many today feel was a momentous discovery. Partly obscured by dense under-growth around South Shore Cove, it proved to be nothing less than an equi-lateral triangle, ten feet on each side, which somebody had fashioned of large beach stones. From its base, a vertical arrow of smaller stones ran toward the triangle's apex. With enough already on their plate, however, and company funds practically depleted, the men appear to have glossed over the bizarre find, the existence of which was completely forgotten until the early 1930s.

The Treasure Company's swan song on Oak Island was an attempt to sink a deep shaft—the twentieth excavated thus far—parallel to the Money Pit and to tunnel in under the presumed iron plate at 171 feet. Fifty feet or so shy of that depth, workmen were driven to the surface by surging water and this shaft was unhappily written off.

The employees received their final paychecks, Captain Welling and T. Perley Putnam totted up their losses, and Frederick Blair bought out the few remaining stockholders. To his credit, Blair had greatly contributed to the sum knowledge of the altogether brilliant design of the Money Pit. Now, it ap-peared that besides the one "pirate flood tunnel" protecting an oak chest or chests at just below ninety-eight feet, there existed a second tunnel presum-ably doing the same for a treasure vault at 155 feet, reckoned by Blair to be of far greater value than the first.

Frederick Blair (aside from his oversight with the stone triangle at South Shore Cove) had borne careful witness to the Oak Island mystery as it moved into the twentieth century. The question now begging an answer, though, was whether it all might be too late.

A pair of ill defined and unrewarding recovery operations were all Oak Island would see for the next two decades. In 1933, though, Blair was back. By this time, wear and tear on the Money Pit was such that its very *location*—as Blair had earlier learned to his chagrin—not to mention that of the alleged treasure vault hidden away somewhere in its murky depths, were matters of considerable dispute. William Chappell, the drilling expert of the Oak Island

Treasure Company who had been responsible for bringing the 1897 parchment to light, thought it high time to pinpoint locations. Having prospered in association with his brother Renwick during the intervening years, Chappell now had the time and the money to pick up where he had left off.

Chappell had no intention of getting fancy; he was a capable man with a drill and he would stick to what he did best. The two brothers kicked in $40,000 of hard-earned real estate profits between them and determined to dig until the money ran out or they struck pay dirt—"whichever came first!" Aided in the endeavor by their two sons, Mel and Claude, the men went down to a depth of 150 feet in the Money Pit—fully forty-seven feet past the deepest re-excavation shaft sunk to date—and along the way came upon a number of curious finds.

The "Chappell Shaft,"[9] so-called, was efficiently drained by electric power (for the first time), using a centrifugal pump connected to the mainland via underwater cable. Between 116 and 150 feet they uncovered a miner's seal-oil lamp, an anchor fluke, a 4 x 4-foot section of oak, chunks of granite, a pick and an axehead thought to be 250 years old.

Ever the studious chronicler, Blair kept voluminous notes:

> These tools, I believe, belonged to searchers who worked there many years ago, and had fallen from a much higher level to where found ... The only reply that I can think of is that there existed an open space into which they fell when the Pit collapsed years ago ... The question now is where is the wood and treasure metal in pieces—which dropped from 100 feet; the iron struck at 126 feet by drillers; the cement and wood drilled into between 153 feet and 157 feet, and the iron (plate) at 171 feet? It appeared as if we had gone past them. They certainly must be somewhere in the vicinity of the Pit![10]

Blair's question was one which William Chappell never managed to answer. After reaching 155 feet in October he drilled laterally and almost lost his foreman, George Stevenson. Water rushing in at this depth had, in Claude Chappell's words, entered through a "round, clearly defined tunnel," precipitating a cave-in. This latest tunnel was thought, possibly, to be the second "pirate" watercourse leading up from South Shore Cove and it probed as deeply into the Money Pit mystery as William Chappell himself would ever penetrate.

Fred Blair met in Gilbert D. Hedden the man he thought most capable of getting to the bottom of the Money Pit mystery. On July 25, 1935 the skilled engineer, vice-president and general manager of the Hedden Iron Construction Company of Hillside, New Jersey, bought Oak Island for a mere $5,000.

By the time work was curtailed in the late autumn of 1936, Hedden and his gold miner partner, Sylvester Carrol, had re-excavated and cribbed the Chappell Shaft to a record depth of 170 feet. Costly turbine pumps with capacities of 1000 gallons per minute powered by a 7500-watt line to the mainland kept the shaft in an unprecedented state of dryness. Still no sign of treasure was encountered.

The following spring, Hedden left his own signature on Oak Island with an excavation bearing his name; the twenty-second thus far and the only one, with the exception of the current Triton Shaft, to last into the 1980s. For all the time and money dedicated to its construction, though, the so-called "Hedden Shaft" produced only an uninspiring series of oak pieces brought up from 150 feet.

More interesting was a find Gilbert Hedden made at Smith's Cove later that summer. Remarking to his friend Blair upon the noticeable erosion of the shoreline thereabouts, the two, upon closer examination, came upon a pair of timbers, the ends of which protruded from the beach at low tide. After the removal of four feet of sand what appeared to be the remains of an "ancient skidway" was revealed. This was made up of timbers set four feet apart and notched at intervals of four feet; each notch held a wooden peg.

The final curiosity which worked to turn Gilbert Hedden's attention away from the supposed skidway (or, as others believed, the original Smith's Cove cofferdam) actually lured him away from Oak Island altogether for a few months in 1938. This was a popular work published in London by one Harold Wilkins, a few years before, entitled *Captain Kidd and His Skeleton Island*.

Upon receipt of this enthralling tract, Hedden sequestered himself alone in his cabin. Throughout the afternoon and evening he remained there and rumors began to circulate that either the "boss" had a woman inside or that he had quietly taken to drink. In fact, Hedden was simply reading up on just about everybody's favorite pirate, William Kidd.

Of supreme interest to him were several reproductions of charts attributed to the legendary brigand, on one of which Hedden identified no fewer than fourteen similarities to Oak Island! Signed WK and labelled "Mar Del," below it were carried the following directions:

18W and by 7E on Rock
30 SW 14 N TREE
7 by 8 by 4

At dawn Hedden's work crew were treated to the rare spectacle of their no-nonsense boss—book in hand and muttering to himself—pacing up and down north of the Money Pit for all the world as if marking off certain measurements in the time-honoured fashion of treasure hunters. Indeed, for the first time in 150 years on Oak Island, someone finally had a "genuine" pirate's map.

Carrying the book, its cover open to the map, Hedden diligently searched the area around the Money Pit. Fifty feet to its north he soon came upon a large granite stone, three feet long, in which a hole two inches deep and 1 1/4 inches in diameter had been drilled. When Hedden hurried to inform Blair of his discovery, he was greeted with the unexpected news that its apparent mate, "marked in exactly the same manner," lay near the beach at Smith's Cove. As it happened, Blair and his partners had stumbled upon it forty years ago but had been baffled as to its possible significance.

Fred Blair's memory can only be described as prodigious since he managed, albeit with some difficulty, to relocate the marvel which, with the years, had become embedded in sand, and the two men immediately set about stepping off the distance between the two drilled stones. The measurement turned out to be approximately twenty-five rods, *the sum of eighteen and seven!* Hedden, of course, was extremely gratified by the arithmetic, all the more so since it pointed to a unit of measurement used by British surveyors of Kidd's day.

Hedden now wasted little time in summoning the Provincial land surveyor, Charles Roper. With the aid of his assistant, George Bates, Roper carefully inspected the moss-covered pair of stones, although he was kept completely in the dark as to the motive behind Hedden's all-consuming interest in them.

Roper and Bates ascertained that the two stones lay 421 1/2 feet apart, nine feet in excess of the exact equivalent of twenty-five rods or 412 feet. Undeterred, they next surveyed a position seven rods from the rock at Smith's Cove and eighteen from that by the Money Pit. Then, experimenting with the chart's directions, they turned southwest, stepping off the distance of thirty rods or 495 feet; this led them to a dense tangle of bushes close to high-water mark on the southern shore. Here, an employee of Hedden's, named Amos Nance, was given the honor of crawling in first and, at his subsequent cry, the others gamely followed suit. Scarcely believing their eyes, before them stood Nance pointing excitedly to a collection of beach stones embedded in the ground. Clearing away the surrounding growth until the whole of its pattern was open to view, Hedden and his companions beheld, with measureless wonder, the very stone triangle which had been uncovered in 1897 by Captain Welling.

> Each side of the triangle was ten feet long. A half circle of stones enclosed its base giving the whole structure the appearance of a sextant. An arrow of stones fourteen feet long connected this curved base with the triangle's apex.
>
> Setting up his transit and sighting it along the line of the arrow shaft, Roper peered through his view-finder. "North," he announced, quickly qualifying his finding by the state-

ment that the direction was True and not Magnetic North. "It points," he exclaimed. "Come, and look for yourselves," he invited. Hedden peered through the view-finder. The arrow pointed directly towards the Money Pit.

The directions, concluded Hedden, led to the Money Pit. But no one could fathom the meaning of the cryptic numbers "7 by 8 by 4."[11]

Over the next five years operations at Oak Island slipped into a desuetude remarkable only for legal haggling and half-baked projects.

An American GI, who had purchased an Oak Island treasure map at auction in New York City, turned up with spade and shovel in May 1946. Later in the summer a crooner from the Broadway stage intended to dig a vast open pit across Lot 18 with steam shovels, only to vanish before following through on his $150,000 proposal.

Colonel H. A. Gardiner had a clever notion of his own. Gardiner, for a measly 10 percent share of the treasure, pledged to crawl through all Oak Island's known tunnels and shafts with a portable radar scanner, a prototype of which had, he claimed, been developed during the last war. With it the Colonel was confident of being able to identify "any and all original excavations and hidden chambers." Hedden was interested but the deal fell through, thanks to objections from Blair who still held the treasure trove rights to the island.

These were quickly snapped up by Mel Chappell upon Blair's death in 1950. Chappell had, earlier that same year, succeeded, by means of a bit of judicial sleight-of-hand, in gaining the deed to Oak Island as well; for the next thirty years (and for the first time) one individual possessed both treasure rights and title to Oak Island.

Chappell likewise witnessed his share of tragedy on Oak Island. In the autumn of 1959 he signed a contract with Robert Restall, a Hamilton, Ontario steel worker better known as half of a death-defying husband-and-wife motorcycle act. Robert and his plucky wife, Mildred, had toured the western world until their final performance in 1956, electrifying audiences with a high-speed sensation dubbed the "Globe of Death." The highlight of this was the couple wheeling in loops on over-powered motorcycles and shaving one another by inches at speeds exceeding 65 mph.

Mildred was happy she had survived it all and settled down with Bob to a normal suburban existence. She truly enjoyed her new life and had no complaints whatsoever. Then her restless husband made a chance excursion to Oak Island as one of over 15,000 annual tourists by now arriving on its shores—and his doom was sealed.

Impatiently waiting his turn for a crack at the fabled Money Pit, Mel

Chappell finally gave it to Restall in October 1959. Restall and his older boy, Bobbie, were quick to set up camp within spitting distance of the Hedden and Chappell shafts, before the onset of winter. Mildred and young Ricky joined them after the spring thaw in 1960. That first year Bobbie and his father built a forty-foot bridge over the Hedden shaft, designed to accommodate the weight of a 1000-gallon-per-minute diesel pump.

Restall had invested the whole of his and his wife's life savings in this Oak Island gambit and he had done a great deal of homework on its history. For Bob Restall's money, it was pirates that had been responsible for the Money Pit's extraordinary engineering—"a sort of 'Fort Knox'"—he believed, "but built by forced labor over a period of twenty years." Restall had heard of alleged pirate banks uncovered in places like Madagascar and Haiti designed in a similar fashion, boobytrap flood tunnels and all. It seems that in his ceaseless prowling of the island Restall had stumbled over a mass of coconut dunnage and a stone (perhaps bogus) with the date "1704" scrawled on it; this provided a circumstantial link to the era of the Le Havre pirates south of Mahone Bay.

August 17, 1965 dawned hot and overcast. Nothing if not persistent, Restall had seen more than a few such mornings in his five years' hard labor at Mahone Bay. Everything he and his wife possessed in the world was by this time riding on the Money Pit. Everything. Fail now and he was a destitute family man. But Bob Restall believed in himself as he likewise believed that he was finally close to breaking the code of the intricate flood system—the *key* to unlocking the jealously guarded secret of Oak Island.

Restall had been working alone that day in a shaft twenty-seven feet deep near Smith's Cove where continual pumping was required to hold the incoming tide at bay. As the former daredevil motorcyclist was climbing out of this shaft in the afternoon Bobbie, who happened to be working nearby, sensed that something was wrong. Racing to the site the young man peered down into it only to spy his father lying face down in the brackish water, whereupon he hurriedly descended the ladder in a vain attempt at rescue. Just then two of Restall's workmen, Karl Graeser and Cyril Hiltz, were jarred from their labors by a piercing scream. By the time they reached the Smith's Cove shaft there were two inert bodies resting on its bottom. Tragically, Graesar and Hiltz repeated Bobbie's error as did a fourth man, Andy DeMont, who arrived at the scene hard on their heels.

It was left to Ed White, a vacationing fireman from Buffalo, himself nearly overcome by the mysterious fumes, to save young DeMont. An anxious knot of tourists had meanwhile collected some distance from the deadly shaft, among them a student group from Phillips Academy, Andover, Massachusetts. When the toxic gas (which was never conclusively identified) cleared away, the young men helped bring the rigid bodies of the four victims to the surface under Ed White's leadership.

What sort of gas it was that took the lives of the Restalls, Karl Graeser and Cyril Hiltz remains a mystery. Puzzled about the unexplained deaths, bitter and angry over the unseemly haste with which the Oak Island search proceeded in spite of the tragedy; eager, in fact, to forget *everything*, Mildred Restall was nonetheless unable to tear herself away from Mahone Bay. She and Ricky moved only a mile from the scene of the tragedy to the tiny village of Western Shore. Later, Bob's grieving widow took a job at a medical clinic in Chester.

Around Canoga Park, California, Bob Dunfield was known as a "hardcharger." The experienced petroleum engineer had been "lying in the weeds" during the whole of Bob Restall's tenure on Oak Island and, while in no way gloating over the Restalls' misfortune, he was nevertheless loath to tarry. In fact, scarcely were the bodies of Mildred's loved ones in the ground when Dunfield secured a one year treasure-trove lease from Mel Chappell.

By mid-October the Californian had contracted a 100-ton "digging clam," standing seventy feet high and capable of excavating 200 feet deep and 100 feet in diameter. Dunfield knew that something was buried on Oak Island and whatever it happened to be, he would get at it soon enough, guided if necessary by the ungentle principles of strip mining.

Getting his juggernaut of a digger out to the island by barge proved impossible so Dunfield set about laying a 600-foot dirt-and-gravel causeway from the mainland to Oak's western shore, a task he accomplished in ten days. First, positioning the digging clam at South Shore Cove in late October, Dunfield ran a relentless two-shift operation costing him and his twenty-five Californian backers $2,000 a day.

In no time at all these efforts produced a seventy-two-foot-deep trench running the length of the cove, within which Dunfield excavated a shaft that rapidly filled with water at sixty feet. A man for whom time meant money, Bob Dunfield quickly confirmed the existence of the suspected South Shore flood tunnel; unfortunately, in the process, he managed to sunder forever the remarkable stone triangle first uncovered by Blair back in 1897.

Bob Dunfield was unabashedly confident of his ability to dig pits deeper, wider, longer and faster than any of his predecessors—and, by sluicing all material brought forth from them, to get to the bottom of the Oak Island mystery in record time. The only serious problem would be in keeping the excavations dry. To that end, the Californian backers provided him with pumping equipment capable of bailing at a rate of 110,000 gallons an hour.

By early December and now working over the Money Pit itself, Dunfield's excavation already measured fifty feet across by 148 feet deep. Then came the winter rains. Hardly less galling had been a string of suspicious mechanical breakdowns plaguing his equipment; these delayed work until Christmas. Then, to top it all, his exhausted crews clamored for a holiday. Returning from the sunshine of Canoga Park on January 2, 1966, Dunfield discovered that during the intervening fortnight, the walls of his pit had collapsed.

Facing the prospect of starting over again, Dunfield determined to pull out all the stops. This time he simply cut an enormous tapering cavity 200 feet in diameter at the top, the better to safeguard against the possibility of cave-ins below. In so doing, his rapacious digging team literally consumed the whole of the original Money Pit.

Certain purists were appalled. Was nothing sacred? Certainly, by the time Dunfield finished, successful or otherwise, the "Mastermind" himself would not be able to recognize the prodigy born of his own inimitable genius. Nor for that matter would anyone else.

Dunfield and Co. pushed on amid growing signs of sabotage. His machinery seemed to be taking an odd sort of beating, a nuisance attributed by some to local fishermen irked that the Dunfield Causeway was obliging them to circumnavigate Oak Island when they followed the coastline south. Thanks to improved security, Dunfield's men eventually managed to reach a depth of 140 feet in the Money Pit without further incident. They then turned right around and filled it all in again, the better to have a stable base from which to drill. Now a giant rig was brought in. Six-inch holes were next bored to 190 feet, one of which brought up evidence of having passed through a two-foot-thick layer of limestone at 140 feet, followed by a forty-foot drop into empty space before striking bedrock. Here, evidently, was the very chamber bored through by a Texan named George Greene in 1955, the same man who had once claimed, during a petroleum survey in eastern Turkey, to have photographed the remains of Noah's Ark atop Mt. Ararat.

Dunfield and Greene independently conceded that the chamber was most likely a natural phenomenon—the Windsor Rock Formation as it was known to geologists—made up of limestone and gypsum, minerals conducive to the preparation of cement. Whether it was the "cement" first encountered by the Oak Island Treasure Company in 1897, that which A. Boake Roberts & Co. Ltd. identified as likely to have been "worked by man," was entirely debatable.

The slight rise upon which the Money Pit lies is a geological drumlin or ridge of compact glacial drift extending to a depth of 150 feet with hard clay throughout. "The significant point," argues D'Arcy O'Connor, "is that in undisturbed areas the soil can be (and obviously was) excavated with hand tools without the use of vertical shoring or the threat of water seepage."[12] Another is that Oak Island may be brimming with sinkholes.

> There is strong evidence to prove that the supposed artificial openings (which originally led to the search) were really but natural sinkholes and cavities formed by the gradual disillusion (sic) of gypsum deposits underlying layers of soft sandstone and shales which gave way under the pressure of the

super-incumbent covering of the glacial drift.[13]

Could the Mastermind not have encountered one or more of these and used them to ingenious advantage?

> Sinkholes or solution caverns are cylindrical and funnel-shaped depressions. They often extend to greath depths and lead to a labyrinth of cavities or caverns. The Carlsbad Caverns and the Kentucky Caves are famous examples.
>
> It would not be surprising for a sinkhole to have formed on Oak Island. The fault which runs beneath the island could account for the underground stream which appears to run through the depths of the Money Pit. Talking to a reporter on March 25, 1966, geologist Robert Dunfield said, "We have sufficient evidence of where the Windsor Formation is, and this is the answer to the water problem." The Money Pit site was, he thought, part of an underground natural rock structure of carbonate, as in minerals such as limestone.
>
> Dunfield believed that the original depositors found a cavity at the bottom of the Pit which they made into a sealed and watertight treasure chamber.[14]

One month prior to this interview, Dunfield wrapped up his operations on Oak Island with an excavation of the Cave-in Pit.

Bob Dunfield had called upon big machinery and high technology; he was fast, brash and, in his way, efficient. When he forever turned his back upon it after one furious year, Oak Island wore the scarred and pitted face of a battleground where, for all the sound and the fury, little had signified.

Triton was Poseidon's son; a minor god, half man, half fish. And such is not a bad description of Dan Blankenship. The Miami contractor has dug farther and dived deeper than anyone before him on Oak Island and, for a Yank at least, cuts a popular enough figure around Mahone Bay. Equally certain is that he and his associates have sunk more dollars (both Canadian and American) into the Money Pit than all their predecessors combined.

Triton Alliance, the syndicate formed in 1969 by Blankenship and David Tobias, a packaging manufacturer from Montreal, is expected to make Bob Dunfield's performance look like child's play. Over $1 million alone have already found their way into the pockets of a battalion of specialists: underground researchers from Ottawa; mining experts from Aspen, Colorado; Toronto geotechnical engineers; a team of Nova Scotia divers; two separate drilling firms; a Cambridge, Massachusetts Carbon-14 analyzing lab; IBM; the Canadian Steel

Company (Stelco); Washington's Smithsonian Institution; archeologists, geologists, security guards and, hardly surprising, more than a few major underwriters.

Triton's associates include a former deputy Attorney General of Nova Scotia, the honorary chairman of one of Canada's largest food-retailing chains, financiers, lawyers, real estate magnates and a past president of the Toronto Stock Exchange.

The current Money Pit dig, which may well prove the last, is reckoned the deepest archeological excavation in North American history and quite probably the most costly. Of the fact that *something* was buried on Oak Island, Blankenship and Tobias, like Dunfield before them, are close to 100 percent certain. The chances of this elusive "something" still remaining there, however, Tobias puts at no better than between 25 and 50 percent.

The two enterprising gentlemen have, nevertheless, dated the Money Pit, at least to their own satisfaction, and, in the course of their diverse investigations into the possible identity of its creator and the function of its workings, have buoyed investors with a string of curious discoveries, among them a "gigantic man-made plug," a grouping of mysterious holes in the ocean, a telltale scrap of logwood; a pair of scissors, a "heart of stone" and even a severed human hand for good measure.

As far as Dan Blankenship was concerned, previous investigators on Oak Island, while on the right track, barely got their feet wet. For his part Blankenship would dive deep within the infamous Borehole 10-X and, on one occasion in the late 1970s, he came within seconds of becoming the latest of the Mastermind's casualties. Blankenship's initial efforts, though, began safely enough with help from Becker Drilling. The results proved extremely encouraging:

> Core samples from several of the holes brought up pieces of china, oak buds, cement, charcoal and metal, anywhere from between 160 and 212 feet down. Some of the holes hit tunnels or chambers that appeared to have been cut through bedrock. In these instances the drill went down through 30 to 40 feet of rock then hit several inches of wood, a thin layer of blue clay, a few more inches of wood, and then dropped into voids six to eight feet deep before again striking the bedrock floor. Samples of the wood were sent to Geochron Laboratories Inc. of Cambridge, Massachusetts for Carbon-14 analysis.[15]

Between 160 and roughly 190 feet Becker Drilling also came upon what appeared to be a circular chamber or cavern hacked out of the bedrock. To his amazement, Blankenship was informed that it was packed solid with puddled blue clay, making up what all tentatively agreed was a massive man-made watertight "plug." Cementlike material brought up from it was also judged "man-made" by experts, while the origin of the charcoal could only be guessed at. Some figured it to be the remnants of oak fires used to heat subterranean forges; others that it was evidence of fires kindled by early workmen for the purpose of cracking large boulders.

> One borehole in the Money Pit came to an abrupt halt at 198 feet. Blankenship and the professional driller operating the machine were positive, because of the high-pitched whining sound, that the drill was biting into hard metal. It required twenty-five minutes for the diamond drill to bore through a half inch of the material. But the core sample was lost before it reached the surface.[16]

Perhaps the biggest surprise of all was provided by the section of logwood which is now prominently on display in Triton's Oak Island Museum. Up to the very moment its analysis arrived through the mail from Cambridge, little was known of the Money Pit's probable age. Now, however, in the summer of 1967, the field narrowed. The simple reason was that, according to the Carbon-14 experts at Geochron Laboratories, the core sample of wood brought up by Becker Drilling dated positively to 1575 A.D., plus or minus eighty-five years.

Naturally, Blankenship was greatly heartened by Geochron's good news and was eager for more. He and Tobias now had what appeared to them to be the "smoking gun"—a section of timber hewn between the years 1490 and 1660. What they would look for next was the hand that had once held it. Perhaps, surmised the two men, at a depth of 200 feet or more beneath the island, there ran man-made tunnels roofed with such planks or timbers. Inevitably, such a premise led them inexorably to Smith's Cove.

Blankenship had to admit that he had never truly bought all those stories surrounding the discovery of tons of alleged coconut husk on Oak Island. He greatly preferred to see some of it with his own eyes. The following summer, 1968, Triton's excavations along Smith's Cove provided him with all he could ever have asked for in the way of "unidentified plant matter." A short time later the National Museum of Natural Sciences in Ottawa had the answer for which he was waiting. There was no question about it: Blankenship was now definitely looking at coconut fiber.

The uncovering of the "filter" material led to the subsequent exposure of the original drains themselves, beneath which were uncovered a pair of "Spanish American" scissors similar, according to Mendel Peterson of the Smithsonian Institution's Historical Archeology section, to those made in Mexico at least three centuries ago. A heart-shaped stone was also recovered nearby which, opined Peterson, clearly showed signs of having been hand chiseled, though at what "early" date he was loath to estimate. Widespread reports reaching Triton that such stones had been removed from alleged pirate banks in Haiti and other Caribbean islands defied confirmation.

Twenty-two years and approaching $10,000,000 later, one might well wonder whether Triton Alliance had been born in 1969 of a will-o'-the-wisp. Certainly, however, the carbon-dated wood, proved to have been cut and worked almost four centuries ago, was a major breakthrough. Harvard botanists agreed that red oaks may live to be over 300 years, further strengthening the case for the existence of the mature specimen sighted near the Money Pit by Daniel McGinnis in 1795. In addition, an analysis of a pollen sample taken from the Pit by Blankenship also indicated that the time frame of the original work predated 1600.

At any rate, the discovery of the old wood crowned Blankenship's overall success with the diamond drill and served to fire the imaginations of important backers who, in turn, brought the big money aboard. As matters fell out, much of it wound up either in the hands of lawyers or down a marvelously designed shaft—the "second" Money Pit—into which railway cars, of all things, would finally be driven.

> One word accounts for all the sorrows, feuds and unhappiness of Oak Island: greed. Whoever owns that pit wants it all. The island had been notorious for this for hundreds of years. Chappell always wanted ninety per cent of whatever was found, his predecessor eighty per cent. But the thing of it is, you have to try to be rational. That's the hardest part— it's so easy to lose perspective because the place is like a magnet, the way it draws and keeps you. But if any of us found anything there, what would we do? I mean what do you really find? Is it trouble for the rest of your life, or is it the end of the rainbow?[17]

Rainbows aside, property disputes have led to considerable trouble for everyone now enmeshed in the Money Pit snare. Precisely what each warring faction has found over the years remains a moot point since both the Nolan and Triton Alliance camps appear to be keeping their best discoveries close to their chests. What visitors to Oak during the 1960s and 1970s found was a treasure island frequently under siege and boasting two separate museums. The first, situated just off the Dunfield Causeway at Crandall's Point, belonged to Frederick G. Nolan.

The Bedford, Nova Scotia land surveyor entered the fray in 1963 after coming upon a heaven-sent anomaly in a property title recorded at the Chester

Registry office in 1935. At that time, the Sellers heirs had sold fifty-two acres of Oak Island, comprising Lots 15 and 9–20, to George Grimm; these were subsequently purchased by Gilbert Hedden, sold by him to John W. Lewis, then sold by Lewis to Mel Chappell in 1950. Nolan, to his delight, recognized that Lots 5 and 9–14, running through the swampy center of Oak Island, had never been legally transferred back in 1935.

He then moved quickly to secure the seven lots, at just the speed one would expect of a property specialist looking at a legal loophole big enough to drive a caravan through. Like a shot Nolan was down in Massachusetts taking tea with several elderly Sellers widows and persuading them to sign quitclaim deeds to the enviable swamp for the reported sum of $2,500. That done, he girded himself to take on the "millionaires," Tobias and Blankenship.

The history of what followed reads like a case study in greed with overtones of violence attended by farce. The highlights are as follows:

1965   Armed guard stationed by Blankenship on Causeway.

1966   Nolan purchases 1/4-acre strip for $3000 on mainland at   Crandall's Point, abutting Causeway, and barricades it.

1967   Both parties now landing men and equipment on Oak Island the only way possible—by sea. Nolan then "salts the wound" by charging Blankenship to cross Causeway. Temporary truce.

1969   Truce shattered by repeated violations on both sides. Nolan chains off Causeway. Triton retaliates by erecting a gate on the island side.

1970   In retaliation for prohibition on use of (Triton) island road, Nolan chains off own road crossing Lots 9–14. Blankenship, now unable to bring workmen to the Money Pit, strikes back by cutting chain. Nolan, using truck boom, blockades own road with boulders. Blankenship threatens to bulldoze. Guns are drawn. Royal Canadian Mounties called in.

A Cold War prevailed on Oak Island for the next fifteen years with neither side willing to so much as blink. In the meantime, Nolan's Museum sprang up on Crandall's Point and the Triton Museum barely 200 yards east across the Causeway. On April 15, 1987, Fred Nolan's claim to Lots 5 and 9–14 was upheld by the Nova Scotia Court of Appeals. To this day neither he nor Triton, for all the endless legal squabbling, have so much as a gold doubloon on display for the tourists paying $2 at either of their two museums. But then neither rival appears to be telling all.

Piled up in a corner of the Nolan Museum is an otherwise nondescript jumble of old spruce stakes—sixty in all. Identical and measuring approximately 2 1/2 to 3 feet long by 4 inches in diameter, they are nevertheless the linchpin of one of Nolan's pet theories: to wit, not unlike the beach at Smith's Cove, the swamp straddling Oak Island's midsection, over which he fought tooth and claw for possession, is in fact man-made.

> It took us three years to find them. They were that cleverly hidden. They were hammered almost all the way into the ground, so that just the little round circles at the top were showing. As I found each one I marked its location on a chart of the island. If you line these points up, they intersect in some curious ways.[18]

It is Nolan's contention that, when sorted out, such lines, with "more crossings than a spider's web," make up a survey map designed by the brilliance of British engineers after the capture of Havana in 1762. This has led him to some fascinating, though only vaguely explained, finds:

> Following some of the survey lines, we have uncovered four different holes shaped in size to hold a chest. We have found remnants of oaken reinforced chests in four holes and nothing in seven others.
>
> Dozens of treasure chests were buried throughout this island that could only be found by using a map. The eleven sites we uncovered were examples of the smaller chests which were probably uncovered between 1875 and 1930 by an unknown party. The real bulk of the treasure luckily is still on the island and under the swamp.

Attempts by Nolan to drain the swamp have met with stiff resistance from Triton Alliance which still maintains certain legal claims upon it.

Quick to defend his belief that the Money Pit may well be a "ruse" designed to divert attention away from the real treasure, Nolan is convinced that a "secret British organization headed by high government officials" was behind the deception. After plundering the immensely rich city of Havana in 1762, Nolan claims that they seized upon the opportunity provided by the fall of French Quebec three years before to secrete their fortune on Nolan's property at Oak Island. "Who," he asks, "would have thought to look in an old inconspicuous swamp that's full of mud and flies and bugs? That's why they buried it there."

For a man who seldom sees eye to eye with Fred Nolan on practically *anything*, Dan Blankenship by no means entirely disagrees. At least part of the treasure, he concedes, may well have been buried in that "inconspicuous old swamp." Furthermore, the possibility that eleven separate caches may have been dug up there does not surprise him either. Indeed, one of the "unknown" diggers—and of this Blankenship claims to be absolutely certain—may have been none other than his mercurial neighbor, Fred Nolan. "Nolan's found treasure in that swamp all right. I'm sure of it. It's just that Fred's not talking."

The Triton Museum offers visitors a variety of its own enigmas. These include any number of small bits of telltale wood and metal, one particularly curious example being a thin piece of "cold-hammered steel," one side of which appears to have once been cemented to wood. Investigators suggest that the steel might have been employed as part of a watertight casing for the treasure chest Triton Alliance hopes one day to encounter deep within the Money Pit—which it believes to be anything but a ruse.

Extensive excavations around Smith's Cove in 1970 provided the museum with some domestic arcana: a hand-wrought nail and two pairs of shoes. One is a prodigious size fourteen, while the smaller pair, sporting metal eyelets, is reportedly identical to those worn in seventeenth-century Spain. Also on display is a sample of gray ash found buried near the beach which has since been analyzed as cremated human bone.

Triton's key discovery at Smith's Cove in 1970 was a set of logs, thirty to sixty feet long by two feet thick, notched at precise intervals of four feet. Beside each notch, some of which still bear the remains of two-inch-thick wooden dowels, are carved Roman numerals. Experts still disagree as to whether it might be part of the original cofferdam or perhaps a slipway for ships. Two other similar structures have also been unearthed on the western end of Oak Island.

It is worth mentioning that, in preparation for Triton's detailed excavations at Smith's Cove, a cofferdam arching 400 feet along the beach, though built by the firm's undeniably professional engineers utilizing modern materials and the best of equipment, soon enough collapsed under the assault of the Mahone Bay tides in the feeble manner of all its predecessors.

Hardly to be overlooked are those famous grainy photographs of Dan Blankenship. Not unlike so many Rorschach blots, designed to elicit varying responses from subjects, no two viewers—at least outside Triton's inner circle—seem to agree upon the significance of Blankenship's highly equivocal images. Photographs taken from a tape monitor, transmitted live by means of a submarine camera floating 230 feet underground, they have been criticized for an unedifying resemblance to those stereotypical UFO pictures one finds in the supermarket tabloids. Such talk struck a raw nerve in Dan Blankenship. "I saw a hand down there, I don't need proof from anybody. No way, no way it was anything other than a human hand!"[20]

Sceptics might please themselves; for his part, Blankenship would eventually descend the ghostly Borehole 10-X to see for himself.

By 1970 Triton had sunk no fewer than thirty-one exploratory shafts around the perimeter of the Money Pit. The number of its boreholes defied easy compilation. Triton's 10-X began innocently enough as a six-inch-diameter hole designed to gauge the flow of water through the 1500-foot-long "pirate" tunnel running from Smith's Cove. Fifteen years later, Blankenship was still concentrating the bulk of his considerable energies on Borehole 10-X, long after Triton Alliance would have preferred that he had forgotten it.

Lounging on a deck chair in the Florida sunshine in 1965, Blankenship had been fascinated by an article in the August issue of *Reader's Digest* recounting the progress of the Restall family's treasure dig on Oak Island. Bob Restall, the ex-motorcycle daredevil, who had worked as unstintingly and, by all accounts, more methodically than anyone before him, was certain that the key to the Money Pit was the pirate flood-tunnel system. Crack that "code" (if Blankenship apprehended him correctly) and you were on your way.

According to the *Reader's Digest,* Restall had assured its editors that, after five years of incessant toil, he was just on the brink of solving the Oak Island mystery. That autumn Blankenship, compelled to make his pilgrimage to the island, brought with him new ideas, fresh funds and the offer of a partnership. He recalls that on a Sunday Restall declined his overtures and the following Monday morning he, himself, was heading back to Miami empty-handed. The following day, news reached him that Bob Restall was dead.

> Oh, everything was there then. The triangle was there and
> the thirty-five and seventy-five foot pits. Between tides, with
> the pumps going, you could walk in the tunnels from the
> Money Pit to the Cave-in Pit. But Dunfield destroyed every-
> thing—he bulldozed it all into the sea.[21]

Blankenship, a burly, muscular man, soft-spoken and strong-willed, had differed with the methods employed by both Restall and Dunfield. Nevertheless, Triton's Borehole 10-X, put down equidistant between the Money Pit and the Cave-in Pit and, by a strange coincidence, on a direct line between the two drilled rocks discovered by Gilbert Hedden in 1937, would most probably have met with the approval of Mildred's deceased husband.

During the summer of 1970 Blankenship's rotary drill hit a series of cavities on its way down, the largest at 230 feet. Compressed air injected into the hole blew several ounces of dull soft metal to the surface; this promptly oxidized and turned brittle as if it had been deprived of oxygen for a very long time. Expert analysis subsequently determined it to be low-carbon steel, probably more than 200 years old. Working an area never before explored, Blankenship now had several suspicious cavities and a fistful of steel—enough to interest Tobias and his money men. In the autumn of 1970 new equipment was called in from Aspen, Colorado and Borehole 10-X was widened and became a "shaft."

In the course of the boulder-strewn excavation, Triton uncovered vast quantities of spruce coated with a pitch-blend preservative; also seashells and bird bones. This was convincing evidence of a floodline running from Smith's Cove beach. With sea water flooding the new shaft at a rate of 500 gallons a minute, however, Triton's sophisticated pumps were hard pressed to maintain a stable water level in 10-X. How then to gain a better understanding of the submarine chamber? Why not, suggested Blankenship, submerge a television camera and sit back and watch?

During August 1971 Triton's preternaturally mobile Project Manager found himself in the unaccustomed position of viewing the action from the sidelines. While the television camera was being carefully lowered in the chamber beneath 10-X, Blankenship ensconced himself in a nearby shed, eyes glued to his tape monitor. No sooner was the equipment suspended in the 230-foot cavity than a partly clenched human hand, later thought to have been severed at the wrist by Triton's churn drill, came into view on Blankenship's screen. Adding in an indescribable manner to the freakishness of such a ghastly, free-floating apparition was the startling fact that—no skeletal organ this—gristled flesh still clung in abundance to its bones.

Mesmerized, it was all Blankenship could do to tear himself away from the spectacle long enough to grope for his flash camera and snap a roll of still photographs. Meanwhile, he had bellowed for his chief driller, Parker Kennedy. In his footsteps followed Triton's security man and all-around factotum, Dan Henksee. Both men agreed that what they saw could be none other than a human hand. As the image hung tantalizingly before them on the monitor, Henksee was despatched to 10-X with instructions for the film crew to maneuver their camera so as to pick up an impression of the hand's palm. Unfortunately, in the attempt the camera bumped against the object, nudging it out of range.

A later probe proved more revealing still. Once again photographed by Blankenship, these images included what appear to be three logs resting on the chamber's floor and three chests, one with a curved top and a handle at one end. Alongside another lies a tool of some sort—possibly a pickax—and, slumped against a far wall, the body of a man, apparently toothless, yet with hair and flesh intact.

Who among the Triton team was not familiar with the fact that pirates, pursuant at least to their extravagant mythology, were inclined to bury a victim along with their plunder—a "guardian" if you will—the better to ensure its safekeeping? One obliging pathologist, pressed by Triton for a professional opinion, even ventured to speculate that, under optimum conditions, a body kept airtight in cold, still, salt water might preserve its physical integrity for a great many years.

For his part, Blankenship rejected the notion that "dumb-assed pirates" could have been capable of pulling off such a titanic feat as the Money Pit operation. Still, he would give his eye teeth for the opportunity to descend 10-X in a wet suit and shake that toothless beggar's good hand.

It did not take an experienced diver to know that descending 10-X was risky. As erosion ate away at the chamber, it took on the shape of a bottle ever widening at the sides, filling in with white rubble at its base. Therefore, it would be particularly dangerous, *away* from the shaft opening. Merely to rub a shoulder against the crumbling anhydrite clay walls of the cavity was courting disaster. Positively obsessed with the mystery of 10-X, five years later on another blustery November morning Blankenship was hanging suspended in a diving suit just above the opening at 145 feet when he came within a whisker of joining his quarry—the toothless votary picked out on a television monitor in 1971.

Blankenship's son, David, was manning the winch on the surface when he heard an ominous rumbling over his telephone headset. "Bring me up; bring me up! Out, out, out, out!" cried his father above the muted roar of a hard rain of imploding debris. The shaft's rugged casing (perhaps ruptured by a Triton-made fault produced by the continual pumping) had suddenly fissured, very much like the shell of a hard-boiled egg!

A man possessed, David jammed the power winch full throttle and, after a frenzied half minute, succeeded in reeling his father up fifty crucial feet. Once enjoying the relative safety of the ninety-foot level, just five feet above the point where the casing had splintered open, Blankenship now peered down from his swaying perch at the raging vortex of spewing mud and sundered casing below. Five seconds more by the clock and 10-X would have swallowed him up alive. After a good night's sleep, Triton's irrepressible Project Manager was back inside the shaft where, thanks to the ravages of the cataclysm, he could actually *stand* at the level of seventy-three feet. Although he was involved for the next two years in various drilling projects around the island, 10-X drew Blankenship back, as if by the force of a charm, in 1978. It was then that he hit upon a clever scheme "inexpensively" to renew his assault on the capricious borehole.

By fits and starts over the succeeding decade, Blankenship and Henksee spent their summer months driving four railroad tank cars inch upon back-breaking inch down the throat of 10-X. Eight feet in diameter by thirty-four feet long, each car was cut open at the sides, tipped on end and, by dint of pick, shovel and jackhammer, eased down into the ground within the circumference of the shaft. As the excavated earth was worked loose and brought up to the surface, the 10,000-pound car slowly settled downward by the sheer force of its own weight and, once set to its full length, a new one was then welded to the tank car beneath it.

By 1987 Blankenship had, to his credit, a marvelous steel-encased shaft reinforced with concrete to 167 feet. Here was certainly Oak Island's most impressive excavation ever, likely to outlast even the tunnels running from Mahone Bay; an echoing, rust-covered monument to faith, toil and—futility. For in the end, Blankenship proved utterly mistaken about 10-X. "The anticipated man-made cavities at 140 and 160 feet were apparently only pockets of loose sand blown away by the original churn drilling, and the still-unexplained metal and wood may have been washed elsewhere by years of pumping."[22]

David Tobias who, for almost a decade, had borne, with unequal measures of loyalty and skepticism, the financial burden of what often appeared within Triton to be Blankenship's single-minded heterodoxy at least where 10-X was concerned, now heaved a $300,000 sigh of relief. Enough good money to date had been thrown after bad down *that* particular hole; besides, a more worthwhile discovery was made during the winter of 1980 which cost Tobias not a penny.

With the waters around Oak Island frozen solid, Tobias one day noticed four holes spaced roughly 150 feet apart, 700 feet off South Shore Cove. Admittedly a skeptic as to the existence of the alleged South Shore flood tunnel, Tobias changed his tune when geologists called in by Triton now conceded that warmer water, "percolating up" from the bottom and doubtless emanating from the Cove, had produced the curious phenomenon. So it was that, in late 1987, Tobias was more determined than ever to put $10,000,000 on the line and tackle the mysteries of the Money Pit from the very point at which McGinnis, Smith and Vaughan had begun with picks and shovels close to two centuries before.

The new Triton Pit—the "pit to end all treasure pits"—should finally strike bottom, and perhaps a fortune as well, more than twenty stories underground. Eighty feet in diameter, lined with steel plate and concrete and costing its Canadian and American investors approximately $50,000 a vertical foot, *this* pit will swallow up just about every other major shaft ever put down on Oak Island in the past 250 years.

The Herculean task is being handled by a crew of thirty men working full time who, before they are through, will displace one million cubic feet of earth. North America's deepest, most extensive archeological dig (and Tobias fondly stresses the adjective), the Triton Pit, though it may never hit the jackpot, is expected at the very least to answer the nagging question of who constructed the diabolically confounding Money Pit in the first place and the reasons why they did so. If David Tobias is to be taken at his word, these two answers alone will justify Triton's seemingly outlandish expenditure in time, energy and cold hard cash. But, as ever throughout Oak Island's dramatic history, new players stand in the wings, content for the moment to watch and wait.

Frederick Nolan acts more like a gratified spectator enjoying the show from a front row seat, a mere 625 feet from the stage, along Triton's western boundary line; he wishes his long-standing nemesis the greatest good fortune. The only irony in his generous sentiment is that it is, by-and-large, true. Nolan feels certain he can well afford the magnanimity, sitting pretty, as he sees it, with his hard-won Lots 9–14, on a fortune whose astronomical recovery bill will ultimately be footed, or so he believes, by Triton Alliance Ltd. In Nolan's view the Money Pit is nothing more than a brilliant and supremely ambitious decoy—the treasure itself, or the great bulk of it, has quite plainly been secreted elsewhere.

It is Nolan's firm belief that the Mastermind, after going to great pains to construct a hopelessly booby-trapped "master" shaft complete with hydraulic seals and triggered flood tunnels, would surely not have squandered his peculiar genius on an empty farce, much less so on a costly joke rigged to backfire upon himself or his confederates. No, the treasure most certainly was not at the bottom of that hole and no amount of digging by the "millionaires" of Triton will make it so. If one is to believe Fred Nolan, what these benighted souls will find at the end of their rainbow is a series of branch tunnels leading far from the Money Pit and slanting up toward the surface along a gentle gradient *heading directly for his own property*.

> The final stage of [the Mastermind's] Grand Design may have been planned to prevent his workmen from knowing the exact location of his cache or caches. This last operation could have been done by a selected few. [The Mastermind] descends into the depths of the (Money Pit) shaft. From its base his men tunnel upwards and outwards to create a cache or caches, beneath the surface, above high-water mark, without disturbing the ground. He may have made several caches. He could return at his leisure with even fewer men, and quickly recover one or more without revealing the whole plan of concealment.
>
> Having made his caches, [the Mastermind] climbed from the shaft, his men refilled it with earth, sealing each platform down to ninety feet, and connecting the water supply. No one could ever go that way again; as they dug down, they would release the air-pressure and the sea would surge up and flood the shaft. The entrance to the treasure's hiding place was forever sealed, [the Mastermind's] defenses impregnable, his treasure absolutely safe. The water would flow as long as the tides rolled up the beach.[23]

The logic of such an argument strikes Fred Nolan—who claims to have already discovered eleven "chest-sized" holes about his "man-made" swamp—as unassailable. Two gentlemen, themselves waiting upon Triton's predicted debacle, have arrived at a similar conclusion. One of them is a Baptist minister from Phoenix; the other a retired engineer living in Vancouver, B.C., and each further argues that a variety of caches probably remain buried on Oak Island.

For the middling sum of $50,000 or even less, the two independently put their services at the disposal of an unforthcoming Tobias. The treasure troves, so each claimed, rested mainly undisturbed no more than forty feet below ground! The secret of their respective locations, again arrived at independently through the diligence of both parties, resides not, they caution, in the brute power of machines but rather in the subtle ingenuity of the human brain. Turn to the "coded map" written ages ago in the stone of an equilateral triangle, some markers and a pair of drilled rocks. There lie the keys, promise an engineer and a man of God, waiting to unlock the Money Pit mystery.

Meanwhile, in January 1988, Dan Blankenship received the go-ahead from the beleaguered Tobias to reopen his investigation of Borehole 10-X. The dig continues.

Postscript

Who dug the Money Pit? After 200 years, telltale physical evidence of any kind is extraordinarily scant. It amounts to little more than a heart-shaped stone, a pair of wrought-iron scissors of allegedly Spanish vintage, coconut fiber, a few odd bits of wood and metal and a minute fragment identified in 1897 as parchment. Gone are the inscribed stone, the pair of drilled stones and the stone triangle. Despite the accumulated wisdom of military historians, engineers, "geo-psychics," hydrologers, map dowsers, seers of all descriptions, academicians, surveyors and cipher experts, no single coherent theory has yet emerged to account for the phenomenon of Oak Island.

But outlandish notions positively abound. Was the Money Pit actually designed as a "seventeenth-century alchemical reactor?" Might it possibly contain religious artifacts of great value, such as the Holy Grail? Is it a UFO base? Did the Incas, or perhaps the Mayans, expert builders with a highly advanced knowledge of hydrology, flee to Mahone Bay before the onslaught of the Conquistadors and painstakingly design the Money Pit as a treasure house against better times?

Those seeking an explanation for lost royal treasure speculate Oak Island might possibly guard the wealth of Scotland's St. Andrew's Cathedral or even the church plate and valuables allegedly spirited out of England during the Protectorate of Oliver Cromwell. Then again, for those to whom logic is no impediment, the Money Pit contains the crown jewels of Marie Antoinette and Louis XVI guarded by a booby trapped vault.

To certain literary sleuths, such riches pale to insignificance beside the mysterious disappearance of the Shakespearean manuscripts. Eminent scholars and artists have long pointed to Francis Bacon, an Elizabethan Renaissance man with a stunning breadth of knowledge, as the most likely author of the immortal plays and sonnets. The argument goes that, for a variety of reasons, not the least of which being that play writing in those days was hardly a pursuit worthy of a Lord Chancellor and Keeper of the Great Seal, Bacon wrote them under the pseudonym of an obscure actor.

Nevertheless, some Baconians hold that their man arranged matters with the connivance of a select following so that the full scope of his genius would eventually become apparent to future generations. Bacon's published interest in complex word ciphers, for example, and the preservation of manuscripts through the agency of mercury, among other perceived "clues," appeared to hint at the possibility that the full flowering of his stunning gifts might have been stored away for posterity.

Seized upon as confirmation of their thesis was the curious parchment fragment brought to light by William Blair in 1897 and the discovery at Joudrey's Cove, forty years later, of an ancient "dump" holding the "remains of thousands of broken pottery flasks," some of which were reported to contain a mercury residue. Moreover, scholars were quick to cite the fact that Bacon (1561–1626) "was among a group of patentees granted colonial lands in Newfoundland by James I."[24]

However fantastic, here is a theory that, at the very least, has stood the test of time, inasmuch as the Carbon-14 dating of the Money Pit (1525–1625) fits Bacon's life-span (1561–1626) like a glove.

Prior to Triton's dating of the wood sample, Oak Island scenarios predicated on the eighteenth-century military history of eastern Canada enjoyed a certain currency. Europe's two prime antagonists had traded power bases there for decades before 1795 and, in so doing, invested manpower, money and material in the protracted tug-of-war. But however logically the Money Pit's *raison d'être* was linked by one theory or another either to French funds earmarked for the construction of Fort Louisbourg in 1744, the accumulated fortune of the Acadians banished from Nova Scotia by the British in 1755 or war monies allegedly diverted from New York to Halifax by British general staff at the height of the American War of Independence, fatal flaws remain.[25]

Again, suggestions that British naval officers occupying Havana after the siege of June 1762 may have extorted a fortune and smuggled it to fellow conspirators in Halifax, leading to the construction of the Oak Island works, likewise founders. The problem is that not a hint of such a contingency exists in any known governmental file, nor has a shred of real evidence ever been unearthed around Mahone Bay to justify it.

Furthermore, D'Arcy O'Connor points out that British artificers and elements of the army's corps of engineers would have been called upon to undertake the mammoth task of constructing the Oak Island works under a veil of remarkable secrecy indeed. Thanks to the fact that the nearby town of Chester was founded in 1759, one can only assume that such an enterprise would have attracted considerable attention from the local populace which would have seen more than Oak Island's mysterious "burning lights."

The existence of the heart-shaped stone notwithstanding, the idea that sea rovers possessed the equipment, patience and expertise to construct such a complex engineering marvel as the Money Pit strikes many investigators as patent nonsense. That would appear to leave the Spanish standing alone in the field.

By the 1550s great fleets of their galleons (the "plata flotas," so-called) were routinely plying the Gulf Stream within several hundred miles of Mahone Bay. D'Arcy O'Connor, who has spent twenty years investigating the Oak Island story and to whom we are indebted for a great deal of historical background and theoretical speculation relating to the Money Pit, has convincingly advanced his own scenario as to who might have been responsible for the Pit.

O'Connor pictures a treasure-laden galleon of some 500 tons outbound from Cuba in the early 1600s. Separated from the main body of the accompanying fleet in heavy weather, her captain judges it expedient to run before the storm. By the time it blows itself out, he and his crew are standing off the Nova Scotia coast; he casts about in desperation for a likely place at which to put in for dry dock and they happen to select Oak Island.

The disoriented captain has saved the lives of his passengers and crew and safeguarded his valuable cargo. Nevertheless, damages to the galleon will mean a delay of several months. Luckily, the captain has the benefit of adequate manpower (he may be transporting black slaves), among whom figure carpenters and riggers equipped with a forge by which to fashion iron fittings.

> The ship's passengers include an auditor representing the Spanish Crown and agents of the Seville merchant who owns most of the cargo ... Their particular concern is for the tons of gold and silver bullion and coins in the ship's hold.[26]

The good news is that the island is reckoned appropriate to an extended stay: it is well timbered with red oak, offers a plenitude of fresh water and is separated from the mainland—discovered to abound in game—by a mere few hundred yards of Bay water. Moreover, it lies snugly hidden behind a group of outer islands and is therefore beyond the line of sight of passing enemy vessels.

The bad news is that the ship's officers agree that, even after major repairs, the galleon's seaworthiness is bound to remain a matter of considerable uncertainty. It is at this point, then, that the concept of the Money Pit is born.

Rather than risk shipping the considerable weight of her precious cargo, the Spaniards devise an ingenious plan. (O'Connor suggests that a mining engineer en route home after a tour of duty at the Potosi silver mines in Bolivia might possibly have provided the technical know-how.) Probes of the island's soil indicate that, as it is claylike and well drained, scant impediment to excavation is foreseen. Favorable, too, is the proximity of Smith's and South Shore Coves.

> The Money Pit is dug first. Separate work crews tunnel out from it at various levels and directions, and large chambers are made at the end of each corridor some distance from the Money Pit. The treasure is placed in these vaults, sealed with puddled clay and crude cement made from the island's limestone. At the same time at least two flood tunnels are dug, one toward Smith's Cove and the other to South Shore Cove.
>
> Other crews have been constructing cofferdams at mean low tide in both these locations. The one at Smith's Cove also serves as the outer wall of a huge dry dock for the five-hundred-ton galleon that's being repaired on the slipway. The stone drains are built and covered over with the ship's coconut fiber dunnage, as well as eel grass, rocks, and sand.
>
> Each vault has been carefully measured and mapped with respect to its position directly below the island's surface. The ship's commander has the valuable map, for it shows precisely where to dig through virgin soil to enter each watertight vault. The stone triangle and drilled rocks are set in place and keyed to the captain's map.[27]

What remains now is the all-important job of covering tracks. Nothing, of course, can be done about the denuded copse of oaks. But all non-burnable refuse is taken offshore in longboats and dumped, the latrine carefully limed and covered over and all tools, down to the smallest chisel, accounted for. Then the cofferdams are dismantled, effectively setting the flood traps and, after four months in the wilderness, the galleon and her crew are away!

So far so good. Lamentably, however, the captain once again runs into nasty weather. This time the unseasoned planks of his patched-up vessel's hull buckle under the strain. Powerless to stop her taking water, he and his men are soon heading to the depths of the frigid North Atlantic and, with them, the map of what three centuries later would be referred to as the Oak Island Money Pit.

Agrihan Island

How will I know
In thicket ahead
Is danger or treasure.
—May Swenson
"Question" (Stanza III)

The history of the Agrihan treasure has come down to us, courtesy of Captain Gabriel Lafond de Lurcy, and been retold by a number of writers since, Maurice Magre among them. Readers interested in the fullest treatment of this highly colorful tale would do well to refer to Lafond's *Quinze ans de Voyages autour du Monde,* vol. 7–8, Paris 1851.

The story is a favorite, thanks to its romantic mix of violence, treachery, greed and love and has doubtless been embellished over the years. Nevertheless, its ruthless protagonist, Captain Andrew Gordon Robertson, did exist and was not only a contemporary of Lafond but an acquaintance as well. Furthermore, Lafond, a great nineteenth-century traveller and connoisseur of the Agrihan legend, managed to interview a number of Robertson's confederates within a few years of his death in 1828.

Andrew Gordon Robertson hailed from a Glasgow naval family and, after completing his enlistment in the Royal Navy, made his way to South America. Hard on the heels of Britain's defeat in the War of 1812 with the United States, he found his maritime experience esteemed by the revolutionary forces of Chile in whose cause he enlisted in 1817. Robertson's raw courage and ambition, untempered, it might be said, by scruple, was not lost upon Lord Cochrane, Supreme Commander of the Chilean Navy, nor by his superior officer, Captain (later Rear Admiral) Guise under whom he served with distinction for nearly five years.

In 1820 Lieutenant Gabriel Lafond, second in command of the American trading vessel *Mentor,* first met Robertson of the man-of-war *Galvarino* on the high seas. The encounter took place not far from Guayaquil in present-day Ecuador. Overtaken by the swift and maneuverable Chilean ship, Captain Gardiner of the *Mentor* suffered his brig to be boarded by a surly First Lieutenant who, in flagrant violation of protocol, was all for disembarking the neutral's crew into the *Galvarino* and submitting the *Mentor* to a search. As Lafond relates, only the timely intercession of an American frigate thwarted the plans of his Scottish counterpart whom he describes in the following manner:

> Robertson was exceedingly bold, his impetuous and fiery character making him often savage and cruel. He was of medium height, with red hair, a wild look, and while he wasn't exactly repugnant, he cut a fearful figure indeed.[1]

Two years later, his ardor seems scarcely to have cooled. At the head of a landing party charged with running to earth a Royalist brigade under the Spaniards, Benavides and Martellin, he reportedly left his mark on the terrified Chilean province of Concepción as well as on the back of a victim identified by Lafond as Pacheco.

Smarting under the lash, the tormented Spanish officer is said to have betrayed the whereabouts of his compatriots whom Robertson subsequently ambushed in a wood near the town of Arauco. Whether or not apocryphal, the horrifying account went about that, in an excess of inhuman theatrics, Robertson's dementia for symmetry led him to hang Pacheco's cohorts, some seventy all told, in a circle the Scot felt compelled to complete with the corpses of a number of Arauco's inhabitants, including women and children.

With the end of hostilities in Chile, Robertson resigned his commission and settled down briefly on the island of Mocha, seventy-five nautical miles south of the Bay of Concepción. Apparently restless and missing the action taking place not far to the north, he soon accepted a new commission, this time in the Peruvian Navy. He subsequently took an active part in the thirteen-month siege of Fort Real Felipe at Callao, Lima's beleaguered port.

Curiously, in his capacity as First Lieutenant in the Peruvian Navy, Robertson would necessarily have been in the vicinity of the hijacking of the *Mary Dyer.* One can only speculate that this celebrated outrage, perpetrated by a fellow Scot into the bargain, may possibly have sown a seed in his fertile and highly duplicitous mind. Be that as it may, Lafond, who met up with him again later in Lima, attributed Robertson's future course to an unlikely infatuation.

Teresa Mendez, widow of a Spanish colonel, was, by all accounts, twenty-one years old, beautiful and troubled. Tainted by her marriage and subsequent involvement as the mistress of the aged Marquis de Montemire, Spanish ex-Governor of Lima, Mendez might well have paid dearly for her Royalist caprices. That she survived the revolutionary purges of San Martín and his rancorous mestizo has been credited to a combination of beauty, guile and the "discreet protection," in Lafond's words, of the chief of the newly established city council, de Cabildo.

Robertson, meanwhile, having attained the rank of captain, settled into the roistering shore life of post-war Callao. Hardly less ambitious than Teresa Mendez herself, he was, however, physically unprepossessing in the extreme, with his shock of red hair, blotched northern skin and carious teeth. Moreover, he violently chafed under the constraints of what seemed an intolerable position. Faithful dog soldier in the employ of the revolutionary forces, Robertson proved himself a fiercely capable foreign mercenary whose personal ambitions, nonetheless, could hardly have mirrored the long-term goals of his ideologically minded superiors. Struggling along on a captain's pay, beset by gaming debts during the years 1823–5, he might look forward to an eventual rear admiralty, though peacetime, as he well knew, was poorly suited to a meteoric rise.

Jostling among the throng at Peru's annual Corpus Christi procession in 1826, he happened to join his fellow officers in admiration of a raven-haired beauty making her way into the cathedral of Lima. Later, on the verandah of Commodore Young's home in Callao, a naval lieutenant named Viera reportedly captivated his audience with gossip currently attaching itself to the lady. She was, of course, Teresa Mendez. Not to put too find a point on it, the unsentimental Scottish captain fell in love and, to the bemusement of the assembled company, brazenly set his cap at the unattainable girl.

Nothing if not bold, the lovelorn Robertson, through his naval connections, soon managed to toast her beauty at a social tea. Wasting little time in declaring himself to her, Mendez, ever the coquette, mockingly reminded the besotted officer of his unimpressive rank and deplorable material estate. Perhaps conjuring up a motive for Robertson's subsequent folly where it may not have existed, Lafond, a son of France, laid it unequivocally at the feet of Robertson's quixotic attachment to de Cabildo's alluring mistress.

In any event, Captain Robertson soon after caused a sensation. Privy to the manifests of ships served by the once again bustling port of Callao, the presence at anchor of the richest of their number shocked him into action. She was the *Peruvian*, a brigantine of English registry about to set sail with a reported 2,000,000 gold piastres crowding her hold. Moreover, enjoying the security of peacetime, she was said to be guarded by hardly more than a dozen men. In the early morning hours of July 16, 1826 Captain Andrew Gordon Robertson took her.[2]

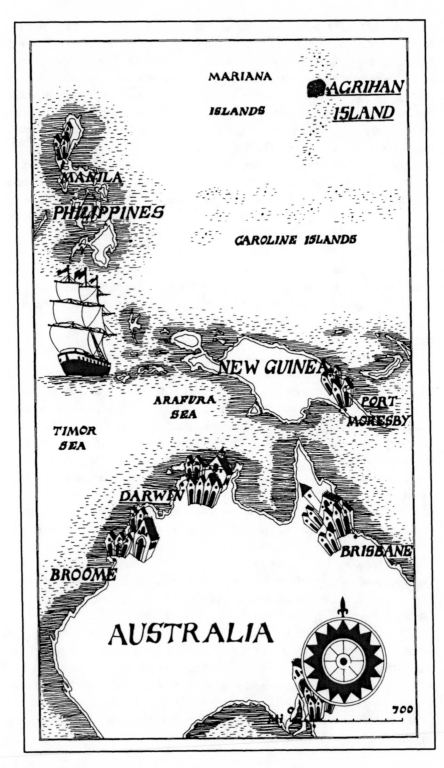

Leading twelve hand-picked followers, veterans all of Robertson's previous campaigns, he stole up upon the *Peruvian* in a longboat and overpowered her bosun before the man could sound the alert. Once well out to sea, the officer and his six disgraced mates were put overboard in the offending longboat and later picked up by a Spanish search party. Left with a positive description of the gang's ringleader, and little else, the authorities put out a hue and cry order for the *Peruvian's* capture and her nonplused owners set a price on the Scot's head.

Robertson would lead them all a merry dance but it was his accomplices who would end up paying the piper. These he had chosen expressly for their pluck and expertise in boarding ships of war. By no means their match, the *Peruvian's* somnolent crew had capitulated to Robertson's brigands without so much as a shot fired. But though his men had served him well, even as he set a course for Tahiti they were destined to be made redundant by half.

Skilled at navigation (as were none of his renegades), Robertson apparently hoped to assure his own indispensability by steering his prize into unfamiliar waters and, at an opportune moment, whittling down her crew. Those remaining, relieved to have survived the cut, might then assuage their sorrows over lost companions with the thought of a future share-out of the 1000 iron-ringed chests stacked below decks.

There, however, the men underestimated their captain's singular aversion to dispensing largesse. As Robertson's far-flung trajectory took him to Agrihan Island, away and then back again, the final eighteen months of his violent existence would read like the ten little Indians which were finally none.

By the time Robertson made landfall at Tahiti, he had taken two favored Irishmen, whose patronymics were Williams and George respectively, into his highly limited confidence. Charging them with remaining aboard ship, Robertson meanwhile invited six ill-fated crew members ashore, ostensibly to join him in a much-touted island debauch. Fuddled to a man by drink, he managed to row them back to the *Peruvian,* jump aboard and leave them comatose in the dinghy. Having carefully instructed George and Williams beforehand to have his ship's sails set at the appropriate hour, he then eased the *Peruvian* out of the harbor and, only hours later, cut the dinghy's painter.

That left the Irishmen and the four remaining sailors. Making a virtue of extreme necessity, they readily assented to handling the now undermanned brig on double watches as she sped, unbeknownst to all but Robertson himself, toward the northern Marianas Islands.

How Robertson seized upon this remote north-south island chain as the repository of his fortune remains anybody's guess. At roughly 18° N. by 143° E., it could hardly have lain more distant from either Glasgow or Lima. Today, though by no means well known by civilians, it is justly famous as the site of pitched battles during the Second World War, positioned as it was along the Allied invasion route to Japan. Its southernmost island, Guam, is home to a major American air base. Lieutenant Commander Edgar K. Thompson, Assistant Naval Attache for Air at the American Embassy in Lima during the war, wryly comments that "had Robertson buried his treasure on Guam, the Navy's fourteen inch bombardment shells might have blasted it out of the ground." Likewise, he says, if Robertson (as some still believe) had chosen nearby Saipan, American GIs "might have dug it out of the bottom of a foxhole."[3]

Seized by Japan in 1914, the Marianas had earlier devolved to the United States, along with the Philippines, as part of the spoils of victory in the Spanish-American War. But for almost four centuries prior to 1898, the islands were held without interruption by Spain and, as they were situated almost directly along the course of her annual fleet run between Manila and Vera Cruz in Mexico, the Marianas may have been familiar to the likes of Captain Robertson.

Whether such may have been the case, in late 1826 the skipper of the hijacked *Peruvian* is credited with singling out Agrihan—a six-mile long by three-and-a-half-mile-wide island—toward the northern tip of the chain.

Though the site of the buried piastres remains a matter of the purest speculation, pundits favor a scenario whereby Robertson anchors his brig off a cove on Agrihan's southwest shore and then moves his fortune in longboat loads—a task requiring as much as a week—up a narrow inlet inland. Lafond, among others, believes that the cache was secreted in this way. All, that is, but for some 20,000 piastres. These, it is posited, were set aside as ready funds—one portion toward expenses, another toward the eventual purchase of a replacement for the obviously compromised *Peruvian* and a third as a means to a new identity. For Robertson, at least, was of a mind to cover his tracks and a good deal of distance as well, prior to a return visit to Agrihan. After all, standing in the way of a magnificent retirement—one that he certainly intended to enjoy without forever watching his back—were six dangerous men.

As the *Peruvian's* jittery crew now headed back on an east-northeasterly course across the Tropic of Cancer, the tension aboard ship can only be imagined. On dry land their lives would probably not be worth spit and they knew it. Throughout the long crossing to Hawaii, for thither Robertson had pointed his craft, they might start at the very thought of it, as if from some evil dream. Even as the men derived a measure of cold comfort from their fleeting indispensability, handling as they did a severely understaffed ship—no conceivable treachery might be ruled out. Thus, contrary to precedent, the night watch aboard the *Peruvian* might be expected to be less than a hardship.

In fact, sleep forfeited en route was soon, in the case of the four odd men out, to be recompensed after a fashion. Privy to Robertson's selective confidence Williams and George were ready when, within striking distance of Oahu, their captain gave them the nod. Inferior in number, but favored by the decisive element of surprise, the three conspirators succeeded in overpowering their hapless comrades. Driven below decks, the men were bound hand and foot and the companionway hatch sealed above them. Then, as the events were related to Lafond, Robertson, Williams and George scuttled the *Peruvian* and made good their escape in a longboat. Drifting ashore a few days hence, having prudently secreted their portable booty, the erstwhile captain convincingly passed off himself and his two pitiable companions as shipwrecks.

Months later, Robertson reportedly turned up in Brazil. Blind chance in the guise of a passing brig had delivered him there, accompanied by his ever-present Irish accomplices. Having signed on as itinerant merchant seamen, a role they apparently carried off word perfect, the three, upon hitting shore, plunged as best they could, given Robertson's eye-catching physiognomy, into the teeming and indifferent docklife of Rio de Janeiro. Tragically for George, when the trio next surfaced it was shy of a man.

Now Robertson made an inspired move. A British convict ship, then in port, seemed just the ticket for a working passage to New South Wales. Whatever the extent of their incognitos, he and Williams looked like able enough seamen and carried the requisite forged papers to prove it. Safely reaching Sydney with nobody the wiser, they proceeded undeterred to Hobart, Tasmania.

There, Robertson struck up an acquaintance with a fellow Glaswegian named Thompson. Down-at-heel and getting along in years, Thompson bore his penury with a show of philosophic disdain. Past skipper of a lucrative whaler, he was, in the hour of Robertson's timely introduction, reduced to trawling for an exiguous livelihood, master of no better than a weather-beaten fishing yawl. Still, there was something about the man which implied he would not come cheap.

For their part, Williams and Robertson were by no means as flush as they might have wished. The lately departed George, it seems, had betrayed, while in his final port of call, a fatal weakness for losing at cards with money not his own. What remained might just do for an overhaul on Thompson's yawl and the man's exorbitant fee. Though they might drop their last piastre on this, the final leg to Agrihan, it bore remembering that the distance was considerable, being roughly equivalent to sailing from Rio to Glasgow. Besides, the South Pacific was known to be studded with islands, reefs and shoals more than a match for even a navigator of Robertson's abilities, negotiating them for the first time. Better, it was decided, to leave the business to Thompson and his young crew.

Naturally, details of the voyage were as rare as pearls. It was made plain to Thompson that for the kind of money he was being paid he might keep his beastly curiosity to himself. Robertson made no secret of the fact that their destination was to be the Marianas Islands. Beyond that he resolutely declined to venture, except for promising the man an attractive gratuity should he deliver them in one piece. Since Robertson had proved loath to share Agrihan's bearings with his long-standing partner, Williams posed no threat from that quarter even if he and Thompson should prove treacherous.

Such, in fact, was what transpired. Robertson was no easy man to live with and now, some two years into their criminal association and becalmed in the torrid doldrums of Melanesia, the strain on Williams began to tell. That, at least, is how Robertson chose to paint the picture to the canny and highly inquisitive Thompson whose bonhomie toward the Irishman was beginning to put out a bad smell. Williams for his part, once in his cups, was simply talking too much and, as his conversations with Thompson could not always be monitored, Robertson's killer instincts were soon aroused. Letting it be known that his friend was prey to delusions, suffered fits and even harbored suicidal tendencies, Robertson now stuck like glue to his man.

Late one sweltering night, as the two men shared the relative cool of the afterdeck, tragedy struck again. Asleep at the time, Robertson could only speculate as to how or why Williams had got himself overboard. All he could say was that, no sooner had he realized what had happened, than the poor demented Irishman was beyond saving.

By the time Robertson's charter sighted the island of Tinian in the Marianas, a day's sail north of Guam, Thompson—neither timorous nor gullible—had made himself thoroughly odious to his client. Having badgered the taciturn Robertson unstintingly, though without success as to the exact nature of their mission, Thompson's own frustration finally boiled over in a flood of Celtic pique. The two men had been sharing a hand of cards at the time when Thompson—his line of interrogation thwarted yet again—snapped that he knew more about the mysterious treasure, thanks to Williams, than Robertson might think. With that, the younger man was suddenly on his feet and kicking out at him so violently that Thompson, unable to maintain his grip upon the foredeck bollard to which he had clung in desperation, found himself tumbled into the sea.

The young crew later swore that, while they prepared to bring the yawl about and come to their captain's rescue, Robertson, armed and threatening, had prevented them from doing so. Instead, they were ordered to hold to course and were thus reluctantly obliged to give up Thompson for dead.

A lifetime's experience on the water had, however, steeled the man to adversity. Still blessed with a powerful stroke and benefiting from a temperate sea, Thompson, keeping a level head, eventually made his way to within several hundred yards of shore. There, luck was with him.

Anchored just beyond the reef, by the greatest good fortune, was a frigate flying the Spanish colors. Hauled aboard by her astonished crew, Thompson, once composed and treated to a set of dry clothes, presented himself in the commander's quarters to the vessel's distinguished guest.

The gentleman in question was His Excellency, Señor Medinilla, Governor of the Marianas. Attended by an officer named Pacheco, Medinilla was, at the time, overseeing an inspection tour of the islands and, after listening to disjointed snatches of the exhausted swimmer's story, determined to act at once. His men ashore signalled back to the ship. Medinilla ordered her anchor slipped and a course set north.

At the very next island, Saipan, he overtook Thompson's yawl. The Australian crew, relieved at the timely intervention, reported that, on spotting the pursuing frigate, Robertson had pulled himself ashore alone in Thompson's dinghy. An armed shore party, sent in hot pursuit, soon cornered him and, surprisingly, Robertson chose to give himself up without a struggle.

He might easily have taken his own life with a single well-placed bullet. That he did not may be accounted for, first, by the fact that he was, at long last, within an ace of Agrihan's treasure and, second, having doubtless spied the frigate's colors, he needed no reminding that, although he had once taken up the revolutionary cause against Spain the hijacked *Peruvian* herself had flown the Union Jack.

Be that as it may, whatever damning information as to Robertson's past Thompson might have gleaned from Williams, the man was surely drowned at sea. The crew, of course, could pose a problem but, at the worst, the late incident on the foredeck would be a matter of his word against theirs. At the very best, who knew but that the youthful Australians, greedy for a promised cut of the fortune, had not set loyalty to their captain aside and kept silent?

Led back to the shore under guard and rowed out to the Spanish frigate, Robertson was in for a nasty shock. For who should be standing on the bridge but Thompson and, flanking him, as if by some evil curse, the very Spaniard he had flogged a decade before at Arauco, Chile. Pacheco it seems, after his country's defeat at the hands of Bolivar's irregulars, had taken up a commission in the Philippines which had remained squarely under Spanish dominion throughout. Ironically, having played his small part in the winning of a war, for which his loyalties proved half-hearted at best, Robertson now found himself fast losing a battle for the prize he had risked all to capture, and indeed, defend.

Justice, in Robertson's case, proved swift and summary. Enlightened by Pacheco and Thompson as to crimes past and present, Governor Medinilla favored the Biblical eye-for-an-eye. Stripped to the waist and bent over a cannon, Robertson reportedly took some twenty salt-dipped lashes of a cat-o'-nine-tails before breaking down.

He alone among them knew the whereabouts of the *Peruvian's* missing fortune. Spare his life, upon their word as officers and gentlemen, and he would lead them to it straightway. Then, rich as sultans, they might take their separate paths. Pacheco had had his revenge; so, too, had Thompson. His Excellency, for his part, should simply be recovering lost enemy specie— no dishonor there. The treasure lay nigh—1000 chests and more of gold piastres—and with a ship's muster of navies to dig it up at that!

It should come as no surprise that Robertson's desperate brief, argued by fits and starts in a choked voice from between clenched teeth, carried the day. Robertson spat out, as if in disgust, the name "Agrihan," like some sweet and long-cherished charm gone suddenly sour. He was then taken below decks and the frigate's mainsail set.

Governor Medinilla, in his official capacity as Inspector General, was familiar with the island and the cove in question off Agrihan's southwestern shore. From there Robertson would be obliged to direct the landing party in person as he owned to having chosen his site, back in 1826, with extreme care.

In fact, he would take its secret with him to the grave. As Gabriel Lafond relates the denouement of the Agrihan mystery, Robertson, shackled with heavy chain and lowered into a lifeboat readied to ferry him ashore, lunged precipitately forward. Sucked swiftly to the bottom, thanks to the weight of his bonds, Robertson breathed his last before the first of the Governor's divers ever managed to reach him.

Left without so much as a clue to the treasure's whereabouts, after a desultory search inland conducted during the following days Medinilla took himself off. Lafond, visiting the Philippines in the 1830s, learned that Medinilla returned to Agrihan on more than one occasion before his transfer and that he engaged, all told, close to 600 natives in combing the six-mile-long island under the watchful eye of a trusted "capataz." To Lafond's knowledge, not a trace did they uncover of the *Peruvian's* gold piastres. Nor, reportedly, has anyone since.

Lord Howe Island

*Fortune brings in some boats,
that are not steer'd*
—William Shakespeare
Cymbeline

An island paradise with subtropical weather, surrounded by a sparkling blue ocean and the southernmost
coral reef in the world. An untouched landscape with no
poisonous snakes or spiders . . . Crystal-clear lagoons free
of sharks and "stingers". An island of unique beauty home
to rare species of flora, fauna and sea life ... The only place
in New South Wales where the sun sets over the ocean.[1]

Captain Rattenbury of the 185-ton whaling brig, *George,* might well have counted
himself lucky to have been marooned at such a place. There was abundant game,
good wing shooting, plenty of turtles and fish and fresh water. Lying 435 miles
northeast of Sydney in the Middle Banks of the Tasman Sea, it had just about everything to console a man waiting to be rescued. The only difficulty was that it gave an
otherwise hard working whaling captain, with a chest of well-earned gold sovereigns in his cabin, the unaccustomed luxury to ... think.

Remarkably, the existence of eastern Australia was not known to white
men until the great Captain Cook, hydrologer extraordinaire, landed at what
is now Sydney on April 29, 1770. En route, he apparently missed a pair of
mist-shrouded peaks rising out of the Tasman Sea. It would be up to an
obscure officer named Ligberg Ball, the man credited with discovering Lord

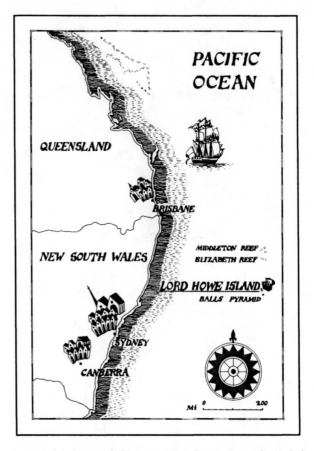

Howe Island, to sight them while serving as lieutenant aboard the *Supply* on a run to the penal colony at Norfolk Island in 1788.

The background to the lost treasure of Howe Island is straightforward enough. The Derwent Whaling Club had lost one of its ships and, in 1828, Mr. Walter A. Bethune was sent abroad to purchase another. On March 27, 1830 he sailed from London in the brig *George* by way of Mauritius where, at Port Louis, she took on a consignment of bananas, liqueurs, eau de cologne and 727 bags of sugar. The *George* carried a crew of seventeen, led by Captain Rattenbury, whose wife and two children accompanied him on the voyage. It appears that Rattenbury intended to start a new life with his family in Tasmania.

At Hobart, the Derwent Whaling Club had the *George* converted to a whaler and then dispatched her to the Middle Banks, the rich whaling grounds lying between New Zealand and Australia in the Tasman Sea. Rattenbury enjoyed early success, so much so that he took the *George* into Sydney where he sold his load of oil to a number of whalers wishing to top up their cargoes. By now £6,000 the better for his transactions—a sum reportedly paid in sovereigns—Captain Rattenbury returned to the Middle

Banks and, while in the vicinity of Howe Island, decided to put in at Boat Harbor just long enough to fill his vessel's casks with fresh water.

Little enough was known of the island at the time, although it was not uncommon for whalers to water there. Such was always accomplished under armed guard as Howe was not settled until 1834 and the mistaken belief that "savage natives" inhabited it (as they did the New Hebrides) was still widely held in the early 1830s.

In the shadow of Mount Gower, which looms mist-shrouded some 3000 feet over Boat Harbor on Howe's southernmost extreme, Captain Rattenbury sent a party ashore in one of the *George's* longboats with orders to return to the ship as soon as they had completed their mission. Meanwhile—depending upon who is relating the story—he either "hove to" or "stood off and on."

Some blame the disaster that soon struck the *George* on a "heavy mist" that swept over the mountains. According to this particular scenario, Rattenbury, sailing by the wind, was moving away from, and approaching, the island when he lost his bearings and mistook Mount Gower for her sister peak, Mount Lidgbird. Others hold that the *George* dragged her anchor when a gust of wind "blew down from the mountains." This would have meant that she was "heaving to" dangerously close to the shore. Captain Edward Knight of the *Alerte,* for one, cautioned against just such a procedure:

> It must be remembered that a vessel is never really secure when anchored off a small oceanic island ... One should always be prepared to slip one's anchor and be off to sea at once should it come on to a blow. It is therefore necessary to lie at some distance from the land, so as to have plenty of room to get away on either tack. If one is too near shore one incurs a great risk ... for even though it be blowing hard outside, one is becalmed under the cliffs or subjected to shifting flows and whirlwinds, so that the vessel becomes unmanageable, and is driven straight on the fatal rocks by the send of the swell.[2]

In either case, onto a fatal rock (which to this day bears her name) the *George* was indeed driven and, in the process, severely holed. Again, versions differ. But whether Rattenbury was forced to take ashore all the stores and valuables he could manage by longboat and finally abandon the *George* to her fate; or whether he managed to beach her on a rocky shore at Boat Harbor, the damage had been done.

Lord Howe was no desert island. Today, tourists will spend good money for a blissful week playing at beachcombing on its idyllic shores. Between the island's plentiful fish and game, and the *George's* salvaged stores, Rattenbury's crew may be expected to have sojourned in relative ease, but for the fear of a native attack. None of them wished to tempt fate by straying off into the dense, subtropical interior and, with the exception of a single investigation of Mount Gower undertaken by Captain Rattenbury and one or more of his four officers, the men preferred the safety of their makeshift camp at Boat Harbor.

After five uneventful weeks, remarkable for neither a tribal assault nor the sighting of a single sail on the far horizon, two ships suddenly put in at the island.

> The government Colonial brig *Mary Elizabeth* on a voyage to Norfolk Island and 40 days at sea, called at Lord Howe Island for water and found the wreck of the ship *George*, of Van Diemen's Land. She brought off Captain Rattenbury and four men. The remainder of the crew were picked up by the London whaler *Nelson*, Captain Davie, 2 1/2 years out, and taken to Sydney, from whence they finally reached Hobart.[3]

Strangely enough, no reference was made in the reports filed by either Captain Davie or his counterpart aboard the *Mary Elizabeth* to the large sum in coins lately in Rattenbury's possession. Clearly, the gentleman was keeping his counsel, and wisely so, since he was apparently strolling the decks of a prison supply ship heading for a notorious penal colony in Norfolk Island without so much as two pennies to rub together.

The question of how Rattenbury explained the wreck of the *George* and the disappearance of 5,000 gold sovereigns to Walter Bethune and his partners in the Derwent Whaling Club remains unanswered. In any event, Rattenbury managed to clear his name and then wasted no time in leaving Hobart while the going was good.

Once back in Sydney he struck up an acquaintance with a sympathetic whaling skipper by the florid name of Edward Primrose Tregurtha who was good enough to sign him on as first mate of the *Caroline*. At some strategic point in their brief association Rattenbury obviously confided in his man. No doubt news of the *George's* disaster was, by this time, general; particular to her erstwhile captain, however, was the truth behind the fate of the gold sovereigns at Boat Harbor.

If the Lord Howe story is to be credited—that sometime during his unanticipated five weeks on the island Rattenbury succumbed to avarice and buried his employers' gold on the shore below Mount Gower—speed must now have been of the essence. According to Tregurtha's ship's log, the *Caroline* did not weigh anchor until November 1831. That meant that close to a year had passed since the *George* was holed, enough time for any of Rattenbury's accomplices to steal a march on him back to the treasure site.

Precisely one month later the *Caroline* approached Lord Howe Island. The extent to which Rattenbury confided in Tregurtha is a mystery but it is a matter of record that, after giving the mists and winds of Boat Harbor the widest of berths, they landed together on Howe's southern shore. But what awaited them there? Some accounts, including that published in *Vanished Fleets* by Alan Villiers, quote Captain Edward Primrose Tregurtha in the *Caroline's* logbook as follows:

> In November we set out and shaped a course for Howe's Island. My mate had assured me of some whaling treasures he knew of being buried there, which would only cost us the trouble of taking away ... On the 15th we sighted Howe's Island, and at 10 A.M. lowered the two quarter-boats, in which the mate and I proceeded for the shore. It took us, pulling and sailing, 7 hours to reach the beach, where on landing we shot a quantity of bronzewing pigeons, which were so tame they would not go away until we killed 60 or 70. Some persons had removed the gear we sought.[4]

Max Nicholls, however, in a work commissioned in the 1950s by the regional government of Lord Howe Island, quoted Tregurtha's log thus:

> In November we set out and shaped a course for Howe's Island. My mate said he knew where a treasure was buried. On 15th December we sighted the island and landed two quarter-boats. It took us seven hours to reach the shore where we found a great number of bronzewing pigeons. We shot about 70 of them but were unable to find the treasure as the country seemed to have altered considerably.[5]

Whichever of the two versions is correct, the story got about that Rattenbury led Captain Tregurtha to the place on the beach at the foot of Mount Gower where he had hidden the sovereigns, only to find to his horror that a landslide had covered it over with tons of debris.

The better to cloud the record, the Lord Howe Island story presents further anomalies. For example, the question arises as to whether the sovereigns were more likely to have been Spanish dollars which reportedly enjoyed wider currency in Sydney in the early nineteenth century. In any event why is there no mention anywhere of Rattenbury's fellow officers having sought them?

In the end, one may only safely reckon that the legend of Lord Howe Island can neither be proved nor disproved. But if the landslide account is true, a treasure possibly worth £400,000[6] lies to this day buried in the shadow of Mount Gower.

Gardiners Island

If I call for it and it is gone,
I shall take your head, or that of your son.
—CaptainWilliam Kidd
Gardiners Island, June 1699

For the Scottish preacher's son, life may truly be said to have begun at forty. Though a relative newcomer to New York, William Kidd seemed to be making all the right moves. Only a matter of days after the death of her second husband, the well-to-do widow, Sarah Bradley Cox Oort, took out a marriage license in Manhattan with one "William Kidd, Gentleman," dated May 16, 1691. His young wife's dowry included properties on Wall, Water, Pine and Dock Streets, a two-story brick house on the corner of Hanover and Pearl, as well as an interest in the Sawkill Farm at what is today 74th Street, in addition to a country place in "the Harlem."[1]

Thanks to the emoluments of trade and licensed privateering, Kidd's mercantile connections allowed him to lavish upon his discerning bride a wealth of exotic wedding gifts, among them the first "Turkey carpet" in the New World. Moreover, he ingratiated himself with New York's rising Anglican faction by contributing tackle from his vessel, the *Antigua,* toward the construction of Trinity Church on Broadway. Upon its completion, Sarah and William later purchased a pew alongside those of Robert Livingston and New York's newly installed Governor, Benjamin Fletcher.

A man of unblemished reputation, at least for those troubled times, Kidd was happily married and twice a father. Whatever beguiled him away from such comforts makes for one of the enduring mysteries of the most notorious brigand in history.

Neither a ruthless man, nor a desperado, the extraordinary arrangement he nonetheless entered upon some years later in London with a privileged syndicate of England's political figures, linked to a most influential silent partner, King William III, finally led Kidd to a small private estate in Long Island Sound off East Hampton—known to this day as Gardiners Island.

The man who seems to have persuaded Kidd was the ambitious, silver-tongued entrepreneur, Robert Livingston. In the autumn of 1695 he guided Kidd through the rites of passage to the powerful Whig Junto[2] in London and to a privateering contract engineered by the Earl of Bellomont, soon to be Governor of Massachusetts. Simply stated, the terms empowered Kidd to harry both the French and any pirates operating on the high seas, the fruits of such enterprise, once legally "condemned" in a Boston court of Admiralty (as overseen by Bellomont), to be divided among the syndicate's various signatories. Kidd's crew, whose ranks he was entitled to "beat up" along the voyage as the need arose, were to receive no more than a quarter share of the takings on a "no prey, no pay" basis. Should gross profits exceed £100,000, Kidd and Livingston would be further rewarded.

His vessel was the 284-ton *Adventure Galley,* equipped with thirty-four guns and manned by 150 hardened men, many of them ruffians recruited from the bars of the Thames docks and Lower Manhattan where the *Adventure Galley* briefly laid over during the summer of 1696. Also among the crew was Samuel Bradley, Kidd's brother-in-law. From there, Kidd made the crossing to Madeira and then hauled south for Madagascar—to late seventeenth-century brigands what Lourdes was to the halt and the blind. Since the cost of so lengthy a voyage to a fare-paying passenger was otherwise roughly £100, there figured among Kidd's crew men who had shipped aboard in New York for no better purpose than a free ride to the Mecca of Indian Ocean piracy at the syndicate's expense.

Perhaps for that very reason, Kidd gave Madagascar a wide berth and, after a profitless run through the Comoro Islands in the spring of 1697, headed for the trade route of the Grand Mogul's fleet. It was in August off the port of Aden at the mouth of the Red Sea, fully one year after he had departed New York and with nothing to show for his pains, that the *Adventure Galley's* restless crew apparently pressured Kidd into crossing the line. After a bungled assault upon the East Indiaman *Sceptre,* Kidd tacked eastward for the Malabar coast, pillaging en route the humble Moorish vessel *Mary* of a sack or two of coffee, a bale of pepper, some rice, myrrh and about a fistful of gold dust.

Battered by two of the Viceroy of Goa's men-of-war off Karwar on September 12, the *Adventure Galley* watered at Calicut then sailed for the Laccadive Islands where her riotous crew, fired by a trading deal gone awry, proceeded to brutalize the oft-abused native population. The following month off Cape Comorin at India's southern tip, Kidd aroused the ire of his men by strenuously objecting to the capture of a Dutch trader, the *Loyal Captain.*

In a related incident on October 30 Kidd, enraged at what he took to be threats by the *Galley's* chief gunner, William Moore, cast about for a ready cudgel and seized upon the nearest thing to hand; this was a wooden bucket bound by iron bands. Hurling it towards the seated figure of Moore, who was sharpening a chisel at the time, the unlikely projectile landed a direct hit against the gunner's skull. Oddly enough, Moore's death served, at least temporarily, to lay the ghost of impending mutiny. Then, too, the next few months provided a lucrative distraction for the *Galley's* chastened crew. In November they took the 280-ton *Rouparelle* of the French East India Company's fleet (whose captain was summarily relieved of his French "pass") and, in December, a Portuguese trader brimming with butter, rice, opium and iron.

But the best was yet to come.

Known variously as the *Quedagh Merchant,* the *Quetta, Kara* and the *Kedah Merchant,* she was an exceedingly fine prize by any other name. Outbound from Calcutta where her French "pass" had been notarized by none other than Francois Martin, at Chandernagore on January 14, 1697, founder of Pondicherry and father of the French "empire" in India,[3] her diverse cargo included gold, silver, diamonds and pearls, spices, cloth, opium and saltpeter to the value of around £100,000. She carried a number of Dutch and Moorish passengers, was skippered by an Englishman named Wright, and her treasures were owned by an Indian consortium, one of whose members, Coji Babba, was aboard when Kidd challenged her. Babba later testified that Kidd spurned his offer of a 20,000-rupee ransom for the goods and tossed all the *Quedagh's* bills of lading overboard in an effort to obscure the nature and value of her cargo.

Kidd may rightly have spoken the truth when he later claimed to have taken her under duress, since the prisoners aboard, before being marooned, all agreed that he later attempted, over the violent protests of his crew, to return the *Quedagh Merchant.* Be that as it may, her owner, none other than the Grand Mogul of India, was not surprisingly outraged when he heard of this outlandish English assault upon his shipping.

Kidd was thought to have reached Madagascar in early April in fine fettle. Now two years out of Plymouth, he had finally made good. With at least £100,000 profits on his books, he might look forward, after some explanation, to a warm welcome from Bellomont and his backers. If he had committed a few minor transgressions along the way, they would surely be papered over by his powerful friends on both sides of the Atlantic. And, though he had tarried, in a pinch there was always good King William—an interested party himself.

Such did not prove to be the case. Not only had Kidd greatly offended India's Grand Mogul, Aurangzeb, thereby risking the English East India Company's future on the subcontinent, but peace in Europe—the bugbear of international privateering—had but recently "broken out" with the signing of the Treaty of Ryswick in a little village near the Hague on December 30, 1697. Kidd's humanity may have been gratified by these sudden tidings of European harmony but, as an English privateer who had taken at least two French prizes (the *Quedagh Merchant* and the *Rouparelle)* several months after the cessation of hostilities, he was undoubtedly nervous.

Granted, word of the peace had not reached the Indian Ocean until April, 1698 and, pursuant to Article X of Kidd's privateering commission, such a contingency was covered for captures made "beyond the line [the Equator] within six months of the signing of the Peace." Nonetheless, the timing of his depredations remained unfortunate, particularly since he had overrun the deadline of his commission by more than a few months.

Kidd had plenty of time to ponder his predicament at Ile Ste Marie, off Madagascar's northeast coast, where he chose to lay by for fully five months, "waiting," as he later testified, upon a "fair Wind." In the meantime, the better to round out his skeletal crew which had abandoned him by droves, Kidd was reduced to signing on passengers of one sort or another. Among them was Captain Edward Davis who brought with him the truly alarming gossip that William Kidd had lately been declared by King William as an "obnoxious Pyrate."

Having torched the battered *Adventure Galley,* Kidd weighed anchor in the *Quedagh Merchant* that November, setting a gingerly course for the Caribbean island of Anguilla where he landed in April 1699 to the disheartening news that a hue and cry order had been issued against his capture. More ominous still, the General Amnesty for Indian Ocean pirates, offered by King William to sailors surrendering to the proper authorities in or before April, specifically excluded him. To add to a rising sea of troubles, upon reaching St. Thomas and the limit of his patience, Kidd marooned his wife's ailing brother, Samuel Bradley, long a critic of his actions. Bradley would take his revenge for such cruelty by surviving the ordeal; the thoroughly unflattering deposition he subsequently swore against his brother-in-law made for yet another nail in Kidd's coffin.

Kidd now found himself in urgent need of a good friend with sound advice and a fast boat. He was determined to head without delay for a parley with governor Bellomont. An Antiguan merchant, Henry Boulting, was unfettered by the fine points of the law and seemed just the man. Meeting up with him on tiny Isla Mona between Puerto Rico and Hispaniola (the Dominican Republic), Kidd handed over bills of exchange plus "dust and barr gold" toward the purchase of Boulting's sloop *San Antonio.* He then scuttled the *Quedagh Merchant,* possibly near Isla Catalina east of Santo Domingo, after transferring a good part—though reportedly not all—of his treasure to the *San Antonio.* Whether Kidd secreted a portion of it in the vicinity of Isla Catalina (as he steadfastly maintained) is a mystery which has never been satisfactorily resolved. Be that as it may, once the necessary preparations for his departure were set in hand, Kidd sailed north and, after brief stays in Delaware and on Rhode Island, he arranged for a clandestine meeting with his attorney.

James Emmott was a crack Admiralty lawyer who knew how to skin a cat nine ways. Not surprisingly, Emmott was no friend of the reform-minded Governor. In a night-long session aboard the *San Antonio* quietly anchored in early June off Oyster Bay, New York, Kidd unburdened himself of the highlights of his successful, though impossibly compromised, voyage.

The home news, said Emmott, was, if anything, worse. His client might as well dismiss the hope of cutting a deal with the syndicate as it had since disappeared under a cloud. To make matters worse, on both sides of the Atlantic the "Kidd business" had become nothing less than a *succes de scandale. This* scandal was an ideal vehicle on which the Tories might ride back to power and the Whig Junto, reeling under the onslaught of its implacable rivals in Parliament, was proving craven in its haste to distance itself from the beleaguered figure responsible for all its current woes. Kidd, as he would learn to his horror, was up to his eyes in, of all things, politics.

Putting out to sea at dawn, he was a man with a fortune below decks and yet a bleak future before him. One of his lifelines—his pair of French passes—he had handed over to Emmott; the other he determined to bury, as the most hopeful of bargaining chips, at a dot on the New England map called Gardiners Island.

In disgrace, near despair and struggling for dignity, the Governor of Massachusetts, meanwhile, sat beleaguered in Boston. His man was cruising somewhere on the Long Island Sound and, were he but able to lure him in from the cold, Bellomont was fully prepared—indeed pledged—to toss him to the wolves. A scapegoat was wanted here; the treasure for the moment be damned! And as if to comply with the terms of a tragic fate, Kidd had surrendered up his two French passes to Emmot who was now en route with them in hand to the Massachusetts capital. Kidd, as it turned out, would never set eyes on them again.

Captain Kidd,

Mr. Emmott came to me last Tuesday night late, telling me he came from you, but was shy of telling me where he parted from you, nor did I press him to it. He told me you came to Oyster Bay in Nassau Island and sent for him to New York. He proposed to me from you that I would grant you a pardon. I answered that I had never granted one yet and that I made myself a safe rule not to grant a pardon to anybody whatsoever without the King's express leave or command. He told me you declared and protested your innocence and that if your men could be persuaded to follow your example, you would make no manner of scruple of coming to this port or any other within her Majesty's Dominions; that you owned there were two ships taken but that your men did it violently against your will and used you barbarously in imprisoning you and treating you ill most of the voyage, and often attempting to murder you.

Mr. Emmott delivered me two French passes taken on board the two ships which your men need, which passes I have in my custody and I am apt to believe they will be a good article to justify you, if the peace were not, by the Treaty between England and France, to operate in that part of the world at the time the hostility was committed, as I was almost confident it was not to do. Mr. Emmott also told me that you had to the value of 10,000 pounds in the sloop with you and that you left a ship somewhere off the coast of Hispaniola in which there was to the value of 50,000 pounds more which you had left in safe hands and had promised to go to your people in that ship within three months to fetch them with you to a safe harbor ...

Your Humble Servant,
Bellomont[4]

By his own account, rendered on July 17, 1699 before Lord Bellomont and the Boston Council, John Gardiner, third Lord of the Manor, had awoken one day in late June to the sight of a sloop of six guns riding at anchor off the island bearing his name. Oddly, over the course of two days and nights, neither he nor the unknown party deigned to communicate. Gardiner was unable to glean the smallest clue as to his visitors' numbers, nationality or intent. Marauding Spanish brigands had been known on occasion to terrorize settlements along eastern Long Island and thus strangers in sloops, much like that of Kidd's, were greatly feared by local residents.

At last, nerves ravaged by the bizarre standoff, his native caution was conquered by a sudden onset of daring. Gardiner broke the ice. Striking out for the mystery sloop in his dinghy, the Lord of the Manor approached her stern in the late afternoon. Out of the sloop's stern companionway appeared a well dressed individual who leaned over the taffrail and greeted him warmly with a "How do you and your family do?" Such an opening gambit on the gentleman's part, after two days of ominous silence, Gardiner found disconcerting in the extreme, no less so when the stranger familiarly introduced himself as Captain William Kidd, a name with which he, Gardiner, later claimed to have been thoroughly unacquainted.

After a round of drinks and cordial, though insubstantial conversation, the gentleman reportedly came round to the point. He was, Kidd confided, on his way to Boston on an errand of the utmost importance and desired to lay by off the island, with Gardiner's permission, and to entrust to him certain valuables:

> Kidd was going to my Lord at Boston and desired the Narrator to carry three Negroes, two boys and a girl, ashore, to keep till he the said Kidd or his Order should call for them, which the Narrator accordingly did. That about two hours after the Narrator had got the said Negroes ashore, Captain Kidd sent his boat ashore with two bailes of Goods and a Negro Boy, and the morning after, said Kidd desired the Narrator to come immediately on board and bring Six Sheep with him for his the said Kidd's Voyage for Boston, which the Narrator did, when Kidd asked him to spare a barrel of Cyder, which the Narrator with great importunity consented to, and sent two of his men for it, who brought Cyder on board said Sloop, but whilst the men were gone for the Cyder, Captain Kidd offered the Narrator several pieces of damnified Muslin and Bengalls as a Present to his Wife.[6]

Tipping the four bearers of the cider keg each with a piece of "Araby Gold," in addition to a variety of "Muslins for neck-cloths," the Captain bade Gardiner farewell, fired off a four-gun salute in his host's honor and stood away for nearby Block Island. Three days later Kidd was back. Having been summoned to the *San Antonio* by New York's irrepressible coroner, Thomas "Whisking" Clarke, Gardiner was now prevailed upon by Kidd to render him a further service:

> The said Kidd was going to my Lord at Boston and desired the Narrator to take on shore with him and keep for him ... a Chest, and a box of gold and a bundle of Quilts and Four Bayles of Goods, which box of gold the said Kidd told the Narrator was intended for my Lord (Gov. Bellomont); and the Narrator complied with the said Kidd's request and took on shore the said Chest, box of quilts, and bayles of Goods.
>
> And the Narrator saith that two of Kidd's crew, who went by the names of Cooke and Parrot, delivered to him, the Narrator, two baggs of silver, which they told the Narrator weighed thirty pound weight, for which he gave receipt. And that another of Kidd's men delivered to the Narrator a small bundle of gold, and gold dust of about a pound weight to keep for him, and did also present the Narrator with a Sash and a pair of worsted stockings. And just before the Sloop sayled Captain Kidd presented the Narrator with a bagg of Sugar and then tooke leave and sayled for Boston.[7]

Before doing so Mrs. Gardiner, acceding to Kidd's request, roasted him a suckling pig. In gratitude, having dined off salted meats at sea for better than two years, he made her the gift of a pitcher and a "cloth of gold," a fragment of which to this day hangs framed in the Gardiner manor house.[8] Stories current on eastern Long Island well into the twentieth century that Kidd comported himself like a beast while John Gardiner's "guest"; that, while inebriated, he pursued the terrified man around a mulberry tree, tied him to the same and then slashed him; that he dropped pearls in wine, ran amok in the Manor house scattering money and wreaking havoc on Mrs. Gardiner's feather bedding with a cutlass; that he buried a portion of his treasure in a swamp at Cherry Harbor and threatened to take his host's head or that of his son were the treasure tampered with; and that Kidd finally "willed" Gardiner the fortune—are all an amalgam comprising unequal parts truth, inspired fiction and distorted history inevitably attaching itself to Kidd's legendary ill fame.

That Kidd's men buried treasure on Gardiners Island, that at least a portion of it was recovered, perhaps all but one "dull, uncut diamond," is a matter of historical record. That Kidd made free with his pearls and Gardiner's wine in the manner described is doubtless fancy. Finally, as to Gardiner being tied to a mulberry tree and physically abused, that tale relates to a true episode that occurred in 1723 when Spanish pirates attacked Gardiners Island. John Gardiner at the time was sixty-seven years old, thrice married, and did suffer his wrists to be slashed by a Spaniard's cutlass—though he survived.

Although Gardiner, thanks to an incident involving the "Kidd diamond," earned a reputation for timidity, the facts seem to have been otherwise. His island home, being the "first station on the way to New York," was most certainly frequented by pirate elements before and after Kidd, ferrying their illegal booty into Manhattan. Indeed, Kidd acted very much like many another Red Sea pirate and it is unlikely that Gardiner was ill accustomed to dealing with their kind.

Married four times in all, the lusty red-headed farmer was a prodigious lover of Indian women. "A man of large appetites and rustic manner ... he fathered innumerable Indian half-breeds, spoke the Montauk language, and according to John Lyon, his great-great-grandson, "came to their wigwams to eat fresh fish and liked the young squaws of the old sachem breed."[9]

His grandfather Lion Gardiner, first Lord of the Manor, bought the 3300-acre island, with its spectacular sweep of white sand beaches, stands of white oak and towering cliffs, from the Montauk tribe in the early 1630s. With them he chose to ally himself against the warring Narragansets. The close relationship, thus cemented, was well nigh unique in English colonial history. Once, when the daughter of Chief Wyandance was kidnapped by Narraganset braves on her wedding day, John Gardiner prudently put up part of the money for her ransom. For services rendered Wyandance, upon his death, bequeathed Gardiner thousands of acres on the Long Island mainland.[10] In 1639, what Indians had referred to for generations as Manchonake, the "Island of Death," was chartered (originally in the name of Isle of Wight) to "Lord" Gardiner by King Charles I. Gardiner's daughter Elizabeth was the first English child born in what is today New York State.

Fourth of July 1699 dawned unremarkably enough for most of the denizens of Boston Bay, the better part of a century prior to their riotous dumping of East India Company tea. The Governor, however, happened to be poorly. Pressure to relinquish his high office over the infernal "Kidd business" was proving inimical to his health—he hoped to see Kidd hang for it. Bellomont unstoically bore a world of medical complaints, most vexing among them an accumulation of uric acid in the blood—commonly associated with alcohol dependence which manifested itself in a painfully inflamed great toe. Simple pacing was intolerable, yet the Governor could scarcely restrain himself, exasperated as he was by Kidd.

Although Bellomont declined to see Kidd privately, the two had met across a table at one of several meetings of the Boston Council, at which time

Kidd had undergone an examination of his movements over the past two years. Among the meetings' express priorities was an attempt to untangle the financial muddle into which Bellomont's erstwhile syndicate had fallen; the Governor was under pressure from several quarters to make good the damages. Meanwhile, Kidd seemed content to temporize, pleading for more time on the grounds that he needed to reconstruct his journal before he could readily answer to the details of his voyage.

Kidd may well have been entertaining second thoughts as to the wisdom of falling upon Bellomont's mercy. He had, after all, only to fly to the *San Antonio* and, after a brief stopover at Gardiners Island, head for the open sea once again. The Governor realized that, should Kidd suddenly turn skittish and do so, whether his man was later apprehended or not would prove immaterial; Bellomont must simply bring the fellow to heel himself or suffer irremedial damage to his reputation. On Wednesday July 5, spurred to action, Bellomont sent out his constables with orders to arrest Kidd on sight. The following afternoon they surprised him entering the house of the wealthy Boston merchant, Peter Sargeant.

Lord Bellomont to the Board of Trade, Boston, July 8, 1699.

My Lords,
I have the Misfortune to be ill of the Gout at a time when I have a great deal of business to exercise both my head and my hand.

It will not be unwelcome News to your Lordships to tell you that I secured Captain Kidd last Thursday in the Gaol of this Town with five or six of his men. He had been hovering on the Coast towards New York for more than a fortnight, and sent to one Mr. Emmott to come from New-York to him at a place called Oyster-Bay in Nassau Island not far from New-York ... Emmott told me that Kidd had left the great Moorish Ship he took in India (which Ship I have since found went by the name of Quidah-Marchant), in a Creek on the Coast of Hispaniola, with goods to the value of thirty Thousand pounds: That he had bought a Sloop, in which he was come before to make his termes: that he had brought in the Sloop with him several Bailes of East India goods, threescore pound weight of Gold Dust and in Ingotts, about a hundred weight of silver and several other things which he believed would sell for about ten Thousand pounds ... I am manning out a Ship to go in Quest of the Quidah-Marchant left by Kidd on the Coast of Hispaniola; by some papers which we seized

with Kid, and by his own Confession, wee have found out
where the Ship lyes; and according to his account of the Cargo
we compute her to be worth seventy thousand pounds. The
Ship that carries this is just upon Sailing, and will not be persuaded to stay any longer; so that I cannot send your Lordships the Inventories of Goods brought in by Kid, nor the
Informations we have taken about him from his own men, till
next opportunity. I am, with Respect,

My Lords
Yours Lordships most humble
and obedient Servant
Bellomont[11]

By the end of July Bellomont was pleased to have the following official
inventory drawn up and sworn to by William Kidd:

Boston. New England. July 25, 1699

A True Accompt of all such Gold, Silver, Jewels and Merchan-
dises, late in the Possession of Captain William Kid, which
have been secured by us underwritten, pursuant to an order
from his Excellency, Richard Earl of Bellomont, Captain Gen-
eral and Governor in Chief over his Majties' Provinces of ye.
Massachusette Bay &c. bearing date July 25, 1699 (vizt):
@In Capt. William Kids Box:
One Bag qt. Fifty three Sillver Bars (357 oz)
One Bag, qt. Seventy nine Bars and pieces of Silver (44 1/2 ozs.)
One Bag, qt. Seventy four Barrs Silver, 421 ozs.
One Enameld Silver Box gilt in which are four diamonds
set in gold, Lockets, one diamond loose, one large diamond
set in a gold ring.
Found in Mr. Duncan Campbell's House:
No.1. One Bag, qt. Gold (58 1/2 ozs.).
No.2. One Bag, qt. 94 Gold ozs.
No.3. One handkerchiefe, qt. 50 gold ozs.
No.4. One Bag, qt. 103 ozs.
No.5. One Bag, qt. 38 1/2 ozs.
No.6. One Bag qt. 19 1/4 ozs.
No. 7. One Bag, qt. 203 silver ozs.
Also Twenty Dollars, one halfe and one quarter
pieces of eight, New English Crowns, one Small Barr of
Silver, one Small Lump Silver, a small Chaine, A Small

bottle, A Corrall necklace, one p's white and one p's of Chckquerd Silk.

In Captain William Kid's Chest, Two Silver Basons, Two Silver Candlesticks, One Silver Porringer & Som small thing of Silver, qt. d. 2 oz; Rubies, small and great, Sixty Seven, Green Stones two, and one large Loadstone. (69 Precious Stones and Jewells.)

Landed from on Board the Sloop Antonio, Capt. Wm. Kid late Commander: 57 Bags of Sugar, 17 Pieces of Canvas, 38 Bales of Merchandize.

Received of Mr. Duncan Campbell Three Bailes Merchandize whereof one he had opened being much Damnified by Water qt. Eightyfive p's of silk, Rumals, and Bengalls, sixty p's of Cauicos and Muslins.

Received the 17th inst of Mr. John Gardner,

No.1. One Bag Dust Gold, qt. 60/3 gold ozs.

No.2. One Bag Coynd gold, qt. 60 gold ozs.; and in it Silver 123 ozs.

No.3. One prcl dust Gold qt. 24 3/4 ozs.

No.4. One Bagg. qt. Three Silver rings, Sundry Precious stones 4 7/8 ozs.; One Bagg unpoolisht Stones qt. 12 1/2 ozs. One p's of Cristoland Bezer (bezoar) Hore. 2 Corneion rings, 2 small Agats, 2 Amethests.

No.5. One Bagg Silver Buttons and a Lamp qt. 29 silver ozs.

No.6. One Bagg Broken Silver. qt. 173 1. 2 ozs.

No. 7. One Bagg Gold Barrs qt. 355 1/4 ozs.

No.8. One Bagg Gold Barrs at 238 1.2 ozs.

No. 9. One Bagg Dust Gold. qt. 59 1/2 ozs.

No. 10. One Bag Silver Barrs qt. 212 ozs.

No. 11. One Bag Silver Barrs qt. 309 ozs.

1111 Gold ozs. 2353 Silver ozs.

The whole of the Gold Above-Mentioned is a Eleven hundred and Eleven ounces Troy Weight. The Silver is Two Thousand three hundred and Fifty three ozs. The Jewells or Precious Stones weighted are 17 oz; and (town MS) in ounces and Sixteen stones by Tale. The Suger is contained in 57 Baggs. The Merchandize is contained in 4 Bailes; The Canvas in Seventeene Pieces.

Signed. Sam Sewall, Nathal. Byfield, Jem. Dumer, LAW. Hammond, Holdr., And Belcher.[12]

As assessed by Sewall and Byfield of the Gardiners' Island investigation, Kidd's treasure—the "Rubies, small and great," the silks, Rumals and

Bengalls, 2353 ounces of silver and the 1111 Troy ounces of gold—came to roughly £14,000. This was a huge sum for the year 1699. Nonetheless, there was certainly more of it about and the Governor meant to track it down.

Kidd never returned to either Gardiners Island or Hispaniola. Clapped into sixteen pounds of irons, he passed the harsh winter of 1699 in Boston's Stone Prison. A nervous Governor Bellomont transferred him there from less secure confinement after firing one gaoler for negligence and hiring a second out of his own pocket at forty shillings a week.

In time, Kidd offered Bellomont "fifty or three score thousand pounds" he swore he had hidden in the Caribbean; the Governor had only to allow Kidd to conduct him to it. However tempting the proposition, Bellomont declined to be led up the garden path, or—God forbid!—beyond, barely trusting as he did his prisoner to the dank walls of Stone Prison. Instead, as good as his word, he and a group of wealthy friends sent a crew through the Florida Straits in the *San Antonio* in the hope of coming upon evidence of the *Quedagh Merchant* off the coast of southern Hispaniola. Reportedly a failure, the voyage did result in the arrest of Henry Boulting whose suspect testimony, as to the fate of the *Quedagh Merchant,* led him in due course to the Old Bailey.[13]

Word of Kidd's capture, as reported in Bellomont's July 8 letter to the Board of Trade, galvanized the London public and sent Westminster's politicians scurrying, some for cover, others to the Admiralty. Within a matter of days, HMS *Rochester* was called into service to bring the renegade home. Departing Southampton in early September, she was driven back by raging seas to the stormy protests of the Tories. So highly charged was the political atmosphere surrounding the "Kidd Affair" that the failure of the *Rochester* to weather the autumn gales of the North Atlantic prompted allegations of conspiracy against the Junto and, in turn, increased the pressures upon Governor Bellomont to secure his prisoner at all cost.

As he was already in sufficiently bad odor at Westminster, the very possibility of Kidd's escape was enough to turn Bellomont's bowels to ice. Thus Kidd could look forward to precious little intercourse with the outside world from Stone Prison, but for the dreaded visitations of Cotton Mather, the hysterical preacher of Boston's Old North Church. Breathing fire and brimstone into the Captain's frigid cell, Kidd would find the Reverend Mather's dubious spiritual ministrations extremely trying and cold comfort indeed in the dark autumn and winter months of his solitary captivity.

Two of Kidd's crewmen, likewise behind bars, nevertheless fared a good deal better. Joseph Palmer and Robert Bradenham, ship's surgeon, were no friends of Kidd since they had both deserted him at Ile Ste Marie and were, by the same token, warmly enough embraced by Bellomont. Bradenham so distinguished himself in the Governor's eyes by agreeing, as did his shipmate Palmer, to testify for the prosecution, that, from being one of the "most hardened" members of the *Adventure Galley,* he was rehabilitated over-night into an "upright" witness and respectable man of medicine. The pair, thus anointed to carry the prosecution's case on their shoulders, were ac-corded immunity from prosecution; it was young Palmer who delighted Bellomont with the revelation of Kidd's aggression by bucket upon the chief gunner William Moore.[14]

The *Advice,* in command of Captain Wynne, set sail from Boston Harbor in mid-February 1700, thirty-one alleged pirates chained together along the walls of her gun room. Attended by a servant, William Kidd was held under close guard in a steerage cabin. At Greenwich on April 8, the Royal yacht *Katherine* came alongside and whisked him off to the Admiralty. There, a specially convened maritime panel was waiting to take his full statement.

Physically and morally shaken by a harsh captivity and cheerless crossing, as his personal effects, chest and papers were taken from him Kidd broke down. Begging for a knife with which to end his suffering, he reportedly fell into a "fitte" from which he only partially recovered later that day. After dictating two depositions and glumly watching as the last of his private documents were bound with white string and removed, Kidd dazedly handed over a gold sov-ereign he hoped would be forwarded on his behalf to Sarah. Then he was led away by a warder to his new home in Newgate Prison.

On March 27, 1701, much the worse for his year in Newgate, Kidd was summoned to a packed House of Commons and put through two grueling examinations. The following day, while he paced his cramped cell, the legal-ity of his privateering commission was hotly debated by House members and a motion carried to impeach several of the Junto for their complicity in the "Kidd Affair."

Recalled to the Commons on the twenty-ninth, a recommendation was then sent to the King calling for the "speedy trial of Capt. Kidd." The morn-ing following, the Admiralty sacked Kidd's jailer for allegedly permitting Lord Halifax (who would resign over the affair) access to the prisoner's cell. Finally, Kidd was once more examined on the floor of the Commons, on March 31, at which time he steadfastly maintained his innocence and like-wise implicated no one. His trial was later set for May 8.

The prosecution had spent much of the previous year preparing the case and their witnesses, Palmer and Bradenham, were, by the morning of Kidd's trial, word perfect. As two witnesses were required for conviction, they had only to stick to their guns—no hardship when their mutinous lives depended upon it—and Kidd was a dead Scot. Cross-examination was expected neither to tax the pair's credibility nor their mother wit; on the contrary, the burden would be all Kidd's. Under English law of the day, the defendant, seldom if ever versed in such a refinement, was nonetheless obliged to conduct the cross-examination of witnesses himself, the role of defense counsel being limited to the contention of points of law rather than of fact. Furthermore, the defendant was barred from testifying on his own behalf and, since Kidd's crew on the *Adventure Galley* stood with him as co-defendants under the indictment of piracy, neither might they take the stand in his defense.[15]

Against this battery Kidd could muster no better than a pair of woefully slender reeds—the obscure team of Dr. Oldys and Mr. Lemmon. Pursuant to the law of the land, £50 had been provided to cover Kidd's legal expenses and the Captain had thus retained counsel in early April. Uncharitably, Lemmon and Oldys declined to confer with their client until such time as the £50 was firmly in their possession. Since the sum in question, due to be forwarded any day by the Admiralty, did not manifest until the eve of the trial, Kidd received scant value for the money. To make matters worse, although they aided him at his first trial, the two left Kidd to shift entirely for himself at the second, for which they inexplicably failed to appear.

Sorely battered throughout by the overwhelming forces ranged against him, Kidd soldiered on in the mistaken belief that his two French passes would ultimately win him a victory over disgrace and death. Having repeatedly petitioned the Admiralty for his personal papers, though without effect, Kidd was finally and grudgingly granted access to them in April, only to discover, to his horror, that those he most coveted were conspicuous by their absence: the passes themselves and Bellomont's letter of June, 1699 acknowledging their receipt.

The prosecution's opening remarks, on the morning of May 8, proved devastating. As Kidd sat stunned by the sheer scope of the indictment against him, Dr. Newton for the Admiralty proceeded deftly to guide his star witnesses through their well-rehearsed paces. Not a hint of mutiny had ever, to their knowledge, been so much as whispered aboard the *Adventure Galley* whose crew, but for the deviltry of her captain, was the very embodiment of humanity and dedication to duty. Chief gunner William Moore was an irreproachable seaman, loyal and uncomplaining; Kidd, a scheming, ill-tempered ruffian.

Predictably enough, Kidd fumbled his tortuous way through an artless and unfocused rebuttal. Crew members, burdened with their own indictments of piracy, were either unable or unwilling to rise to his defense. Kidd could only bestir himself to a half-hearted attempt at vindication, by no means enhanced by a despairing and procedurally ill-orchestrated cross-examination. At one point he exasperated the presiding Lords Justice by interrupting the testimony of the *Adventure Galley's* surgeon thus: "Mr. Bradenham, are you not promised your life to take away mine?"

When the case had run its legal course Dr. Newton addressed the court at length, winding up his sweeping attack upon the defendant with a final gush of florid invective:

This, Gentlemen, is the Crime he is Indicted for; the growing Trouble, Disturbance and Mischief of the Trading World; the scandal and reproach of the European Nations, and the Christian Name, (I wish I could not say, that the Kidd's and Avery's had not made it more particularly so of the English) amongst Mahometans and Pagans ... This is the Person that stands indicted at that Bar, than whom no one in this Age has done more Mischief; or has occasioned greater confusion and Disorder, attended with all the circumstances of Cruelty and Falsehood, and a Complication of all manner of Ill.

If therefore these facts shall be proved upon him, you will then, Gentlemen, in finding him Guilty, do justice to an Injured World, the English Nation (our Common Country) ... and lastly, to your selves, whom the law has made Judges of the Fact.[16]

Kidd was found guilty on five separate counts of piracy and one of murder. Short of a last-minute pardon, his only real hope now was either to rekindle interest in Hispaniola or plead for the firing squad instead of the gallows he so greatly feared. Both proved vain hopes.

Paul Lorraine, the "ordinary" of Newgate Prison, was there to see to it that the Lord Almighty did His best by the condemned and they, of course, by Him. And if the Lord, as it is written, works in mysterious ways, so too did his servant, the Reverend Lorraine. For when not otherwise engaged upon his spiritual rounds at the notorious jail, Lorraine toiled as a "stringer" for the *Post Boy,* one of London's penny dreadfuls whose readers thrilled to "inside" crime stories of cutthroats, thieves and corrupters of youth.

Out of the celebrated figure of Captain Kidd, Lorraine hoped to fashion an apotheosis of his dubious stock-in-trade: sworn evil, hypocrisy and redemption before God's altar. The man was, after all, the talk of London—a "monster" in the words of Governor Bellomont and "the greatest liar in the world." Judged thus, the scenario called for tears, contrition and, at the proper moment, confession of base crimes—in the shadow of the gallows—against God, man and the Admiralty. As matters fell out, William Kidd would only imperfectly oblige.

Lorraine's vocation, among the desperate and the damned, was neither a pleasant nor an easy one. So wretched was life within Newgate Prison in the year 1700 that it might easily have served for one of Dante's circles of Hell. The Old Bailey adjoined Newgate and the sundry prison odors were said to so permeate that venerable place that spectators commonly took with them sprays of flowers, offered for sale outside by peddlers, which the more impressionable among them might press to their nostrils during the court's lengthy proceedings.

Inside the prison itself, the atmosphere, as one might imagine, was immeasurably worse. To the uninitiated, the pestilential stench of Lorraine's chapel was simply overpowering. Were it not for providential clouds of cheap tobacco smoke, said constantly to hang over it like a pall, the doing of the Lord's good works, even by a man as resilient as Paul Lorraine, might have proved a vain hope indeed.

If contemporary reports are to be credited, for every convict eager for spiritual succor more than a few at Newgate were inclined to show their gratitude to Lorraine by copulating on the Chapel's benches, defacing its walls and relieving themselves in its recesses. It is worth noting that, among Lorraine's diverse charges, were a number of criminally insane—men who had either entered Newgate in that benighted state or, more likely, been driven to it as to a refuge by the nightmarish conditions of the prison. William Kidd was not insane; indeed, his very criminality remains open to dispute. Some historians prefer to pose the question of his being either a highly principled man or a plain fool. Perhaps Kidd was both. More to the point, he was clearly among the least favored of the alleged pirates convicted that month in the Old Bailey, for all but a crewman of the *Adventure Galley,* named Darby Mullins—and Kidd himself, were eventually pardoned.

On May 21, 1701, his final pleas having gone unanswered, Kidd suffered his penultimate ceremonial. During two special Wednesday services held at Newgate Chapel by Paul Lorraine and to which, with his blessings, turnkeys had charged admission to the curious, Kidd was seated in the first pew among his trio of fellow condemned—John Dubois, Peter Manquinam[17] and Darby Mullins. Treated to sermons tailor-made to the dire consequences that awaited them, they were seated facing a coffin on the altar draped in black serge.[18] On Friday they were due to hang together along the Thames.

Kidd had learned that the wages of sin—in his case, piracy and aggression upon an English seaman—was death. What he could not have known was that the cost of trying him—specifically, his trial, execution and "exposure"—would come to slightly less than £154. Such was the budget granted John Cheeke, the Admiralty's Marshall for the "Kidd business." And after all was said and done, and Cheeke had left the condemned's "mortal coil" picturesquely set in chains along London's great river for the edification of the pious and as mute warning to children and malefactors alike, just enough of that sum would remain to drink to Captain Kidd's health, 19s 3d worth, "at a tavern at Wapping, and at the Horne Tavern, after our Return."[19]

Public hangings, far from being occasions of solemnity and private reflection, naturally enough generated a kind of carnival air, often fraught with undertones of savagery. The condemned, as he passed through the London streets on his way to the scaffold, might, depending upon the character of his offense, be hailed by some, though more often he was spat upon, mocked, jeered at and abused.

Executions conducted by the Admiralty at Wapping were rare. The majority of condemned prisoners went to their public reward at Tyburn; few pirates had ever been hanged by the Admiralty before Kidd and fewer still would follow his example. In future, pirates captured abroad—particularly in the "English Plantations of America"—would be dealt with there or on one of Her Majesty's men-of-war on the seas.

Thus, May 23 was a red-letter day for Thames merchants, the London rabble, Coji Babba, the East India Company and the Admiralty. If Kidd half expected a reprieve, he was greatly mistaken. His was to be an example, not so much to the London public as to the shareholders of the East India Company and India's Grand Mogul. The Admiralty was determined to show that piracy—especially in the Indian Ocean—would not be tolerated.

At 3.00 P.M. on Friday, May 23, Kidd was taken from his cell, marched into the late spring sunshine, then helped inside one of two awaiting carts. As the procession eased away from Newgate and the Old Bailey, it was led by the deputy Marshall, the "short silver oar" of the Admiralty held high on his shoulder; a second carriage followed, bearing the imposing figure of the Marshall himself, John Cheeke. Bringing up the rear, and surrounded by constables, were two rickety carts within which jolted the four condemned men.

Out along Cheapside where the throngs had already gathered, Kidd in his humiliation was conveyed past London Bridge and beneath the keep of the Tower, then down through the squalor of Katherine Street. Trailing behind a rag-tag escort of street urchins, the procession moved on through the cheerless marsh that was Wapping, beyond its forlorn sailors' tenements in full sight of the river traffic and, finally, across the dreary mud flats toward Execution Dock.

Here another milling crowd awaited: gentlemen and ladies snug in their carriages, high-ranking members of the Admiralty, representatives of the East India Company, judges and politicals cheek by jowl with the Great Unwashed of common sailors, tavern keepers, street sweeps, stable boys, clerks, carters, whores and jugglers, one and all present on that late afternoon in May for a look at the infamous Captain William Kidd.

> This was an age in which dying was an event attended by one's friends and relatives, whether at home in bed or in public at the end of a rope. In fact, the condemned felon hoped they would attend. For the hangman would carry his victim up a ladder and at the proper moment toss him

off. Because the drop was not sharp, it was possible to survive and hang there, choking and suffering, for a long time.
If this happened, the victim's friends would rush forward,
jump up and grab the dangling body, and pull down on it
to break the neck and end the misery.[20]

Kidd would suffer his own bizarre torment on the scaffold that day.
Having freely imbibed along the route, courtesy of the roistering London
crowd, Kidd lurched out of the cart at Execution Dock drunk as a lord. Thus
"inflamed with Drink," as chaplain Lorraine despairingly described his
charge in *The Only True Account of the Dying Speeches of the Condemn'd Pirates*
(a sample of which appeared on the London streets the following morning),
Kidd, shaky on his feet, was in an "ill frame of mind" and wildly unsuited
for the "great" work at hand.[21]

Repentant, Kidd was not. Rather, in his rambling and slurred speech
to the assembled, he cautioned sailing men, and particularly their captains, to beware of politics, and lamented that he should be forced to
leave so shamefully his lovely wife and two young daughters. One
minute Kidd's head was placed in the noose; the next instant he lay in a
heap on the ground.

> Here I must take notice of a remarkable (and I hope a most
> lucky accident) which then did happen, which was this, that
> the rope by which Capt. Kidd was tied broke, and so falling
> to the ground he was taken up alive, and by this means had
> opportunity to consider more of that eternity he was launch-
> ing into.[22]

A new rope having been hastily secured, Kidd, thoroughly stunned, was
once more borne up the ladder by the Admiralty's shamefaced executioner,
Lorraine reportedly clinging to the condemned man's ankles. Kidd now
proved infinitely more tractable and, to the Reverend Lorraine's great relief,
swore that he was sorry before the Lord. Let go a second time, this time it
was Kidd's neck that snapped.

The body was cut down and then, pursuant to the Admiralty's precept,
infra fluxum et reflexum maris,[23] chained to a post and left for the Thames
tide to thrice ebb and flow over it. In a further indignity, and as a final warning, the Marshall then had Kidd's bloated body removed to Tilbury Point, in
sight of Gravesend and every passing vessel on the great river. There, smeared
with tar, the remains were chained into a gibbet. Hung rotting in the air, sea
birds that summer stripped them clean to the bone.

Postscript

Coji Babba, the City of London and the East India Company all filed claims for Kidd's Gardiners Island treasure. Only Coji Babba's was ever taken seriously. "The proctor of the Admiralty Court sent commissions to Bengal, Isfahan (Persia), and Surat to collect evidence. The court waited three years for the documents and when none appeared, Babba's case lapsed."[24]

The recovered treasure was condemned and sold for £6473 on November 27, 1704. Shortly thereafter, the trustees of Greenwich Hospital filed a claim for the money, one that met with the approval of both the Admiralty and Queen Anne. When a Greenwich estate came up for sale, the trustees purchased it and transformed the splendid mansion into Greenwich Hospital, a legacy of William Kidd's brush with Lord Gardiner of New York.[25]

Gardiners Island remains to this day much as it did in that of Captain Kidd, its privacy enjoyed over the years by Ernest Hemingway and Bror Blixen, husband of Karen (Isak Dinesen), both of whom indulged their passion for wing shooting.

If any of William Kidd's treasure eluded the agents of Governor Bellomont, the Gardiner family have had the leisure to search for it. Though its title is currently being disputed in the New York courts by two rival factions, Gardiners Island is owned by Robert Gardiner, the outspoken "sixteenth Lord of the Manor." It remains America's oldest estate held through the male line.

Gasparilla Island

It is, it is a glorious thing
To be a Pirate King.
   —W. S . Gilbert
    Pirates of Penzance

For centuries the barrier islands off Florida's southwest coast attracted a curious, and by no means gentle, breed of habitué—gun runners, slavers, rum runners, Conquistadors and a motley host of pirates. The islands' genesis has been rugged in the extreme. Riding the geo-physical cutting edge between land and sea, the islands are the product of a fortuitous meeting. Here, a relentless triad of wind, surf and churning sand rushes headlong against miles of mangrove swamp whose tangled roots serve to anchor the constantly shifting Gulf floor.

This remains today a primal world, picturesque and not a little daunting, with its labyrinths of sheltered coves, tortuous estuaries and misting bays. Even where a measure of dry land exists, water seems ever to intrude in the form of ponds, lagoons and tidal flats. Renowned for its wildlife, the region has long provided refuge for the likes of roseate spoonbills, marsh rabbits and pelicans, along with more primitive species, the loggerhead turtle and the alligator among them. Reclusive American Indians had long carved out for themselves an isolated home here. Around 1517, to their considerable peril, Europeans became fast acquainted with the truth of this fact. Ponce de León led his men to an early grave, thanks to a clever ambush sprung by the Caloosa Indians. Himself wounded in engagement, de León was left to bury eighty Conquistadors under the Cross of the Christian faith and, forever with them, Spanish pretensions to colonization in the region.

After Ponce de León other Spaniards came to the Caloosahatchee region, for it was harbors that Spain desired to control for establishment of a base near Havana from which to conquer what is now the United States ... By 1564 when Spanish treasure ships sprang leaks or were wrecked, the Caloosa mercilessly killed the men, captured the women and pre-empted the stolen gold and silver. More desperately than ever Spain need to dominate the sheltered deep harbors and lower coasts of Florida.[1]

Insofar as Caloosa territory was concerned, Spain never succeeded in doing so and the next white men to inhabit it, two centuries later, were pirates—the scourge of the Spanish Main. Within a few decades of de León's death Spain had enormous success in the New World of Central and South America. To be sure, few Indian tribes would henceforth live to relish the spectacle of marauding Spaniards cutting and running in disorder before a rain of poisoned arrows, as had the victorious Caloosa. One by one the hemisphere's great native powers—Mayan, Aztec and Inca—fell in rapid succession before the furious Spanish horse like so many bowling pins. As to the survivors, they soon learned that the dreaded intruders were most certainly around to stay.

By dint of incomparable boldness, unbridled ferocity and outrageous fortune, a mere handful of Conquistadors had carried the day for Spain. Left to her would be the onerous business of holding Eldorado against all comers for three bloodstained centuries. To that end, England, France and Holland—have-nots and come-latelies to the field—were ruthlessly denied so much as the smallest claim upon South America. From the coral reefs of the Bahamas to the icefloes beyond Cape Horn all came to be regarded by pirates as the Spanish Main. Excluded from a share in the riches, adventurers from across Europe, some carrying letters of marque and others not, outfitted vessels with the aim of harrying Seville's far-flung and vulnerable monopoly.

There lived a legendary Spanish mariner of the late eighteenth century who entered upon a career dedicated to combating the evil of piracy on the high seas. Sworn to serve his God and Majesty in that noble cause, he utterly disowned both and remained, to the end, defiant in his bitter apostasy. His name was José Gaspar, the so-called "King of the Florida Pirates."

Gaspar's surname remains unknown. Born to upper-class parents near Seville around 1755 he abducted a wealthy young lady while still in his teens and held her for ransom. Caught and handed over for trial, his father's good connections saved him from the rigors of the *calabozo*[2] and he promptly enlisted in the Spanish Navy. Remarkably gifted, José Gaspar distinguished himself fighting privateers and, in no time, climbed to the rank of admiral, the youngest man of his generation to so aspire.

Propelled upon a meteoric rise, during the late 1770s Gaspar enjoyed all the trappings of a brilliant appointment to Madrid. Raffishly handsome, charming and well bred, though given to recklessness, he was destined for a life of further distinction when his ever-ascending stock at court suddenly took a headlong plunge. A frivolous liaison with a high-born lady had turned rancorous and she; spurned by the dashing young admiral, unleashed her Furies. Rising late one morning, as was his custom, Gaspar was astonished to find himself framed in the theft of certain priceless royal gems.

A furious King Charles, convinced of the charge's merits, demanded the scoundrel's immediate arrest. Alerted by his friends at the eleventh hour, Gaspar slipped away in disguise to the coast, enlisted a band of dissolute ruffians, commandeered one of His Majesty's ships and, standing away from the port of Cadiz, pointed her toward the high seas. There his exceptional naval skills stood him in good stead, as did his extensive experience with pirates. Such was all to the good for José Gaspar.

By the time chroniclers again picked up Gaspar's trail around 1795, it was liberally strewn with the jetsam of fired and scuttled ships at sea. According to his diary, a copy of which unaccountably found its way back to Spain, their toll had reached no fewer than sixty. Moreover, the unkindest cut, prominent among them were vessels flying the standard of Spain! Omnivorous in the best pirate tradition, Gaspar's prodigious appetites were apparently gratified by preying upon his own kind, doubtless as a means of avenging the wrong he had suffered at court. Gaspar's only ill luck is that he found his calling so late in the pirate era.

By the turn of the century, though rumored to be rich as Croesus, he found the pickings of Caribbean shipping unwholesomely slim and the authorities increasingly active in the suppression of West Indies' privateering. Thus, Gaspar determined to haul for the freer waters of the Gulf of Mexico. Off the Florida coast he discovered a tiny island he named Gasparilla, not only an ideal site on which to secrete his fortune but a strategic base from which to harry Gulf commerce.

Strung out in a north-south axis along the mouth of Charlotte Harbor, the barrier islands form a right hook curving shoreward. Gaspar claimed the northernmost island for himself and constructed an admirable dwelling there. Landbound now for the first time in years, Gaspar protected himself against surprise attack by encouraging pirate settlements along his flanks. Direct beneficiaries of this politic course were his most loyal captains—King John Brubaker with his following at Bokeelia to the southeast and the towering ex-slave, Black Caesar, at the head of his own to the south on Sanibel. Lesser lights carved out their own pirate havens at Cape Haze, Placida and Bocilla Islands.

Gaspar ran, if not a tight ship, certainly a well-secured one at Gasparilla. At pains to distance himself from the ruffian elements so necessary to his

calling, yet repugnant to his
personal tastes, he left his men
to shift for themselves in a
shambles of a colony down-
wind from his home—known as
"Low Town."

Whereas Gaspar's forebears
in the New World had had a genius for colonization, promptly
erecting their Christian edifices
over the rubble of sundered native temples, laying out broad
avenues leading to handsome
plazas, each bordered by a pre-
fecture, a counting house and a
hospice for the weary traveller,
"Low Town" was simply everything the name implies. Its one
noisome main street led nowhere. What, after all, was the
good of a plaza without gentle-
women, children and the elderly to enjoy such an amenity?
In Low Town one encountered
a sprawl of rude palmetto structures, practically indistinguish-

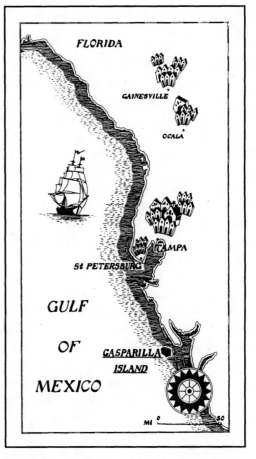

able one from another: taverns, shacks, gambling dens and brothels. Rough
justice may be expected to have been administered at any time of the day or
night—and without recourse to a prefect. As to counting houses, a man did
better to bury his boodle unseen and hope that he never boasted of it while in
his cups.

To a pirate, one of the prime virtues of land was that, though it might not
in the end receive his bones, the earth would serve as a handy repository for
the ill-gotten gains of a life at sea. Herein lies the allure of Gasparilla since any
number of its resident brigands are reckoned to have left behind them a
legacy of buried pots, casks and leather chests stuffed with coin.

This is not to say that the life of a Florida brigand was a matter of pure
sport. They were the survivors of a dying breed and, whether aware of it or
not, living on borrowed time. The thieves' economy of Gasparilla depended
upon a steady influx of commonplace articles: dry goods for the stores; supplies such as molasses, rum and powder with which to trade with the local
Indians for beef; whiskey, tobacco, canvas and cloth. Sustaining a man's spirit,

though, was always the hope of ducats, jewelry, stones and, best of all, ingots of Spanish silver and gold.

Gasparilla's enviable location made it a springboard for many an ambitious outlaw. To the west lay the bustling port of New Orleans. Yankee flatboats brought its way the fruits of French exertions, such as timber, furs and hides, from as far afield as the Rocky Mountains and Canada. Transferred to seagoing vessels at the mouth of the Mississippi River these, along with valuable cargoes of sugar and cotton—though perhaps unglamorous—were nevertheless attractive spoils for the pirates of Gasparilla. Hardly less so was the incoming commerce heading for the Louisiana Territory and the pleasure-loving citizens of New Orleans: silk, bales of damask, cloth by the bolt, powder, arms, wine, lace, china, minted coins and slaves. Negotiable items all, they might be traded, auctioned, sold outright or even ransomed.

Still bigger fish begged to be netted—though not without considerable danger—a few degrees south around the Florida Strait. Two great Spanish fleets sailed out from Cadiz every year for the Spanish Main. One made for Cartagena de Las Indias where it took on rich consignments of Colombian gold as well as pearls snatched from the deep by slavediving crews off the Atlantic coast. Its next stop was Puerto Bello, Panama. There it waited upon the arrival of heavily protected mule-trains bearing silver mined over the previous twelve months from the fabulous Potosi Mines in Alto Peru. The treasure came across the isthmus stamped in the form of ingots and bars, each bearing the Royal Seal and swathed by the hundreds in rough hides.

The second fleet sailed straight for Vera Cruz. Its business was to receive precious metals, gems and spices freighted across the Pacific on the annual plate ship run from Manila. Off-loaded at Acapulco, this immensely valuable cargo was then borne, once again by mule-train, over vertiginous trails cut into the Sierra Madre and, barring the unforeseen, arrived at the port of Vera Cruz in midwinter.

The entire operation usually took six months. Arriving in late autumn, the fleet laid by for the winter and loaded their cargoes in the spring. May could be a merry month for pirates as the two fleets met in Havana for the hair-raising dash through the Florida Strait. The dream of every brigand worth his salt was to catch one of these lumbering, wide-beamed galleons as it straggled, or was perhaps blown off course. Although there was nothing remotely simple about taking such a prize, accomplished Gasparilla pirates owned the great advantage of being able to slip through the Florida Keys and haul the quick run back to a safe haven at Charlotte Harbor.

In 1801 Gaspar is said to have waylaid a Spanish vessel sailing from Vera Cruz. Having sent her terrified crew forthwith to their unhappy reward, he then took aboard his sloop an unspecified cargo, along with a certain "treasure" he would certainly live to rue.

She was a great beauty by the name of Josefa de Mayorga, daughter of the former Vice-Admiral of Mexico, and, in her train, were a dozen noble-women en route to a convent education in Spain. Safely back at his island lair, Gaspar shared out the pitiable virgins among his rapacious captains, reserving Señorita de Mayorga for himself. Much taken with her, he treated the young lady not with brutality but, rather, in the manner to which she had surely been accustomed in the upper reaches of Spanish society. Some thought, only partly in jest, that the King of the Florida Pirates had finally found in her his "queen."

In any event, much to the amusement of his vulgar following, Gaspar took it upon himself to woo her after the fashion of a Spanish "caballero," although to precious little avail. His overtures were treated to the iciest disdain from the stalwart Josefa. Time and time again he was seen cutting a most dejected figure as he rowed back to his solitary home in the moonlight, following yet another humiliating rebuff. According to legend, the rebuffs took place on what is today called Useppa Island where the pirate King kept his beleaguered Queen under lock and key.

In the end, unrequited passion is said to have got the better of Gaspar's imperfect gallantry. Forcing himself upon Josefa one evening, he received for his pains an unladylike broadside of spittle whereupon, in an excess of blind rage, he reportedly drew forth his cutlass and smote her a mortal blow to the heart. Gaspar's brush with Señorita de Mayorga, while further clouding his already dark view of women, did have its silver lining.

Brigandage no longer being what it was, thanks to increasing surveillance from the Great Powers, shifting for a dishonest living at sea increasingly called for imagination. Thus, inspired by his nemesis, Gaspar extended his repertoire of villainies to include a lucrative trade in ransomed females. Henceforth, women passengers aboard captured ships were whisked away to Gasparilla's sister island of Captiva and there held hostage in a semi-circle of twelve rough palmetto cells. With a loyal guard to keep the fox, as it were, from the henhouse, Gaspar consigned his prisoners to a purgatory of heat, filth and disease until such times as his harsh terms were agreeably met. The fate of the women hinged entirely on payment of ransom and negotiations were handled through the unsavory offices of a disreputable attorney in Havana. As for the pitiable creatures who happened, through the ambivalence of loved ones, to wear out their welcome, a shallow jungle grave awaited.

In the meantime, Gaspar and his followers continued to make the most of an Old World in collision and a New World not yet come of age. Even as the flood of South American gold and silver threatened to swamp Europe's economic base, Spanish hegemony from Mexico City to Santiago, Chile was being sorely tried by a diffuse host of Liberation armies. Reeling under the strain of revolution, her once absolute military might was now attenuated to breaking point. Spain faced the desperate burden of siphoning off what were destined to be the final precious fruits of her Eldorado. Overwhelmed by the crisis at hand, riding hard on the Gasparilla renegades would have ranked low on her list of priorities. Such a state of affairs naturally favored Gaspar, as did the lack of a competing power in the Gulf of Mexico.

Well after Bonaparte had sold off the Louisiana Territory which gained, at the stroke of a pen, the strategic mouth of the Mississippi river at New Orleans, the United States could boast little better than a second-rate navy, over which few Florida pirates can possibly have lost much sleep. Only when the War of 1812 made a virtue of necessity did the United States become a maritime power with the means and the will to police the Gulf. Once victorious over the British, however, the United States moved quickly to consolidate its gains and when, in 1819, Spain ceded Florida, the brigands at Gasparilla were forced to take stock of the situation.

At a parley convened later that same year on Sanibel Island, sentiment among the hundreds of assembled pirates ran overwhelmingly in favor of getting out while the going was good. Alone among his captains—but for Black Caesar and King John—José Gaspar reckoned he would stand his ground—at least for a spell—and test the water of Uncle Sam's new resolve in the Gulf.

The deserters now applied themselves to careening their vessels, mending sails, stowing provisions and retrieving decades of buried loot which came down to the ships anchored at Charlotte Harbor like summer harvest. Standing away from Gasparilla Island, some of the very last freebooters to ply the western seas finally sailed off toward whatever fate might await them in the Indian Ocean.

Meanwhile, at the behest of Washington, a special anti-piracy strike force had been mobilized and was soon camped on Gaspar's doorstep in the Florida Keys. Now largely undefended on his flanks, Gaspar wisely concluded that he was a marked man. Clearly, the time had come to beat a strategic retreat and so, in the early months of 1821, the remaining Gasparilla outlaws turned to an unaccustomed round of house-cleaning. There were stores to be stripped, a dry dock to be dismantled and, according to Francis Bradlee in his 1923 work, *The Suppression of Piracy in the West Indies,* no less than $30,000,000 in accumulated booty to round up.

Bradlee believed that the treasure of Gasparilla was dug up that spring from six different locations around the island and that, in the course of the excavations, a fateful event occurred. From atop an observation tower erected years before on Cayo Pelao (Bald Key), over an ancient burial mound measuring 400 feet in circumference by fifty feet high, a sentinel sighted what looked, for all the world, like a large if ordinary British merchantman.

Confident of his ability to take her, and no doubt convinced she would be the final prize ever to come his way in Florida waters, Gaspar chose thirty-five of his best men and stood by to attack. In the late afternoon he and his crew dashed through Little Gasparilla Pass in the *Florida Blanca*. With Gaspar closing fast on her wake, the merchantman appeared to hesitate before the wind and then, quite suddenly, struck her colors—one of the oldest pirate tricks in the book. Her captain ran up, in their stead, the Stars and Stripes!

She was no British merchantman! But was she, perchance, the USS *Enterprize*, Lieutenant Lawrence Kearney as commander?[3] Whoever she was, she was not what she seemed and to prove it, the aft gunner whipped aside the camouflage sheathing his artillery piece and spat a peppering fire into the teeth of the oncoming brigands.

Another mortifying surprise lay in store for José Gaspar, courtesy of the Yankee helmsman. Bringing his craft tightly about, he then laid her abeam the *Florida Blanca* whereupon the chief gunner brought his superior firepower to bear in a crippling broadside cannonade. Down in a crashing rain of splintered timber came the *Blanca's* main mast as sea water flooded through a gaping breach in her port side. Struggling for a footing on her listing deck, Gaspar was quick to read his fate and, on the instant, a watery grave held all the merits a swing from the Yankee yardarm plainly lacked. Furiously winding a length of the *Blanca's* anchor chain about his waist, the King of the Florida Pirates cursed his assailants and flung himself overboard—thus skipping an appointment, kept by his crew, with the hangman.[4,5]

The lone exception proved to be a cabin boy, Juan Gomez. Thanks to his having been kidnapped at a tender age and pressed unwillingly into Gaspar's domestic service, young Gomez was spared. Imprisoned for a time in New Orleans, he later earned a reputation around South Florida watering-holes as a double-fisted drinker and colorful raconteur. Indeed, more than one treasure map of Gasparilla Island doubtless owes its provenance to the trembling hand of this scalawag who came to be known locally as "Panther Key John."

Shortly before his death in Palmetto, Florida in 1875 he recounted a story to a crew of railway engineers which has intrigued treasure hunters. According to Gomez, the pirate, Jean Lafitte, sought refuge at Gasparilla Island after the burning of Galveston in 1814. Furthermore, Gomez claimed that, on that afternoon in 1821, Lafitte was supporting his host, Gaspar, in the *Pride*. Seeing that Gaspar had been duped and hopelessly outmaneuvered, Lafitte quickly tacked about and headed for the Manatee River whose shallow waters were certain to offer his shallow-drafted sloop safe passage inland. At dawn the *Pride* was found scuttled across the river's mouth. She was empty of valuables and her crew long gone.

What became of the treasure of Gasparilla Island remains to this day a mystery. Some believe that $11,000,000 of it was stowed aboard the *Florida Blanca* before she was sent to the bottom. Whether true or not, she lay visible in the waters off Barbel Buoy for some thirty years until, at last, she was obscured forever beneath the shifting sands of the Gulf.

Galveston Island

He left a Corsair's name to other times,
Link'd with one virtue and a thousand crimes.
—Lord Byron
The Corsair

"He was six feet and two inches high," recalled an admiring Texas colonel named Hall in 1821,

> and his figure one of remarkable symmetry, with feet and hands so small, compared with his large stature, as to attract attention. In his deportment he was remarkably bland; digni-fied and social toward equals; though reserved and silent to-ward inferiors, or those under his command. He received visi-tors with an easy air of welcome and profuse hospitality. He wore no uniform, but dressed fashionably, and was remark-ably neat in his personal appearance. On board of his vessel he usually wore a loose coat, with nothing to distinguish him from his subordinates. He spoke English correctly, but with a marked French accent, that at once indicated his nativity, though it imparted additional interest to his conversation. He possessed superior conversation powers and entertained his guests with the rehearsal of many original and amusing anec-dotes. He had a remarkable habit of closing one eye while in conversation, and keeping it closed so much, many who had but a slight acquaintance with him were firmly impressed with the belief he had the use of but one eye.[1]

Jean Lafitte was indeed a remarkable man. Lauded by one sitting president James Madison; first vilified as a "bandit" then later hailed as a hero by another, Andrew Jackson—Lafitte is reputed to have once shot a certain Grambo through the heart for referring to him in jest as a pirate. "Privateer" is how Lafitte preferred to describe his calling and he carried letters of marque from the altogether dubious Republic of Cartagena to prove it.

Thought to have been born in Bayonne, France about 1780, some said Bourbon blood ran in his veins; others that he was an intimate of Napoleon Bonaparte. Perhaps no less apocryphal are tales of daring exploits in the Bay of Bengal which Lafitte carried out in command of La *Confiance*. Was he the brilliant naval tactician who, heavily outgunned, captured the British merchantman *Queen* off Sand's Head on the Indian coast before sailing away with a fortune in ivory, palm oil and gold dust?[2] Or was it true, as his detractors claim, that Lafitte suffered from seasickness and "did not know enough of the art of navigation to manage a jolly boat"?

What is known is that—handsome, bold, ambitious and thirty—he arrived at New Orleans about 1809 with his elder brother, Pierre, and promptly set up business. For one of the last of the great European privateers (and certainly one of the most dashing), it is difficult to say just which was the less glamorous: his manifest occupation or the thinly disguised nature of his real stock in trade. Indeed, two more improbable and elegant ironmongers can hardly have administered a forge in all the Louisiana Territory. Still, this is exactly how the brothers began, as proprietors of a blacksmith shop on the north side of St. Philips Street between Bourbon and Dauphin.[3] Nevertheless, by night, their rounds were likely to take them among the wharf company of pirates and slavers and Creole smugglers, all of whom were instrumental in making the Lafittes among the wealthiest gentlemen in New Orleans.

The brothers' clientele came to include respectable merchants, planters and society matrons; their accomplices were the waves of French refugees, fellow privateers and native islanders of Dominique and Guadeloupe, lately taken by the British Navy. Dealing in stolen goods was their trade and, for serious competition in their heyday, the brothers had none in the entire Gulf of Mexico.

The Lafittes can by no means, of course, be said to have introduced smuggling into Louisiana. Well before their arrival on the scene, plantation agriculture and restrictions upon free trade had fostered it; the political atmosphere of the Gulf had prompted it; the topography of the Bayou had favored it and nobody but Governor W. C. C. Claiborne seemed to mind. What they *did* was brilliantly to capitalize upon these altogether fortuitous conditions and eventually produce that *ne plus ultra* in financial enterprises—the monopoly.[4]

Pierre handled the New Orleans end. He wined and dined the heads of the great commercial houses, disposed of merchandise, mollified the politicians, secured contracts and dealt with the courts when necessary. A sort of politician-

agent-broker-fixer and public relations man rolled into one, he left to his younger brother the job of overseeing upwards of 1000 privateers and brigands at their new headquarters on Barataria Island just west of the Mississippi Delta.

They were a mixed bag to say the very least. Among their company were former soldiers in Napoleon's defeated armies, deserters from the American Navy, Spanish-speaking soldiers of fortune, Portuguese and Dutch tars, drifters from Cuba and Santo Domingo, and French privateers driven out of Guadeloupe by the forces of Admiral Rodney in 1810. Men of all races and dispositions, they harried the Gulf of Mexico in Lafitte's ships, delivered the plundered goods to his door, received his pay and answered to his justice.

Hardly idle was Jean Lafitte's boast that he made half the merchants of New Orleans rich. There was no class of chattel he could not, or would not, provide and, although privateering was by his day generally moribund, he and his brother helped to keep it very much alive for a few years longer in the Gulf.

"The times," as J. Frank Dobie wrote in the autumn 1928 issue of the *Yale Review*, "were propitious to privateers." Thanks to an endless series of revolts across Spanish South America, Lafitte could count upon easy letters of marque from self-styled republics like that of Cartagena and, later, of Venezuela and Mexico. France turned a blind eye to privateers acting against her enemy,

England, while the latter, hamstrung by the Napoleonic Wars, could do little to assert herself in the Gulf.

As for the American Navy, "tinpot" was a word often heard to describe it in Washington in 1809—Yankee politicians made few friends down on the Bayou. Powerless to police the Gulf, they strained Southern loyalties by endorsing the Embargo and Non-intercourse Acts, so-called, which proved thoroughly repugnant to Louisianians. Gatekeepers of one of the world's great waterways, New Orleans' citizens chafed under the restraints upon free trade. Life was expensive in the city and it was Uncle Sam who was to blame; fortunately for the brothers Lafitte, his legal hand lay but lightly upon them.

While Governor William C. C. Claiborne was American to the core, his constituents were anything but. Prominent among them were Creoles, both French and Spanish, whose backgrounds were strongly rooted in Europe. Then there were the Cajuns who had emigrated to the Isle of New Orleans from Acadia (late Nova Scotia) after being drive out by the British in 1775. Rounding out the population were refugees from a dozen Caribbean ports; Cubans, Choctaw and Creek Indians; a smattering of English colonists left over from the War of Independence, some Germans, some Swiss and even the odd American.

By the early nineteenth century New Orleans and the Louisiana Territory had a good deal of the "hand-me-down" about them. During the previous 200 years they had been traded back and forth between Spain and France, finally being sold by Napoleon Bonaparte to President Jackson's representative, Robert Livingston, on May 2, 1803 for $27,267,622 including interest.[5]

Having in a sense been "orphaned" with such frequency, and the land beneath their feet so often bought, sold and ceded, it is hardly surprising that Cajuns and Creoles alike were strongly inclined toward a standard of charity and loyalty that began at home. New Orleans, after all, was a *French* city; Jean and Pierre were French. The brothers offered the widest possible selection of duty-free goods at rock-bottom prices with no questions asked. For customers who brought their gold to Barataria, everything from silk, cut glass, champagne and perfumes to gunpowder, hides and salt beef, were readily available. So reasonable proved their prices that buyers might purchase Lafitte stock and then turn right around and export it at a profit.

If there were a dozen approaches to Barataria Island from the sea, there were a hundred ways out through the Bayou. As the duck flew, New Orleans lay roughly sixty miles to the north through tidal marsh and pampas grass tall as a man. Inland this gave way to branch upon forking branch of bayous, inlets, shaded lagoons and lake-chains bordered with cypress, scrub oak and palmetto. Lilies and hyacinths carpeted these still, brown waterways, while gray Spanish moss festooned the arms of gnarled trees stretching out like canopies above. Through this nether world—peopled with trappers, moss-gatherers and shrimping folk—moved the feluccas of Lafitte's pirate band as well as the vessels of French and Spanish merchants and planters, loaded with gold cloth, casks of wine and slaves, purchased for a song from the Master of Barataria Island.

Barataria is actually two islands in one. Grande Isle lies to the east; Grande Terre to the west. Between them runs the shallow Barataria Pass. Lafitte is believed to have fortified either end of Grande Terre with a battery numbering twenty guns in all. Here, from atop its walls, sentries might intercept smoke signals sent up from the north shore of the bay announcing the arrival of foreign elements to Lafitte's stronghold. About his dwelling, which was constructed on the Spanish principle with wide verandas and shade trees, ran a high brick wall and, beyond that, a welter of rude palmetto-roofed shacks belonging to his minions.

Beyond the island, roughly six miles from the open sea, lay a secure harbor which communicated with a labyrinth of lakes and canals leading to the Mississippi River on one side and Bayou Lafourche on the other. Spies and lookouts, ranged about the Bayou and delta, kept Lafitte well informed at all times.

Secure in his pirate lair, he was free openly to conduct his commercial affairs. These were primarily accomplished at the "Temple," a high clam-shell mound once thought to have been a place of worship for an extinct race of Gulf Coast Indians. Here the diverse plunder of his ships was exhibited to buyers.[6]

"From all parts of Louisiana," reported Major A. Lacarriere Latour, Principle Engineer in the Seventh Military District of the United States,

> people resorted to Barataria, without being at all solicitous to conceal the object of their journey. In the streets of New Orleans it was usual for traders to give and receive orders for purchasing goods at Barataria, with as little secrecy as similar orders were given for Philadelphia or New York. The most respectable inhabitants of the State, especially those living in the country, were in the habit of purchasing smuggled goods coming from Barataria. The frequent seizures made of these goods were but an ineffectual remedy of the evil, as the great profit yielded by such parcels as escaped the vigilance of the Custom House officers indemnified the traders for the loss of what they had paid for the goods seized, their price always being very moderate, by reason of the quantity of prizes brought in and of the impatience of the captors to turn them into money and sail on a new cruise. This traffic was at last carried on with such

scandalous notoriety, that the agents of the government in-
curred very general and open reprehension, many persons
contending that they had interested motives for conniving
at such abuses, as smuggling was a source of confiscation
from which they derived considerable benefit.[7]

The famous Bowie brothers, Rezin and Jim, were no doubt aware that this
was so. Later, from Lafitte's second headquarters at Galveston Island, they were
themselves party to his nefarious trade in smuggled African slaves. After pur-
chasing them from an obliging Lafitte at $1 a pound the Bowies would then
turn them over to the U.S. Customs House. By so doing, the public-spirited
brothers earned a reward equal to half the value of the "contraband." Under
the law, the U.S. Marshall at New Orleans was obliged to offer the slaves at
public auction. Having purchased the Africans *back,* the Bowies were then entitled to sell them openly within the United States at a handy profit.[8]

Shortly after Louisiana officially entered the Union as the eighteenth
state, Governor Claiborne issued a proclamation in the spring of 1812 con-
demning activities on Barataria Island. It was there, he fulminated, that:

a considerable number of bandits, composed of individuals
of different nations, have armed and equipped several vessels for the avowed purpose of cruising on the high seas,
and committing depredations and piracies on the vessels of
nations at peace with the United States and carrying on an
illicit trade in goods, wares and merchandise, with the inhabitants of this State, in opposition to the laws of the United
States and to great injury of the free trade and of the public
revenue.[9]

The exasperated Governor besought his constituents to:

rescue Louisiana from the foul reproach which would at-
tach to her character should her shores afford any asylum,
or her citizens any countenance, to an association of individuals whose practices are subversive to all laws, human
and divine, and of whose ill-begotten treasure no man can
partake without being forever dishonored and exposing
himself to the severest punishment.[10]

Despite the forceful language, the Lafittes were welcomed into New
Orleans society, openly strolled the streets of the city when it pleased them

and may even have rubbed shoulders with the Governor during the ball season. Their popularity, for a time anyway, outstripped that of Claiborne's whose zeal finally exposed him to the worst sort of public ridicule. By now at his wit's end, the Governor issued a second proclamation in November of the following year offering a $500 reward for Jean Lafitte's capture. The very next day, a rival proclamation hit the streets of New Orleans, much to the amusement of local residents, offering a $500 reward for the capture of Governor W. C. C. Claiborne, signed "J. Lafitte."

Even as Claiborne was exhorting the State Legislature to take prompt action against the pirates of Barataria, the Lafittes let it be known that on January 24, 1814, an auction of 450 slaves was to be held at the Temple. An inspector of revenue, by the name of Stout, felt duty bound to disrupt the proceedings and was shot for his pains. Wounded with him were two fellow agents; the remainder of the hapless posse was taken prisoner.[11]

Addressing the Louisiana General Assembly on March 2, Governor Claiborne sought authority "to raise by voluntary enlistment a force of not less than one captain, one first lieutenant, one second lieutenant, one third lieutenant, one drummer, one fifer, and one hundred privates"[12] whose mission would be to assault the pirate's den at Barataria. To Claiborne's dismay, however, this proposal did not appeal to his phlegmatic colleagues and the matter was soon dropped.

One result of the Governor's broadsides was a "presentment" against Pierre and his brother set before a Grand Jury in July under the aegis of the U.S. District Court. No sooner, however, were the various writs attested and delivered to the District Attorney, John R. Grymes, than the estimable lawyer promptly traded hats and headed the defense of the accused! Ably assisted by another prominent member of the Louisiana Bar, Edward Livingston, whose ancestor, fittingly enough, had figured among the financial backers of Captain Kidd, this potent legal team so arranged matters that their clients never even had to appear in court. Later, Grymes passed a memorable week as an honored guest at Jean Lafitte's luxuriously appointed home at Barataria. Feted like a Royal, he came away with nothing but praise for "the most honest and polished gentleman that the world ever produced," as well as a chest full of gold to the value of $40,000.[13]

Lafitte was believed to have buried portions of his enormous profits which, by custom, he converted to gold, beneath some of the numerous shell mounds studding Barataria Island. If true, he may well have been wise to do so, for storm clouds were gathering. The United States was now in the midst of war with Great Britain and Lafitte's strategic enclave at the mouth of the Mississippi River was beginning to cause grave concern for both camps. The first to approach him were the British, represented by Captains Lockyer and Percy of H.M.S. *Sophia* and *Hermes* respectively. The pair bore documents penned by their superior officer, Colonel Nicholls at Pensacola, and were addressed in complimentary fashion to the "Commandant of Barataria."

Nicholls, by turns, wheedled, threatened, flattered and suborned, dangling a "post captaincy" before Lafitte plus a cash consideration should he "enter into the service of Great Britain." Otherwise, he pledged to "carry destruction over the whole of Barataria."[14]

Stalling for time, the "Commandant" kindly begged leave to sleep on the magnanimous British proposal, then immediately sued for peace with the Americans. In an emotional letter, dated September 4, 1814, Lafitte sought rapprochement with his long-standing nemesis, Governor W. C. C. Claiborne, referring to himself at one point—perhaps disingenuously—as "the stray sheep wishing to return to the fold."[15] Lafitte soon enough discovered that, by simply spurning his British suitor, he had not put himself in the good graces of the Americans. Mistakenly, he reckoned upon being welcomed back to that "fold" from which he can hardly have "strayed," never having been a loyal member of it. Moreover, trust, not to mention forgiveness, was at a premium in the Governor's mansion.

On September 16, under orders from Washington, Commodore Patterson of the American Navy, with Colonel Ross and a contingent from the U.S. Infantry, sailed into Barataria with cannons blazing. Besides the schooner *Caroline,* Patterson could boast an escort of six gunboats and a launch. On their approach, Lafitte mustered ten vessels and formed them in a line along the harbor.

In a seemingly equivocal gesture, no sooner had Patterson run up a white flag reading "Pardon to deserter," than he saluted his pirate hosts with a salvo of well-aimed broadsides to Barataria's fortress walls. Spying smoke billowing from two of Lafitte's schooners—these having been scuttled by their crews—the Commodore now gave chase to the remaining craft which flew before him in disarray. Taken in the ensuing engagements were several of Lafitte's private vessels, among them the schooner, the *General Bolivar,* carrying an eighteen-pound, a six-pound and a pair of twelve-pound guns.[16]

Barataria's telegraph and all its stores and warehouses were destroyed. Lafitte's sumptuous home was leveled. The jubilant strike force then returned to New Orleans on September 24 amid a "peel of guns" from Fort St. Charles.

That Lafitte's men chose discretion over valor, by fleeing with him up Bayou Lafourche while Patterson's troops rifled houses at Barataria, was significant. It simply spoke volumes for the rising, though by no means dominant, power of the U.S. Armed Forces in the Gulf and, conversely, the imminent decline of privateering. Doubtless, at a critical moment, Lafitte determined to throw in his lot with the Americans, come what may. Neither to be overlooked is the likelihood that he and his hundreds of followers preferred to dig up as much of their buried loot as they could in a short time and make a run for it while the going was good. In any event, Commodore Patterson and Colonel Ross allegedly recovered $500,000 in merchandise and gold from the Barataria storehouses, a fact that rankled with Lafitte to his dying day.

From a redoubt on Last Island near the mouth of Bayou Lafourche, Lafitte renewed his petitions to the Americans. General Andrew Jackson, soon to be the man of the hour, was having none of him. Stationed at Mobile, Alabama, Jackson's public response was larded with vintage hauteur:

> I ask you, Louisianians, can we place any confidence in the honor of men who have courted an alliance with pirates and robbers? Have not these noble Britons—these honorable men Colonel Nicholls and Captain W. G. Percy, the true representatives of their royal master—done this? Have they not made offers to the pirates of Barataria to join them and their holy cause? And have they not dared to insult you by calling upon you to associate, as brothers, with them and these hellish banditti? Confident that any attempt to invade our soil will be repelled, the undersigned calls not upon either pirates or robbers to join him in the glorious cause.[17]

Nevertheless, soon after arriving in New Orleans, "Old Hickory" Jackson was whistling a different tune. Remarkable, indeed, was the sea-change wrought upon his prejudices by word of 12,000 British troops reportedly making straight for Louisiana, and the appalling prospect of facing them with a rag-tag army of irregular militia. Now it was painfully clear that every man Jack would be called upon in the defense of New Orleans, the General emptied her jails and then turned for succor to her "favorite son." Following an interview with Jackson, during which Lafitte and his top officers pledged full support for the American cause, Barataria's residents were transformed overnight from "hellish banditti" into "privateers and gentlemen."

The rest, as the saying goes, is history. At Chalmette Plain, on January 8, 1815, Lafitte and his men covered themselves in glory. Worthy of special praise were artillery units under Lafitte's favorite gunner, Dominique You, which fought that day with singular distinction.

By a proclamation dated February 6, 1815, signed by President James Madison and acting Secretary of State, James Monroe, the "privateers and gentlemen" of Barataria were granted:

> a free and full pardon of all offenses committed on violation of any act or acts of the congress of the said United States, touching the revenue, trade and navigation thereof, or touching the intercourse and free commerce of the United States with foreign nations, at any time before the eighth

day of January, in the present year one thousand, eight hundred and fifteen, by any person or persons whatsoever, being inhabitants of New Orleans and the adjacent country,
or being inhabitants of the said island of Barataria.[18]

This was no trifling recompense for a day's labor. Nonetheless, it was Lafitte's
ardent desire to return to Barataria and to be reimbursed for the property of which
Commodore Patterson had lately relieved him. At the amnesty, however, Uncle
Sam's gratitude ceased. Washington now became steadfastly unwilling to suffer
the intolerable presence of Barataria's pirates on America's shores.

Casting about for a new base, Jean Lafitte finally found it in 1816, 400
miles to the west of New Orleans at Isla del Serpiente. Lately renamed
Galveston Island (possibly in honor of Bernardo de Galvez, the Spanish colonial administrator), Lafitte chose it neither for its comforts nor its beauty—
not for nothing had the place once been called "Snake Island." Nevertheless, it possessed a number of virtues. As Mexico was now in full revolt
against Spain, the island was a no-man's-land and its position greatly suited
Lafitte's designs; it was near enough to his old clients in New Orleans and
yet beyond the jurisdiction of the United States. He would be working from
territory officially claimed by the Spanish.

Spain, embroiled in an increasingly menacing revolution, was, on the
one hand, ill equipped to dislodge Galveston privateers while, on the other,
loath to admit such inability by inviting the U.S. to take the upper hand. In
the meantime, Lafitte, with well-measured doses of bonhomie and guile,
wooed the Mexican authorities in the hope that they might incorporate
Galveston into the Republic of Mexico. Toward that end he found it politic
to snuggle up to the revolutionaries without, however, harbouring much
genuine sympathy for their cause.

On the east of Galveston Island, which is roughly twenty-eight miles
long by three miles wide, Lafitte set up his headquarters at what he called
"Little Campeche," after its more ancient counterpart on the Yucatan
Peninsula of Mexico. A shallow inlet through which only light-drafted
vessels might pass, separated it—much to Lafitte's advantage—from the
mainland at Point Bolivar. To the west lay scorching miles of bleached
wasteland composed of shell fragments and sand. Breaking the monotony
was the waving green of shoreline stretches of marsh grass. Shade being
at a premium, the single most favored patch was provided by what the
Karankawa Indians referred to as "The Three Trees." It was beneath these
that they occasionally met to form hunting parties and, to this day, of all
the sites mentioned as being likely to have held Lafitte's treasure, none
is more notorious than these live oaks.[19]

Little Campeche was a good deal more hospitable than the rest of the island. Partly as a precaution against snake bite—for which abomination Galveston was indeed famous—Lafitte established himself atop a narrow ridge of sand and shell banked up through the ages by tempests blowing across the bay. These, in time, would prove infinitely more inimical to Lafitte's settlement than the snakes.

On the bright side, fresh water was plentiful and the climate, thanks to refreshing onshore breezes, reasonably salutary. Marsh rabbits and a pleasing variety of waterfowl were a boon to the hunter; the abundance of marine life around Galveston Bay, an angler's dream. Lafitte's neighbors, too, with a few notable exceptions, proved friendly. While physically imposing, the Karankawa Indians—though allegedly given to the occasional weakness for human flesh—were generally tractable and, in time, would provide Lafitte with valuable furs, exchanged for archetypal bits of white men's cloth and beads.

Odd though it may seem, many of Lafitte's following saw fit to set up housekeeping with their wives at Galveston Island. Black, Indian, Caribbean, Latin and Cajun, after marauding on the Gulf for weeks at a stretch, were pleased to return to the simple domesticity of hearth and home. Indeed, word of the advantages to be gained from living under Lafitte's firm, but not unbenevolent hand, went forth and Campeche's population quickly multiplied. By January 1818, at least 1000 souls—equal to Barataria's population at its height[20]—were attached to the Campeche settlement which boasted 200 structures in all, numerous vessels, a dry dock and a shipyard. A dispensary with a French physician in residence saw to the basic health needs of the sailors, their wives and small children.

The pirate Louis-Michel d'Aury had left behind him an unfinished mud fort which Lafitte's followers greatly improved by shoring up its earthworks and topping up its walls.[21] Within an area covering roughly 10,000 square feet, they constructed a heavily masoned two story house in flaming red of the finest stone and hardwoods for the island's "Governor." Known as the "Maison Rouge," it was crowned with an imposing watch-tower from which poked the barrels of a pair of cannon. Its great rooms were luxuriously furnished in silk hangings, mahogany furniture and a wealth of silver plate. Here, Lafitte entertained on a grand scale, offering his guests the choicest cuisine and the best in purloined wines.

Nearby he erected the "Yankee Boardinghouse" in which resided the captains of the Galveston fleet. Lafitte admiringly referred to them as his "Generals" and usually chose Americans to fill their ranks; in his frank estimation, no better skippers plied the seven seas. The crews of these Yankee brigands, as in the Barataria days, hailed from virtually everywhere and were at liberty to make their own domestic arrangements at Little Campeche. Such dwellings were commonly informed by the unvarnished tastes of their rough-and-tumble lives; as often as not they elected to live about the island in a welter of rude shacks and canvas tents. This was the life of the grasshopper rather than the ant—those, like Lafitte, who had built to last, were the greatest losers in the summer of 1818.

Just as he had laid the firmest foundations for his magnificent Maison Rouge, Lafitte fully intended to build a lasting community around it on Galveston Island. The architect of so bold a design, Jaô de la Porta, remained from the days of d'Aury. An albino with unsightly white-splotched skin and a brilliant and enlightened mind, he persuaded Lafitte that the settlement's best hopes of longevity resided in the commune system. Impressed, Lafitte agreed that the Galveston enterprise would operate on a share-and-share-alike basis whereby each and every sailor received a guaranteed piece of the action in the form of a regular monthly "dividend." In return, he swore allegiance to the community and deferred to the jurisdiction of a criminal court as well as to a court of admiralty, both quietly under the thumb of Citizen Lafitte. Justice was swift and sometimes terrible, particularly when the most heinous offenses of robbery, murder, mutiny and, yes—piracy, were concerned.[22]

The court of admiralty was established to redress this last evil and to discourage fraud in the accounting of prizes taken at sea; it was openly administered by Lafitte himself. No vessel might deal with him unless her captain produced the proper documentation, the contents of which the Governor of Galveston pored over with the finest-toothed comb. These must include letters of marque issued by republics other than that of Cartagena which had, but recently, been taken back by Spain. Utterly abjuring piracy in all its wicked manifestations, and straining, perhaps somewhat unconvincingly, for a legitimacy that ever eluded him, Lafitte submitted seafarers to the minutiae of his own legal scrutiny and to a jurisdiction recognized by no republic or monarchy on earth.

However equivocal his reputation abroad, Lafitte was every bit the leader at home. By early 1818 his operation was better and grander and richer in every respect than that of Barataria at its prime. Business throughout the year 1817 had been extraordinary and for their exertions his men were receiving as much as $159 *each* per month, an unheard of sum for that day.[23]

If a problem existed, it was said to be the charred hulls of plundered merchantmen which were beginning to dot in profusion the shallows around Galveston Island. These were impossible to sell on the Texas coast and such was the inconvenience of towing them out and, indeed, the waste of scuttling them, that the matter moved Lafitte to thinking. Would it not be preferable to return captured ships to their captains? "If we permit these ships to return to sea," he is reported as informing his Generals, "they might find new cargoes the which we can capture. The more merchantmen, the better our business ..."

If such a novel precedent may have gratified certain of the Gulf's large shipowners, many New Orleans merchants seemed less than pleased. Lafitte had become so powerful that the city's increasingly legitimate businesses were suffering from a disturbing fall in prices, thanks to the volume of goods and the bargains available at Little Campeche.

In peak months Lafitte's warehouses groaned with merchandise. Depending upon the hauls brought in at any given week, these might include a variety of silks, virgin alpaca wool, consignments of spices, gem stones, dyestuffs like the valuable indigo, tea, coffee, hardwoods, port and madeira, porcelain and china, firearms, canvas and, most unfortunate of all, human beings. So numerous were the buyers that flocked to Lafitte's auctions that a Turkish gentleman by the name of Selik made his own fortune on the coat-tails of privateering by setting himself up as an innkeeper on Point Bolivar. There, in its homely parlor, Governor Lafitte, ever on the lookout for spies and infiltrators, interviewed prospective clients with a firm handshake and a keen eye.

In no way alarmist by nature, Lafitte took precautions for all the right reasons. Once more, Uncle Sam was on his trail. Boldly contravening the terms of a Spanish-American treaty prohibiting the commissioning of privateering vessels in U.S. ports, Pierre Lafitte had outfitted a murderously sleek black schooner in 1817. Said to be the swiftest craft of its kind in the entire Gulf of Mexico, sufficient numbers of merchantmen had looked down the barrels of the *Jupiter's* thirty-two-pound swivel guns to call down an eternity of evil upon Lafitte's head.

Lafitte had quite simply become a victim of his own success. Already legend throughout Louisiana were stories of his enormous income and of the treasure he had buried at a dozen sites around Galveston. One frontiersman—having been a guest of Lafitte's at Little Campeche—took his story to a New Orleans newspaper which detailed lurid highlights of Lafitte's opulent life at Maison Rouge.

The Governor of Galveston was now on the receiving end of a bad press. The bloom had largely faded from his rosy image as a war hero as New Orleans fast settled into an inexorable process of "Americanization" inimical to his foreign background. Worse by far were stories circulating in the New Orleans' dailies of ships under his command being involved in depredations upon vessels flying the Stars and Stripes. But Lafitte was about to meet his match. In the summer of 1818 he suffered the wrath of God.

It came in the form of a hurricane and the devastation visited upon Little Campeche could hardly have been more complete. The shantytown of tents and palmetto-thatched huts simply blew away like so many leaves before the wind, as did taverns, stores and warehouses. Lafitte's arsenal was left a shambles and the dockyard dealt a blow from which it never recovered. Against such an emergency Lafitte had constructed Maison Rouge two years before of the stoutest timbers and the heaviest masonry. Little could he have suspected that, by shepherding Galveston's women and children within the refuge of its sturdy walls (while he and his Generals anchored offshore in the *Saragosa*), he had mistakenly led the panic-stricken flock to its violent death.

In the terrible wind, the *Saragosa* simply keeled over like a child's toy though, thanks to the shallow waters of the harbor, she did not fully sink. By dint of this small miracle all aboard her survived. Quite impossible to make out over the tumult of wind and pounding surf, however, were the shrieks of those trapped inside Maison Rouge who first suffered the cave-in of its massive walls and then the final abomination of cannon tumbling about their ears from the collapsed tower above.

Once he had fought his way to shore, Lafitte acted with admirable dispatch, tirelessly directing all aspects of the rescue operation. Throughout subsequent weeks he put a brave face on the disaster, vowing at every turn to rebuild Campeche from the ground up. He pledged to restore it to its former greatness and even to improve upon *that*. Reassuring words these might have been and well-laid plans indeed; in truth, Campeche slid into a decline. So many of its surviving brigands drifted off that, by the following year, its population stood at less than 400. Suddenly much reduced in estate from one tempest, and fearing the vicissitudes of another in this most hurricane-prone locale, those who remained were not inspired to mount an extensive rebuilding program.

Lafitte himself soon acquiesced to the situation. Salvaging what valuables he could from his beloved Maison Rouge, he stowed them aboard the *Saragosa* which, though righted, remained listing on the Galveston Bay shallows. There he made a remarkably comfortable home for himself during the remainder of his stay at Galveston.

Lieutenant McIntosh U.S.N., putting ashore from the *Lynx* in October 1819, spied a curious looking structure opposite Point Bolivar at Little Campeche. Five brigands under the leadership of a certain Brown had recently been accused of pillage at the Lyons Plantation and it was now up to McIntosh to see that justice was served. The desperadoes were known to call Galveston home and the youthful lieutenant, his sense of foreboding difficult to mask, now girded himself for a custody battle with the legendary Jean Lafitte. Luckily, McIntosh need not have worried. The curious looking structure turned out to be a gallows and gibbet from which hung a man. The man's name was Brown.

Furious over the incident at Lyons Plantation, which could only do his tarnished reputation further harm, Lafitte had been only too happy to extract harsh justice. With a flourish, he handed over to McIntosh the four remaining prisoners, accompanied, however, by a strongly worded protest.[24]

In spite of the initial rebuke, Lafitte was on his best behavior. Capable of charming the birds from the trees, he now regaled his young guest with the full treatment. By day the two hunted wild geese together in the marsh-lands, swam in the warm waters of the Bay and angled for garfish. The cool evenings they passed comfortably ensconced in the sumptuous stateroom of the *Saragosa*, lingering over Spanish port and Cuban cigars. All the while, Lafitte had striven to impress McIntosh with the fiction that he was a true representative of the Mexican Republic and that his Galveston operation was legitimate in every respect.

The gambit earned him a friend and, for a little better than a year, bought him a reprieve. In the meantime, Lafitte carried on his privateering with a watchful eye toward miscreants. He sentenced a sailor named Francis to death for "piracy," put down a mutiny at Little Campeche and continued to take the last of his booty from the Gulf of Mexico.

By late 1820, Lafitte was fast losing control of his men; France, Spain and England were clamoring for his head. Whether true or not, he stood accused of harrying the vessels of all and sundry. So strongly, for example, did opinion run against him in Seville that her ministers only condescended to approve a treaty hammered out between President Monroe and Don Luis de Onis on condition that the Frenchman and his followers be forcibly re-moved from Galveston Island.

The final straw came with the capture of an American vessel in Matagorda Bay. Plundered and scuttled by pirates whose style had all the hall-marks of Campeche about it and whose trail led precisely *there*, Wash-ington now determined to act. Early in 1821 their man in the Gulf, Lieuten-ant Lawrence Kearney of the U.S.S. *Enterprize*, anchored off Galveston Is-land and awaited Lafitte's pleasure.[25]

Received with a hospitality perhaps no more genuine, but certainly no less warm, than that accorded McIntosh before him, Kearney spent days with his affable host during which time he did not once breathe so much as a single word on the exact nature of his visit. Equal to the charade Lafitte too, kept his counsel. Only on the day of departure did Kearney show his hand: Uncle Sam would see to it that Lafitte departed Galveston Island in perpetuity. He might enjoy ninety days in which to see to his affairs and then he must leave—on pain of arrest.

Kearney made his return to Campeche aboard the Enterprize in May. As good as his word, Lafitte had passed the previous months dismantling his operation and, to prove it, conducted the American officer on a guided tour. Still intact was the very gibbet that had accommodated the miscreant Brown not so many months before and, swinging from it, were the remains of a sailor. What, Kearney was curious to know, was the nature of this man's crime? With that characteristic closing of the eye, Lafitte informed the

Lieutenant that, in his penultimate act as a Governor, he had hanged him for rogue piracy upon a vessel of the United States to which he extended, for the last time, his undying loyalty. Kearney than took his leave of Lafitte with a shake of the hand.

That evening, the Lieutenant and his officers gazed in astonishment from the bridge of the *Enterprize* as Campeche burned to the ground. The following dawn, Lafitte's battered headquarters were now a wasteland of cinder and windblown ash. Gone from the harbor was his flagship, the *Pride*. After bidding farewell to Lieutenant Kearney, Lafitte had simply sailed off into legend, leaving behind him nothing so much as a smoldering monument to the transience of the pirate era.

How the "Savior of New Orleans" finally met his end, no less than where and when, remains a mystery. Generations of superstitious Cajuns, however, were convinced that his peripatetic ghost prowled the islands and bayous around Barataria and Galveston Islands. Some believe he never left but, rather, was killed engaging a U.S. revenue cutter up the Lavaca River in Texas; others that he died delirious of fever in a lowly fisherman's shack on Mexico's Yucatan coast. In 1976 Justice Price Daniel of the Texas Supreme Court, in possession of a Lafitte family Bible and a 257 page journal of memoirs allegedly penned in Lafitte's own hand, advanced the novel theory that the Frenchman had adopted the alias of "John Lafflin" and had died at Alton, Illinois around 1854.[26]

Had Lafitte lived to be an old man of seventy-five, and had he secreted but a pittance of the enormous quantity of treasure attributed to him, a lifetime could scarcely have been sufficient for its enjoyment. Contemporaries, it is said, debated only half in jest as to whether or not a solid gold bridge might be built over the Mississippi River with his fortune; or of the likelihood of wiping out, by means of the same, the national debt of 1821.

Lafitte—so the legends go—was a sober, stern and, above all, practical soul with a mania for burying treasure. Where it all might have ended up is, of course, anybody's guess. After all, "dead men," true to the saying, "tell no tales." Such falls to the lot of the living and Lafitte's surviving compatriots, swapping colorful yarns for strong drink in a multitude of Gulf taverns, may have done much to gild the lily.

Between the shell mounds of the Barataria Temple and "Lafitte's Grove" on Galveston Island lies country once criss-crossed by the bandits of the coast. Lake Salvador, Bayou Lafourche, the Trinity River, Turtle Bay, Goose Creek, Port Lavaca … all have held, at one time or another, their pride of place on the treasure hunter's map. *Here,* Lafitte was known to have cached five bearskins of gold; *there,* a pair of brass cannon brimful of pieces of eight. Nor has a shortage existed of oaken casks, urns and strongboxes. Men there were aplenty in Louisiana and Texas willing to squander their youth and even gamble their lives tracking down clues to Lafitte's lost treasure, clues often no more substantial than a set of crossed pegs driven into a lone cedar up a half-remembered swamp.

Like a lightning rod, the burning desires of others were drawn to the famous legend of the "Jacob's Staff." Chancing upon one of these in the wild spelled the greatest good fortune since, as any fool knew, it was one of the sure trademarks of the wily Jean Lafitte. A rod it was—fashioned of brass and with a socket atop used by surveyors of that day in place of a tripod. Believers had it on the best authority that Lafitte once buried a seaman's chest packed with jewels in the salt marshes of Galveston Island. Directly over the spot he set up a Jacob's Staff, into whose socket he carefully fitted a compass. Taking bearings from two nearby clumps of trees, he drove the rod down so that its socket protruded no more than shin high above the ground in a veritable sea of waving grass.

According to the tale, one day years later a field hand was grazing horses in the area. Thinking to catnap through the heat of a particularly sultry Texas afternoon, he cast about for something handy with which to secure his mount and, in doing so, happened to stumble over a spike set securely in the ground. Pleased that he could secure his horse to it, the field hand settled down for a siesta, only to be shaken out of his slumbers by the neighing of his mare. Skittish—though he knew not why—she had worked herself free and, in a panic, galloped off. After being led, groggy with sleep, on a merry chase through the waist high grass, the field hand eventually succeeded in catching up with her. Dangling from her reins was a yard-long rod the likes of which he had never before seen. Baffled, and somehow loath to toss such a curiosity aside, the fieldhand brought it home to the ranch that evening.

No sooner did his foreman lay eyes on the rod than he was taken aback. Here, before him, like a miracle out of his Sunday Book, was Jacob's Staff. This time tomorrow he was sure to be one of the richest men in the entire state of Texas! At dawn, however, the foreman was simply one of the most *irate*. Fearful of owning up to a dereliction of duty, and verily confused— half asleep as he was—by the events of the previous afternoon, the befuddled field hand could not for the life of him retrace his steps to the fateful spot. Round and round for days they searched the meadow but, so thoroughly had its coarse grass been trodden by horses' hooves, that the pair got nowhere. Finally fearing for his sanity, the foreman gave up the search in disgust, left only with a memento of his trials—a Jacob's Staff perhaps touched long ago by the hand of Jean Lafitte.[27]

Isles of Shoals

Only two people know where the treasure lies,
the Devil and myself, and he who lives the longest may claim it all!
—Edward Teach (Blackbeard)
Ocracoke Inlet, North Carolina,
November 29, 1718

The kind of news reaching Bridgetown, Barbados, in the spring of 1717 would ordinarily have scarcely raised an eyebrow. Years of lawlessness on the high seas, coupled with the carnage of the War of the Spanish Succession (1702–17), had done much to inure her citizens to shock. All the more curious, then, that reports of a string of attacks on merchant vessels off the distant Virginia Capes should create such sensation.

Three of the vessels taken—Glasgow's *Anne,* the *Young* out of Leith and the Bristol trader *Endeavour*—had been plundered of their respective lading but otherwise released and undisturbed. It was the fourth, however, Bridgetown's own *Turbot,* which was singled out for especially harsh usage. Moreover, the brigand responsible for looting and then burning her to the waterline, was positively identified as one of Barbados's prominent sons, Major Stede Bonnet.

Characterized at his trial eighteen months later, by a hostile Lord Chief Justice Trot, as "a gentleman ... man of letters" with the "benefit of a liberal education," no less likely individual ever outfitted a pirate brig. Retired some years from the Army and turned planter, Bonnet had shown himself to be, by his every word and deed, an honored member of Bridgetown society. He was esteemed by all and sundry—with but one notable exception. Squire-at-large, the poor Major seems to have been a virtual pariah at home.

Not unlike many a pirate before him, Stede Bonnet enjoyed a short, if incandescent, season. There, however, comparisons cease. Accustomed to command, though entirely innocent of the ways of ships, navigation and the sea, Bonnet is reckoned unique in the annals of piracy in that he actually purchased, armed, manned and provisioned a fully equipped pirate brig entirely with his own funds. Carrying ten guns and a motley crew of seventy, she left Bridgetown harbor in early 1717 and headed north for the American Colonies.

Bonnet called her the *Revenge* and word of her predations as far north as New England convinced his scandalized neighbors that their lifelong friend had lost his reason and was pursuing a demented vendetta against the good name of his much despised spouse. Certainly, Bonnet's methods had, on occasion, the stamp of madness upon them.

Once, cruising off Virginia, he boarded a merchantman straining to the seams with a cargo of ladies' toilet articles—combs, mirrors, needles, pins and the like. Plundering the lot to the last hair ribbon, the Major then turned right around and matched the favor after his peculiar fashion. Ordering his crew to part with two barrels of their best ship's biscuit, plus another of pork, Bonnet magnanimously presented this thoroughly unappreciated largesse to his bewildered victims and sailed off.

Stede Bonnet waxed by turns gallant and cold-blooded in his altogether capricious dealings with captives. He is credited with introducing a personal idiosyncrasy into the folklore of piracy. Commonly known as "walking the plank,"[1] it was no more representative of his newly adopted calling than black eye patches and peg legs. In any event, Bonnet's savage diversion later earned him the enmity of a hanging judge who happened to be adamant on the subject of the Second Commandment.

The Major's peregrinations took him at one point in his short career as far north as Long Island Sound. He may well have gone slightly further—to the Isles of Shoals. To be certain, he is on record as having looted a sloop outbound from New York to the West Indies after crippling the hapless vessel; he had the noblesse to disembark her crew on Gardiners Island.

By the time the *Revenge* again made her way south ahead of the winter weather, a committee of outraged Carolinians had organized to meet her. On September 27, 1718 Colonel William Rhett, commanding two ships, the *Henry* and the *Sea Wolf,* which carried between them better than 100 men and sixteen heavy guns, caught Bonnet's crew careening their newly renamed *Royal James* at the mouth of the Cape Fear River near Wilmington, North Carolina.

Although the ensuing engagement cost him a dozen sailors killed and eighteen wounded, Colonel Rhett returned to Charleston on October 3 triumphant, his dapper prisoner in irons. Held under house arrest in the custody of Provost Marshal Nathaniel Partridge, Bonnet acted the model prisoner. Gracious, handsome and dignified, society matrons saw in the much pitied captive a Southern gentleman wronged and proceeded to make of him a cause célèbre.

Then quite suddenly, just three days before his scheduled trial on October 28, with a "pro-Bonnet faction" lobbying Charleston for his release, the Major absconded in the night. Stepping once again into the breach, a hastily pledged reward of £700 now riding on his efforts, Colonel Rhett took special pains to recapture his man after a brief shoot-out on Sullivan's Island. This time held securely under military guard at the Watch House, Bonnet was brought to trial and condemned to die on a single count of piracy and murder, though thirteen other similar charges were leveled against him during the proceedings.

If, at the end, the Major's courage and dignity utterly failed him, his eloquence clearly did not. In a letter received by the Governor at the eleventh hour and signed "Your Honor's most miserable and afflicted servant," Stede Bonnet gave new meaning to the world "compunction":

> Honoured Sir,
>
> I have presumed, on the confidence of your eminent goodness, to throw myself after this manner at your feet ... [and] I beseech you to think me an object of your mercy ... For God's sake, good sir ... I entreat you not to let me fall a sacrifice ... [If] you'll permit me to live, I'll voluntarily put [wickedness] ever out of my power by separating all my limbs from my body, only reserving the use of my tongue, to call continuously on, and pray to the Lord, my God, and mourn all my days in sack cloth and ashes to work out confident hopes of my salvation ... I humbly beg you will ... send me up to the farthest inland garrison or settlement in the country, or any other [place] you'll be pleased to dispose of me ... [and] I implore you to consider me with a Christian and charitable heart.

Major Stede Bonnet was hanged on November 12, 1718 and his body buried between high and low tide at White Point, Charleston, South Carolina.

A second outlaw considerably more notorious than the "miserable and afflicted" Stede Bonnet is commonly associated with the treasure of the Isles of Shoals. Grossly intemperate in all things, his unbridled sexual license and operatic flair were the hallmarks of a truly feral nature. Nevertheless, he was competent to treat with officialdom and, thanks to well-cultivated connections and horse sense, made his fortune through a series of clever deals hammered out in a Southern governor's mansion.

Should the notion of a girl's ghost haunting his treasure in the bleak North Atlantic strike modern sensibilities as hopelessly quaint, it may be said that the legend, ennobled by a small but tantalizing discovery of silver bars and "cob money,"[2] close to two centuries ago, has enjoyed remarkable staying power.

Edward Teach, Bristol born, outlived his sometime partner, Stede Bonnet, by only a matter of weeks and, despite his richly deserved infamy, proved neither more nor less than a shooting star in the eighteenth-century pirate galaxy. He found his calling sometime around the year 1716 in the West Indies, and a *nom de guerre* to go with it—"Blackbeard." Both occupation and name were courtesy of an ex-privateer with the colorful name of Benjamin Hornigold.

Not known to have distinguished himself as a licensed privateer, although at complete liberty to harry French shipping during the War of the Spanish Succession, Teach took to piracy like a natural under Captain Hornigold's tutelage. During an inspired run in early 1717 the two men waylaid ships between Havana, Cuba, Bermuda and the Virginia coast, capturing their foremost prize off the southern Bahamas, a French Guineaman bound for Martinique. Prudently retiring from the game upon the arrival at Nassau of the legendary Woodes Rogers, Hornigold consigned himself to the Governor's mercy while his protégé carried on.

Renaming his Guineaman the *Queen Anne's Revenge,* Teach mounted her with forty guns and, cruising off St. Thomas, took the formidable *Great Allen*. Engaged shortly thereafter by a British man-of-war despatched to apprehend him, his counter-attack was so successful that H.M.S. *Scarborough* was obliged to withdraw to Barbados. This unprecedented stand-off nevertheless proved a sobering triumph for Teach who would henceforth limit his predations to easier and less remunerative coastal shipping.

Sailing south he plundered everything he could get his hands on, from a Boston trader, the *Protestant Caesar,* scuttled off the Gulf of Honduras, to a turtler near Grand Cayman Island. After briefly hunting for Spanish wrecks in the Bahamas, Teach made north for the Carolinas where he fell in with Major Stede Bonnet. Lying off the bar at Charleston the following year, Teach and his men so dominated the waters that they virtually closed down the port.

If Teach's career subsided into a pattern of highly remunerative, if pedestrian, hauls—these amounting in the main to hogsheads of sugar, molasses and rum (to which the fickle captain faithfully maintained an abiding love), cotton by the bale, slaves and armaments, plus sail cloth, clothing and the jewelry and assorted personal wealth of captured passengers and crews—he took them with inordinate ferocity and brokered them with skill.

In the manner of the early Celts, who treated their skin with dye before doing battle, Teach, though of imposing build and strength, drew for added effect upon his own peculiar brand of psychological warfare. His loose baggy apparel—the better in which to maneuver—was jet black, as were his extraordinary locks and beard. Indeed, it is said to have been a matter of great difficulty to determine just where the one began and the other left off. Teach's copious beard, which fell untamed clear to the buckle of his belt, was twisted into strands and festooned with multicolored ribbons. These he then drew upward (in order to deny an enemy at close quarters purchase) so that the crude braids completely obscured his now well-protected ears and, in the most astonishing of weaves, met up with the coarse matted wool of his hair.

Ranging in kneeboots across the listing deck of a ship, Teach was nonetheless light on his feet and moved with admirable agility, despite the triple brace of pistols he bore in sashes criss-crossing his chest and the variety of firearms and daggers tucked for ready access in his belt. Capping this ponderous ensemble, beneath the brim of a floppy hat he stuck hempen cords, soaked in saltpeter for slow burning, so that, charging forwards, he looked like an adversary's worst flaming nightmare. In fact, he used these "matches" to devilishly good purpose for, as if to prove himself no mere illusion, Teach was likely to preface his onrush with a flurry of homemade grenades—"case bottles filled with powder and small shot, slugs and pieces of lead or iron, with a quick match at the end of [them], which, being lighted outside, presently ran into the bottle to the powder."[3] These sowed confusion and carnage at a stroke.

Vivid illustrations of Teach's gratuitous pyromania and exceptionally volatile temperament surfaced at the trial of his surviving accomplices. A favorite jest of his, it seems, was to ignite stinkpots of brimstone and pitch (with the hatch shut) while his companions lounged below *Queen Anne's* decks. "Let's make a hell of our own!" he is once claimed to have challenged, reveling—though himself unstirred—in the uproarious spectacle of his hardened crew battling through the suffocating smoke and stench for a desperate purchase on the companion ladder.

On another occasion when one of his officers, Israel Hands, happened to nod off over a game of cards, Teach brought him "to" with a bang. "Here," roared his enraged Captain, "is a little something to remember me by!" whereupon Teach snuffed out the candles, drew a pistol from his belt and proceeded to discharge it blindly beneath the table. One of his kneecaps blown away, Hands was put ashore near Bathtown, North Carolina, where the authorities arrested him on suspicion of piracy. Although crippled for life, the horrifying incident later saved Hands from an otherwise firm date with the hangman.

For all his savagery, Teach enjoyed friends in high places and, through their venal offices, managed to convert his diverse plunder into a fortune. Whether or not North Carolina's Governor Charles Eden was corrupt, he certainly turned a blind eye to considerable malpractices, including the fiscal interest his Private Secretary and Collector for the Province, Tobias Knight, had in the disposal of Teach's innumerable hogsheads.

By early 1718 Teach, now a wealthy man, successfully petitioned the Governor for clemency and even secured title to his pirate barque, the hugely compromised *Queen Anne's Revenge*. Settling into a short-lived retirement near Ocracoke Inlet, Teach again turned to Eden for a courtesy, this time prevailing upon the obliging Governor to betroth him to his sixteen-year-old bride.[4] Only later did reports circulate that Teach had exploited the girl most barbarously, prostituting her on occasion in front of him for the pleasure of his drunken and unruly companions at Ocracoke.

In June Teach took to the seas again. It is during this period, with the good people of the Carolinas up in arms and Virginia's Governor, Alexander Spotswood, making threatening noises, that he is thought to have either sailed east to Bermuda or northward to the Isles of Shoals, New Hampshire. If he sailed north in search of a safe, temporary and accessible spot at which to secrete his treasure—or that portion of it he deemed best kept out of harm's way—Teach may have singled out Smuttynose Island, so named for the black ledge of rocks jutting out from its western shore.

The Smuttynose legend notwithstanding, Teach and his men are known to have operated off Cape Hatteras and Pamlico Sound that summer and with their accustomed impunity. Pushed to the wall, a secret delegation of exasperated North Carolinians, lacking faith in their own governor, met with Alexander Spotswood in Richmond, Virginia. Two frigates chanced to be lying at the time in the James River. At a council of war, Lieutenant Robert Maynard of the *Pearl* was appointed head of a volunteer force whose mission was to ambush Teach in two borrowed sloops equipped with small arms and ammunition but without mounted guns.

What must have looked like a suicide squad left Kicquetan on the James

River on November 17. One week later the Virginia Assembly issued a proclamation offering rewards to be paid by the Treasurer of the colony:

> For Edward Teach commonly called Captain Teach or Blackbeard,
> one hundred pounds; for every other commander of a pirate
> ship, sloop or vessel, forty pounds; for every lieutenant, master
> or quartermaster, boatswain or carpenter, twenty pounds; for
> every other inferior officer, fifteen pounds; and for every pri-
> vate man taken aboard such ship, sloop or vessel, ten pounds.[5]

Maynard would earn his reward. Word of his mission beat the lieutenant south by a nose and, on the night of November 21 at Ocracoke Inlet,
Teach was waiting for him. In the ensuing battle the following morning a
single broadside from the *Queen Anne* accounted for twenty-nine of
Maynard's volunteers killed or wounded. Anticipating a further devastating cannonade, the lieutenant ordered all hands, but for the helmsman, below the decks of the *Ranger* and as Teach and fourteen of his men came
across her bows lobbing grenades before them, Maynard's force, on cue,
burst from the forward hatchway and engaged their antagonists hand-to-
hand. Before falling dead, Teach reportedly took some twenty-five wounds,
five of them by shot, including one which tore through his throat and neck.

Lieutenant Maynard would have Teach decapitated and his blood-caked head
hung from the bowsprit before the *Ranger* limped back to Bathtown, North
Carolina, with her prisoners and wounded. At the trial that followed all "Blackbeard's"
men were convicted and soon after hanged, but for a cabin boy, Samuel Odell,
and Israel Hands. Of no use to the Royal Navy, which was generally quick to
conscript such human dross in its service, Hands made his way to London where
he ended his days as a popular beggar on the streets of Wapping. Later, he
would turn up immortalized as a gunner on the pages of *Treasure Island*.

The inventory of Blackbeard's fortune—that is to say, the chattels recovered
from the Queen Anne's Revenge and from a tent pitched ashore at Ocracoke
Inlet—makes for uninspiring reading: a bale or two of cotton, a barrel of indigo,
twenty-five hogsheads of sugar, 145 bags of cocoa, etc. Left unsolved to this day
are the mysterious whereabouts of his treasure. As late as the Second World War,
the Isles of Shoals were still attracting the interest of organized recovery missions
convinced that Teach had left precious metal, most likely silver, thereabouts.
Even diminutive Londoner Island staked its claim to the Blackbeard treasure.

During the early 1940s author E. R. Snow confirmed that "several government representatives went ashore on Londoner Island and made some interesting discoveries." Snow quotes Mrs. Prudence Randall, daughter of the Reverend Frank B. Randall, owner of the island:

> Government men who went ashore on our island without permission found definite indications that there was a substantial amount of silver still buried on the landing side of the beach facing the Star Island Hotel ... We have been told that Blackbeard buried his loot here ... Captain Haley found the silver bars on Smuttynose Island but never found the pieces of eight ...
>
> The sand shifts so rapidly out there after every storm that, whereas you might know where to look one week, the next week everything might be changed ... The government men gave it up, saying that it would take several thousand dollars for dredges and pumps.[6]

The only known silver connected with the life of Edward Teach was that of his skull. Obtained from Maynard by a citizen of Bathtown, Blackbeard's head was reportedly boiled and the skull lined with silver inside and out. The property of sundry parties over the years, including a university fraternity and an Alexandria, Virginia, tavern, it finally wound up in the possession of Mr. Snow who purchased it for an unrevealed sum in 1949.

Edward Teach, struck down fighting, left for posterity neither dying words nor confession. A famous quote, brought to light at the trial of the nine men who survived him, is the kind of thing, however, that quickens the pulse of avid treasure hunters. On the night of November 20, 1718 Teach is said to have sat up drinking rum with a local contraband dealer and a handful of *Queen Anne's* crew. Anticipating Maynard's arrival, one of the assembled company ventured to inquire as to whether Teach had made any provision against his possible demise. Did the Captain's wife, the individual made bold to wonder, have any inkling as to where he had buried his accumulated fortune? "Only two people know where the treasure lies," Teach retorted, "the Devil and myself, and he who lives the longest may claim it all!"

If Robert Louis Stevenson drew upon the true life comradeship of Stede Bonnet and Blackbeard for one of his classic characters, he seems to have set his famous story on a Pacific island remarkably similar to one claimed by the Republic of Costa Rica. But for its want of a tropical clime, Stevenson might well have chosen the haunting Isles of Shoals.

These nine islands[7] hugging the forty-third parallel north make up an oval three miles north to south and half as many miles east to west. Steeped as they are in treasure lore, they count for a mere 205 acres in total. Straddling the boundary line between two U.S. states, residents of Star Island, for example, pay their taxes to Rye, New Hampshire; those of Appledore to Kittery, Maine.

Smuttynose Island (along with Appledore) is steeped in intriguing treasure lore laced with lurid overtones of the supernatural. Female ghosts abound. It was at Smuttynose, for instance, that a celebrated sea rover named Edward Lowe is believed to have murdered a young woman in 1722,[5] and it may possibly be she who later came to be confused with Blackbeard's last wife. One abiding Shoals legend holds that he marooned his young bride at Smuttynose after a quarrel aboard ship (quite uncharacteristically leaving her behind to "guard" a hoard of silver booty) and that the poor creature's ghost haunted the island for a century. In any event, as a matter of historical record, slightly less than two decades earlier renegade seamen of the privateering brig *Charles* were apprehended at nearby Star island in the possession of a cache of Portuguese gold.

In 1703, with the sweet high smell of corruption still hanging over the scandal of the "Kidd Affair," Governor Dudley of Massachusetts and a consortium of some of Boston's leading citizens plunged headlong into a startlingly similar enterprise. The man unfortunate enough to represent it was Captain David Plowman of the brigantine *Charles*. Licensed as a privateer, the eighty-eight-ton vessel was charged with harrying French shipping in the coastal waters off Newfoundland and Acadia and might have proved successful in that capacity but for the machinations of her crew. Fearful lest his mission proved a repetition of that of Kidd's, Plowman appears to have contracted a case of "cold feet."

Upon receiving her commission on July 13, the fully provisioned *Charles* was riding at anchor off Marblehead on August 1 when Captain Plowman suddenly "took ill." A letter he duly despatched to the ship's owners in Boston regretfully informed his employers that he found himself unable to take command of the mission and that, in order to "prevent embezzlement," they would be wise to make haste to Marblehead and "take speedy care in saving what [they] can."[9]

Plowman waxed increasingly desperate as he impatiently awaited the expected delegation, going so far as to issue a second warning, this time urging his backers against sending the *Charles* to sea under any circumstances, "as it will not do with these people." Arriving too late, Governor Dudley's emissaries were still on the road in a coach and horses when the *Charles* was standing off Cape Cod under the command of her new skipper, Lieutenant John Quelch.

Whether or not Quelch and his fellow mutineers were aware of the fact, England had recently concluded a treaty with Brazil's sovereign, the King of Portugal, on May 16 at Lisbon. In any event, between November 15, 1703 and February 17, 1704 the *Charles* took no fewer than nine craft bearing the Portuguese colors, off the coast of Brazil. Among her haul figured sugar, rice, rum, beer, gold dust, gold and silver specie, as well as a variety of jewelry and personal effects separated from the persons of a host of victimized passengers and crew.

Well satisfied with his take—rich as he was after a mere two months of rapine—Quelch headed for the West Indies. There he shaped a most curious design. He would now sail straightaway to Marblehead and beard the lion (as one chronicler put it) in his own den. The absence of Captain Plowman, who had long since been consigned to the depths of the Gulf Stream, might be readily explained away by the poor man's lingering indisposition. The magnificent spoils would speak for themselves.

During the week of May 15, 1704 the following brief mention of the *Charles's* unexpected return appeared in the Boston News-Letter: "Arrived at Marblehead, Captain Quelch in the Brigantine that Captain Plowman went out in. It is said to come from New Spain and to have made a good Voyage.[10]

However good the voyage, Dudley's backers were still waiting with the keenest impatience to reap the fruit of its enterprise a week later. Exasperated by the open carousing of their disreputable minions, the owners of the *Charles* prevailed upon the authorities to apprehend them, pursuant to a proclamation of May 24 issued by Lieutenant Governor Thomas Povey:

> [These men] have lately imported a considerable quantity
> of Gold dust, and some Bar and Coin'd Gold, which they
> are Violently suspected to have gotten and obtained by
> Felony and Piracy from some of Her Majesty's Friends and
> Allies ... I have therefore thought it fit ... strictly to com-
> mand all Officers Civil and Military, and others of Her
> Majesty's loving Subjects to Apprehend and Seize the said
> Pirates ... and their Treasure.[11]

Events now moved apace. Feeling the noose closing around their necks, a dozen of Quelch's accomplices-at-large promptly decamped with their gold. And, as so often proved the case, the lure of it turned the head of yet another honest New England soul.

Boston News-Letter (undated): "Warrants are issued Forth to seize and apprehend Captain Larrimore of the *Larrimore Galley,* who is said to have sailed from Cape Anne with 9 or 11 Pirates of Captain Quelch's company."[12]

In what would have amounted to "rounding up a posse" in the days of the Wild West, Governor Dudley's agents scrambled a volunteer crew while the trail was still warm. Leading it was Major Samuel Sewall, assisted by a veteran of Governor Bellomont's Gardiners Island Commission, Nathaniel Byfield. Mustered with evident difficulty, in all some forty-two of Her Majesty's loving Subjects were duly prodded into doing their duty. To say that they set out on June 9 in hot pursuit, however, would be an overstatement. Sewall and his men were forced to put to sea in a dead calm and were thus obliged to resort to their oars. Fortunately, the *Larrimore Galley* was not built for speed.

The town of Marblehead, alarmed at the rogues' gallery that their good citizens had been inveigled into bringing to justice, passed two days of extreme anxiety. Meanwhile, after following up a couple of false leads, Major Sewall came upon the *Larrimore Galley* lying off Star Island, Isles of Shoals.

Keeping the main body of his men below the decks of his shallop, and posing as a fisherman, Sewall angled within small-arms' range of his quarry and then suddenly brought his firepower to bear.

Salem, 11 June :

> This afternoon Major Sewall brought into this Port the Larrimore Galley and seven Pirates ... whom he with his Commissioners Surprized and Seized at the Isles of Sholes the 10th. Instant viz. four of them on Board the Larrimore Galley and three on shoar on Starr Island ... He [Major Sewall] also Seized 45 Ounces and seven Penny weight of Gold of the said Pirates.[13]

The whereabouts of the remainder—thanks in large part to tantalizing but inconclusive minor discoveries over the years—became the stuff of Shoals' legend and fueled a controversy, some years after Quelch's trial, between Governor Dudley and the Reverend Cotton Mather who accused His Excellency of "Collutions with the Pyrates of Quench's Company."[14]

Boston, June 17:

> On the 13th. Instant, Major Sewall attended with a strong guard brought to town the Pirates and Gold he had seized and gave His Excellency a full Account of his Procedure in Seizing them. The prisoners were committed to Gaol in order to await Tryal, and the Gold delivered to the Treasurer and Committee appointed to receive the same. The service of Major Sewall and company was very well accepted and Rewarded by the Governor.[15]

John Quelch, for one, took the matter in admirable stride. Laconic in his hour of reckoning, he began: "Gentlemen, 'tis but little I have to speak ... " and, as good as his word, wound up a few brief phases later by doffing his hat to the crowd and bowing right and left.[16]

The Reverend Mather, however, mincing no words, harangued the assembled for better than an hour, reminding those gathered that:

> We, even we also, have every one of us an horrible Fountain of Sin in our Souls. There are none of the Crimes committed by these Miserable Men, or by the worst of those Criminals that go

down into the Pit, but we have the seeds of them, in that Original Corruption, which we brought into the World with us.[17]

The diary of Judge Stephen Sewall, Major Samuel Sewall's brother, records the execution:

> When I came to see how the River was covered with people, I was amazed: Some say there were 100 Boats. Mr. Cotton Mather came with Captain Quelch and six others for Execution from the Prison to Scarlett's Wharf, and from thence in the Boat to the place of Execution about midway between Hanson's Point and Broughton's Warehouse. Mr. Mather pray'd for them standing upon the Boat. Ropes were all fasten'd to the Gallows. When the Scaffold was let to sink, there was such a screech of the Women that my wife heard it sitting in our Entry next to the Orchard, and was much surprized at it; yet the wind was sou-west. Our house is a full mile from the place.[18]

There was no "inside story" printed by the Boston News-Letter concerning the arrest of Quelch and Company at Star Island on June 10, 1704. Celebrated around Boston for a time, the name "John Quelch" was soon supplanted by that of "Blackbeard" Teach. The notoriety of Star Island itself languished among the habitués and sparse population of the Isles of Shoals. Still, the belief that somewhere a great treasure had been buried on Shoals during the early years of the eighteenth century has survived intact into the twentieth.

As smoke may be said to betoken fire, a small but possibly significant discovery on Smuttynose Island is credited with keeping the notion alive. In the process of building a wall on his property at the island's western end around 1820, Mr. Samuel Halley stumbled upon a well-documented cache of precious metal set in the hard earth beneath a large flat stone.

It consisted of four bars of solid silver. No more are known to have ever been discovered and their provenance by common, if probably erroneous, consent, is associated with the irrepressible captain of the *Queen Anne's Revenge.*

Obtained through force, buried with cunning, discovered by chance … only the upright, practical nature of a Yankee farmer could account for the singular manner of their disposal. Not a stranger to the virtues of a neatly constructed wall, Halley sold off his silver bars and erected a breakwater, between his land at Smuttynose and nearby Malaga Island, which was said to have stood for many years against the ravages of the North Atlantic and to the benefit of local fishermen.

Mahé Island

Find my treasure who can!
—Olivier Le Vasseur
From the Gallows
St. Denis, Reunion, July 17, 1730

The Indian Ocean is arguably the cradle of shipbuilding and deep water navigation. Twenty-eight centuries before the birth of Christ, at the time Cheops was erecting his Great Pyramid at Giza, Egyptian mariners venturing down the Red Sea and southward across the Horn's shark-infested waters bore the tidings of their great Pharaoh to the lost kingdom of Punt.

Two millennia later the Phoenicians would explore a different tack. Undoubtedly the finest sailors of antiquity—sufficiently bold to have bartered for Baltic timber with the barbarians of the German Ocean[1]—under King Hirian of Tyre and accompanied on their voyage by observers in the service of Solomon, they traversed the Gulf of Aden in 945 B.C., running before the southwest monsoon toward the land of Ophir.[2]

Throughout much of the next thousand years unsung pilots, guiding long forgotten barks, gingerly tested the Indian Ocean's vast and uncharted waters. By the first century B.C. entire fleets of Graeco-Roman merchantmen traded for the silks, spices and gems of the Hindus, while confidently plying the enormously profitable slave route to and from Zanzibar. By the Middle Ages generations of Persian, Arab and Hindustani seamen could boast of the long southern crossing to Madagascar. The best of them even savored the mysteries of Indo-Malaysia and Cathay. Between this teeming cross-fertilization of languages, creeds and cultures, the Seychelles stood apart.[3]

Situated roughly 1,000 nautical miles east of Mombasa, west of the Chagos Archipelago, south of the Gulf of Aden and north of Mauritius, Mahé was convenient for mariners with a natural predilection for coastal navigation and the monsoon winds. The great Vasco de Gama, essaying what turned out to be an ill conceived short-cut to Malabar, sailed in 1502 to within a few degrees of Mahé, pausing only briefly at the Ilhas de Almirantes (Admiral Islands).

Nevertheless, it was not until the very beginning of the seventeenth century that the first European vessel put in at the Seychelles. She was the British East Indiaman *Ascension,* commanded by Alexander Sharpeigh, and she dropped anchor in Victoria Harbor, situated on the northwest coast of Mahé, on January 19, 1609.

Though it had been long familiar to pirates who came to water, rest and careen their vessels on the island's deserted sands, the first colonists did not reach Mahé until 1770.[4]

> Witnessed by the Council, the extraordinary Criminal proceedings, instituted and undertaken at the request and concern of the King's Prosecutor, plaintiff against Olivier Levasseur, known as the Buzzard, accused of the crime of piracy …
>
> The Council has convicted him and condemns him to make honourable amends by standing before the main door of the church of this parish, in penitent's garb, with the rope around his neck and holding a burning torch two pounds in weight in his hand, there to say and declare in a loud and clear voice that he has wickedly and audaciously followed the pirate's trade for many a year, for which he now feels remorse and humbly begs pardon of God and the King.
>
> Carried out at five o'clock of the evening on the seventeenth day of July in the year of our Lord seventeen hundred and thirty. Signed:
>
> Chassin-Dumas-Villarmoy-Gachet-G. Dumas-de Lanux.

Olivier le Vasseur was born at Calais around 1690 to the report of cannon. Reared on the front lines of the Seven Years War (1689–97), the young man earned a privateering commission from Louis XIV during the height of its bloody sequel—the War of the Spanish Succession. Although much of the fighting took place in Italy, Germany and the Netherlands, le Vasseur's role in the Sun King's solitary struggle seems to have been enacted in the warm, tropical waters of the Caribbean.

The Treaty of Utrecht in 1713 signaled a rapprochement among England, Holland and France that served to stabilize Europe for the next quarter of a century. By its sweeping terms the permanent separation of the crowns of France and Spain was guaranteed and the balance of power in Europe and North America radically altered. The dogs of war finally brought to heel, licensed privateers on both sides of the conflict now found themselves in idleness unsuited to the tastes of all. Among the disenchanted figured Olivier le Vasseur.

Of solid bourgeois stock, intelligent and, by all accounts, well educated, his interests are said to have included astronomy and the classics, particularly Greek mythology. Such cultural refinements notwithstanding, the daring young officer was likewise drawn to the company of desperate men. So it was that, rather than immediately turn over his vessel and

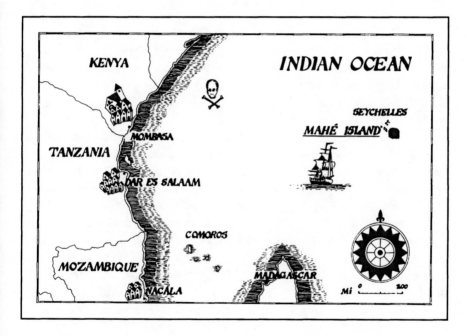

relinquish his command at the war's end as ordered by the French Admiralty, le Vasseur balked.

Instead, he would try his luck at piracy. Along the way he made common cause with two erstwhile enemies of France: one, the renegade British Navy lieutenant, John Taylor; the other, a sometime respectable Irish merchant captain named Edward England. Joining forces in an uneasy and irregular coalition spanning the twilight years of West Indies piracy, together they harried New Spain.

By the time le Vasseur determined to seek his fortune east, he is reckoned to have been a wealthy man. The West Indies had once answered his ruthless purpose but, with Spain's inclusion in the Quadruple Alliance and a united front evolving against lawlessness in the region, piracy was proving an increasingly risky and diminishingly lucrative venture. By contrast, the largely unpatrolled monsoon routes of the Indian Ocean looked like easy pickings.

En route, the French man tried his luck in Africa. In the spring of 1720 le Vasseur's friend, Captain England, called—armed and dangerous—at Ouidah on the Bight of Benin along the notorious Slave Coast, and was surprised to encounter her fort in ruins and her treasury looted to the last guinea. Pressing Ouidah's demoralized garrison as to the agent of their recent calamity, England was referred to a dapper freebooter now going by the incongruous name of La Buse (The Buzzard). The two were fated, as it turned out, soon to meet up again.

The Buzzard's introduction to the Indian Ocean proved inauspicious. Negotiating the reefs and shoals of the Comoros for the first time, he only succeeded in running his vessel, the *Indian Queen,* aground in a storm off Anjouan Island. Holed up there for the month of July while his crew refitted her hull with local hardwood, a lookout one day sighted a pair of sails on the northern horizon.

Against both a possible native attack from the island's wild interior, and an assault from the sea, the Buzzard had ordered a crude redoubt thrown up on high ground fronting Mutsamudu Bay. It was there that he and his followers now hurriedly regrouped, some to shore up the earthworks, others to make ready a line of ship's cannon salvaged from their stricken craft.

Meanwhile, from the bridge of the *Cassandra,* Commander James McRae was covering the *Indian Queen* with his glass, as was also the unarmed chief officer of her sister ship, the East Indiaman *Enterprise.* Whether the Commander had got wind of the Buzzard's predicament or whether this was strictly a fortuitous contact with the "wanted" French brigand, McRae reckoned that he had hit upon a nest of ill-defended pirates which would mean a feather in his cap if he brought their leader to justice. The others he might hang from the yardarm as he deemed fit.

With that end in mind McRae stood into Matsamudu Bay, cannons blazing, only to be surprised aft by two fast-closing brigs. Suddenly caught up in crossfire from both land and sea, the captain of the *Enterprise* lost his nerve and, to McRae's disgust, sheered off to windward leaving the beleaguered *Cassandra* to shift for herself. Credited with holding his own through the worst of the onslaught, McRae finally availed himself of the blessings of the dusk and he and his remaining crew took to the *Cassandra's* lighter. Once safely ashore the exhausted band dug in for a harrowing night in the jungle and then, at first light, made straight for the town of Domoni where they threw themselves upon the mercy of the Chief.

Thankful for the opportunity to lick his wounds and take stock, McRae soon concluded that his position at Domoni was untenable and so was his neglect of Company property. Fearing the worst, after ten days under the protection of the Chief, he surrendered. When he did so, riding peacefully at anchor on Matsumudu Bay were the *Fancy,* the *Victory,* the *Indian Queen* and the *Cassandra;* and there to receive him were the Buzzard and Edward England.

Over the heated protests of his cohort, Lieutenant Taylor (which were echoed by those of the Buzzard himself), Edward England's *noblesse oblige* prompted him to extend an unconditional freedom to his astonished captives along with provisions sufficient for a passage to India. This they were to accomplish—with a bit of luck—in the patently down-at-heel *Fancy* while the *Cassandra* was pressed into England's fleet.

Well before McRae limped into Bombay—the better part of his crew unhinged by thirst—the Buzzard and Co. were indulging the pleasures of rape and pillage at the expense of the oft-abused Laccadive Islanders. The *Indian Queen's* brush with James McRae, who would later become Governor of Madras and pursue her up and down the Indian Ocean, can only be described as providential. Stalked by the "pox" while shipwrecked at Anjouan it was, above all else, the *Cassandra's* medical stores—specifically quicksilver—that the Buzzard's crew most coveted. Naturally enough, once restored to ruddy health, the pirates were free to turn their attentions to the rich plunder of the Indian Ocean.

From the Laccadives, Taylor, England and le Vasseur put in long enough at Cochin to sell the *Cassandra's* mercantile stores to an unscrupulous Dutch trading house for £75,000; they then hauled for Ile de France (Mauritius). It was there, in February 1721, that they learned that Commander McRae was hot on their trail. Punished for his lunatic sense of Irish bonhomie, Captain England was marooned by his shipmates with a water cask, a pistol and a bottle of powder. Nothing if not resourceful, England fashioned himself a raft and drifted on the southeast trades as far as the pirate stronghold of Madagascar where he is said to have died a penniless beggar some years later.

Better things were in store for the Buzzard. He, in the *Cassandra,* and Taylor in the *Victory,* cruised to nearby Bourbon (Reunion Island) where in April great good fortune awaited them. She was the wrecked Portuguese *Virgem do Cabo* and she yielded up a fortune. Described by Athol Thomas in his work, *Forgotten Eden,* as a "floating treasure house," she carried "gold and silver bars, chests of gold guineas, pearls, casks of diamonds, silks, objets d'art and the staff and cross and other valuable religious trappings of the Archbishop of Goa," estimated to be worth some £100,000,000.

Wracked by a fearful tempest during the crossing from India, the vessel had lumbered unsuspectingly into the French port of St. Denis on Bourbon's north coast. In hopes of preventing her from foundering, her crew had reluctantly cast most of her seventy-two cannon overboard. Thus, one of the richest prizes in the annals of Indian Ocean piracy fell into Buzzard's hands without his so much as firing a single round.

So crammed with riches was the hold of the utterly defenseless *Virgem* that Taylor and le Vasseur could well afford to abjure the temptation—inbred in the best of pirates—to ransom her passengers, among whom numbered Goa's Archbishop and the Portuguese Viceroy, the Conde de Ericeira. Such, however, was the limit of Buzzard's chivalry. He proved stone deaf to the Archbishop's plea for a return of his cathedral's most treasured relics. No doubt crowning the list was the diamond, ruby and emerald encrusted "Fiery Cross of Goa"—heavy enough to need three of the Buzzard's men to stow aboard ship.

After a thorough refitting, courtesy of her Portuguese crew, the *Virgem do Cabo,* now under Taylor's command and accompanied by the *Victory* and le Vasseur's favored *Cassandra,* discharged her cannon in a sardonic salute to Bourbon's harried Governor, Joseph de Veauvolliers, and was gone. The combined crews were anxious to put some distance between themselves and their most recent port of call and the sighting of a Dutch vessel, *Ville d'Ostende,* subsequently taken with ease off St. Paul on the island's west coast, delayed the Buzzard's progress but slightly.

Looking forward to the customary share-out, this hugely successful flotilla now made for the safety of Ile Ste Marie where each able seaman is said to have collected no fewer than 5000 gold guineas—and precisely forty-two diamonds per man. Le Vasseur reportedly took his portion in bullion, topped up by a sampling of Church property, including the Fiery Cross. The share-out accomplished to the satisfaction of all, some of the crew retired to the tropical languor of "St. Mary's," as she was affectionately known to the British pirates. Taylor and le Vasseur, however, were apparently in no mood to lower "le joli rouge" just yet.

Before pushing on, they scuttled the *Victory* whose name was forthwith transferred to the *Virgem do Cabo,* then beat 600 miles down Madagascar's east coast. En route, the Buzzard—clearly no patriot—plundered the *Duchesse de Noailles* of the Compagnie Francaise. Advised by sympathetic Malagasy natives that a pirate-hunting squadron was cruising in the vicinity, Taylor and le Vasseur continued south, rounding Fort Dauphin at the foot of Madagascar and then tacking due west for lower Mozambique. Finally, in a singularly bold stroke, they sailed into the Bay of Lourenco Marques in April 1722 and overwhelmed the Dutch garrison at Fort Lagoa.

With tension building aboard the two ships and their respective captains at one another's throats, it was time to part company. Upon returning to Madagascar and a final share-out of their treasure, le Vasseur assumed command of the *Victory*. Taylor, under the influence of an apparent nostalgia for the Spanish Main, careened the *Cassandra* at Ile Ste Marie and then, late in the year, with 150 crew, sailed west. The former British lieutenant reportedly surrendered some time later in the Spanish West Indies and accepted a commission in Spain's navy. Taylor is thought to have died in Cuba.

How did the Buzzard spend the next few years? Almost certainly he passed some months at Ile Ste Marie. From there he despatched an emissary in 1724 to treat with the Governor of Bourbon. The Buzzard's intent was to test the waters of a French amnesty extended to all French pirates in the western Indian Ocean. An attractive option to increasing numbers of brigands who were threatened, as had earlier been their Caribbean counterparts, with extinction, le Vasseur seemed to equivocate.

As a sweetener, the Buzzard made it clear, through his agent, that he was prepared to part with some, but by no means all, of his share of the *Virgem's* cargo. The French government, on behalf of the Archbishop of Goa, as well as itself, remained unmoved. It was clear that the Buzzard's pardon hinged upon the surrender of a considerably grander inventory to include, without a doubt, the Fiery Cross. Finding such terms distasteful, the Buzzard removed himself from the field and the amnesty lapsed.

By this time, around 1725, he may have deemed it politic to retire to the obscurity of the Seychelles. Among the circumstantial evidence lending credence to this particular school of thought is an imperfectly executed map which came to light shortly after the Buzzard's death. Published in Lisbon in 1735, over a rough sketch of what today goes by the name of Bel Ombre on Mahé's northwest coast, are inscribed the words: "Owner of the land ... La Buse."

A few years after his alleged arrival at Mahé, le Vasseur is believed to have been shipwrecked in the vicinity of Ile Ste Marie. He then took up the trade of pilot for a time in Antongil Bay, Madagascar, where his incognito was eventually exposed in 1728 by an employee of the Compagnie Francaise. During a renewed but inconsequential flirtation with piracy in early 1730, Captain L'Ermitte of the warship *Meduse* engaged him off Fort Dauphin. At the height of a pitched sea battle that saw no quarter given, le Vasseur was captured alive and taken in irons to St. Denis where he was remanded in the custody of Bourbon's Governor.

By tradition, le Vasseur went out of the world with a flourish. While being escorted to the gallows on the afternoon of July 17, he reportedly flung a tightly rolled sheaf of documents towards a knot of fascinated onlookers. "Find my treasure," the Buzzard is credited with challenging, "who can!"

The tempest that battered the Seychelles Islands in 1923 may have impressed Mme. Charles Savy and her husband as neither more nor less fierce

than others they had experienced on Mahé over the years. Generations of
their forbears over a century and a half had experienced countless like it.
Notwithstanding the hardship occasioned by such tropical "lows," their
periodic arrival provided a diversion for the Seychellois, acting as a tonic
against the ennui induced by a pleasant yet routine confinement in this equatorial "paradise." But the storm of 1923 worked a sea change on the routine—if not necessarily the fortunes—of Mme. Savy.

Having ridden out the worst of it behind the well-secured shutters of
her comfortable home at Bel Ombre, as soon as the weather permitted she
made her way down to the magnificent palm-shrouded beach at Beau Vallon
for her customary stroll. The storm happened to have coincided with an
uncommonly low tide that year. The effect was to expose to view the tops of
a line of usually submerged boulders covered, as far as Mme. Savy could
best make out, with carvings of some sort. Chipping away an accumulation
of barnacles and bearded sea grasses from one of them, she soon found herself looking at what appeared to be a primitive frieze dominated by, though
not restricted to, representations of various animal forms.

Among them figured serpents, horses, dogs and a tortoise; a man's head
in profile and the rough contours of a female torso. In addition, further clearing brought to light a pair of intertwined hearts, an urn, the silhouette of
what could have passed for an insect's wings; the outlines of a keyhole and,
finally, an arresting depiction of a round "staring" eye.

Discussing the matter with friends, the tortoise and the serpents suggested the
animistic worship of certain East Indian Ocean cultures; while the "staring eye"
struck some as bound up with the arcana of Freemasonry. Nonetheless, not a shred
of scientific evidence could anyone bring to bear supporting the likely colonization
of islands like Mahé, lying north of Madagascar, by Far Eastern peoples, while the
notion of a Masonic connection was dismissed as far-fetched. Thus, interest in her
find might well have ebbed away, even as the march of the Seychelles' tides fast
reclaimed it, but for a second surprising event.

News on an island the size of Mahé travels fast and the discovery at
Beau Vallon was soon brought to the attention of a notary with offices a few
miles away in Victoria. It was the peculiar imagery of the rock carvings as
related to him—the hearts, horse, dog, etc.—which immediately struck a
familiar note. Referring to his files, he came up with a mass of background
material on two eighteenth-century French sailors whose names had been
linked over the years with reputed treasure deposits at one or more of the
islands of Ile Ste Marie, Rodriguez, Mahé, Pemba and Reunion. The first
was Olivier le Vasseur and the second was a licensed corsair based at
Mauritius at the time of the war between France and the First Coalition (England, Spain and Holland) in 1792. His alias was "le Butin" ("the Loot") and
his Christian name in full was Bernadin Nageon de L'Estang.

L'Estang met his end seventy years after the Buzzard. Yet, in a manner cryptic or perverse, their alleged endowments to one or more of the above mentioned islands—endowments rumored to have been immense—appear to have *merged*. That is to say, whether L'Estang "inherited" the Buzzard's famous sheaf of treasure documents and, in so doing, adopted his forebear's method, or whether the inspiration was his own, their respective hoards became so confused that "separating the sheep from the goats" made for an intriguing conundrum.

Among the data in the notary's possession, judged pertinent to the bequests of le Vasseur and L'Estang, were a series of letters, a will, a *rebus* or puzzle, a parchment covered with four unidentified symbols, a double set of bearings and, finally, two cryptograms. One of the letters was headed "Bernadin Nageon de L'Estang to his nephew Justin Marius, 20 Floreal VIII"[5] and read in part:

> My Dear Justin,
> Should death overcome me before we meet, a faithful friend will hand over to you my will and my documents. I urge you to follow my instructions and carry out my last wishes and God bless you ...
>
> I have lost many documents in a shipwreck ... I have already removed several treasures; only four remain, buried in the same manner by the same pirates, which you will find by the key to the combinations and the other papers which you will receive at the same time.[6]

A second letter was addressed to Etienne de L'Estang.

> My Dearest Brother,
> I have been ill since we took Tamatave [Madagascar], in spite of the care of my friend the Commandant. I am weak and the fear of death is upon me. I am speaking to you for the last time, dear Etienne, and impart to you my last wishes.
>
> When I am dead Commandant Hamon will send on to you what little I now possess and have saved during my adventurous life as a sailor. You know, Etienne, that my life's dream has been to build up a fortune to restore the splendor of our house. With the good-will the First Consul has shown me after a glorious feat of arms, I should have managed to do so. But, as God will not permit me to carry out this duty and I feel death approaching, swear to me, dear Etienne, to carry out my wish.

In the course of my adventurous life, before embarking on the Apollo, I was a member of a pirate band which did so much damage to Spain and our enemies the English. We made some fine captures together, but during our last fight with a large English frigate off the coast of Hindustan, our captain was wounded and, on his death bed, confided to me his secrets and papers for finding the sizeable treasures buried around the Indian Ocean.

After first making sure that I was a Freemason, he asked me to use them to arm privateering ships against the English. But I was weary of this wanderer's life and preferred to enroll as a regular and wait till France was at peace to find these treasures and return home. Swear to me that your older son will realize my dream and use this fortune one day to restore our house.

The Commandant will hand over to you the writings related to the treasures. There are three. The one buried on my beloved Ile de France [Mauritius] is sizeable. As stated in the writings you will see: three iron casks and large jars full of minted doubloons and bullion worth thirty million and a casket crammed with diamonds from the Visapour and Golconda mines ...[7]

Of the two cryptograms, copies of which are reportedly catalogued in the Bibliotheque Nationale in Paris and the Archives of Mauritius, one consisted of seventeen lines and was characterized as having been put down in "Masonic cipher." By turns profane, illegible, nonsensical and misspelt, its opening line seemed to mirror the recent discoveries of Mme. Savy: "First: a pair of pigeons draw aside 2 hearts ... head of horse a "kort fil winshient" shield take a spoon half ... " After refreshing his memory, the notary hastened to confer with the Savys. Desultory spadework around the rock carvings at Beau Vallon beach succeeded in turning up a great deal of sand, pebbles and shell but little else.

Then one day workmen digging in the vicinity of the "staring eye" came upon two moldering coffins. Lying next to the skeletons each contained was a single gold earring. The remains of a third male, "buried without ceremony" (which one may take to mean coffinless) were soon discovered nearby. And there the matter rested for the next quarter of a century.

In the early years of the Second World War a Grenadier Guardsman named Reginald Cruise-Wilkins was invalidated out of the British Army and removed himself to East Africa. He made his living as a big-game hunter, safari leader and sometime warden in Kenya until 1947 when recurring bouts of malaria prompted him to convalesce in the Seychelles. After three restful weeks on Mahé in January 1949, during which time he lodged at the Pirates Arms Hotel in Victoria, Cruise-Wilkins was ready to return to work when he learned that the next ship to stop at Mombasa was not expected for three months.

Having the wit to make a virtue of necessity, he promptly moved to a bungalow on the palm-shaded Beau Vallon beach. Living as he did not far from Bel Ombre, his path soon crossed that of Mme. Savy who was pleased to introduce the marooned Englishman to the background of the mysterious rock carvings. Intrigued, Cruise-Wilkins prevailed upon her to allow him the opportunity of studying the notary's documents which had passed into her possession and then lain dormant since the death of her husband.

He was soon struck by two surprising coincidences. The first was the astonishing similarity between the symbol of a keyhole drawn on one of the parchment documents and the keyhole carving Mrs. Savy had discovered years before at Beau Vallon. The second was a reference in one of the crypto-grams to the word "musca"—Latin for fly. Again, Cruise-Wilkins was drawn back to the beach where he could only marvel at the chiseled outline in the rocks of a pair of insect's wings.

Circumstantial evidence at best, it was enough for the former Grenadier Guard. Unlike the malaria from which he only intermittently suffered, the fever to crack this elaborate and masterful riddle never loosened its grip upon him to the end of his days. Arguably the most tenacious and single-minded treasure hunter of this century, Reginald Cruise-Wilkins would dedicate the last twenty-eight years of his life to what he saw as a battle of wits against an implacable foe.

Returning to Nairobi in April, he spent five months poring over copies of Mme. Savy's documents, taking special pains with the cryptograms. Aided by seventeenth-century French and German dictionaries, he managed to translate a smattering of disjointed phrases. One of the documents contained a key in Masonic cipher by which letters a, e, i, o u, m, n and r corresponded sometimes, though not always, to the numbers 1 to 9. On occasion the clues appeared to hint at possible degrees and bearings though, juggle with them as he might, the "message" not infrequently remained as mixed up as a dog's breakfast: "Take the second," advised one. "Go with it close by pqtx then choose L 4 VL FSN2 Close the same ...".[8]

Such apparent gibberish notwithstanding, Cruise-Wilkins soldiered on and sometimes scored a small triumph or two. One that greatly buoyed his spirits was a line from a cryptogram that read: "Provoke a certain woman waterlogged." By this time he had been alerted to the fact that sporadic ref-erences, however jumbled and erratic, recurred throughout the cryptograms in an apparent reference to astronomy, astrology and mythology. Judg-ing his knowledge of such disciplines unequal to the task before him,

Cruise-Wilkins assembled a small library of books and star charts, in thrall as he now was to the wheeling constellations and mythic heroes of Greece.

A Johnny-come-lately to such matters, Cruise-Wilkins found that he had considerable catching up to do where ancient lore was concerned. "Provoke a certain woman waterlogged" ... Might this refer to the constellation Aquarius, the "water-bearer" of the Zodiac's eleventh house? Or perhaps more relevant was the person of Andromeda, the daughter of Cassiopeia, rescued by Perseus as she lay chained, for her vanity, to a rocky ledge on the Ethiopian coast?

On occasion, lucubrating by the light of a hurricane lamp in the heart of Africa, the emergence of a single coherent line made his heart soar. Indeed, his son John would be later quoted as stating that the all-consuming passion for treasure had served to re-educate his rough-and-tumble father who came to view the challenge set before him in the light of a modern-day odyssey.

"Let Jason be your guide and the third circle will open to you." Here was what seemed an obvious allusion to Greek mythology: like a pinwheel it threw out sparks in all directions, one of which Cruise-Wilkins hoped would shed light upon the nature of the riddle before him. It was, in fact, the very clue that would take him far.

The third, and possibly most vital, line decoded from the cryptogram, it seemed to point to the combined fields of mythology, astronomy and astrology. "Let Jason be your guide" ... Almost certainly the subject of the line was the famous captain of the ship Argo whose companions, Orpheus, Theseus, Hercules and other heroes made up the Argonauts. As every schoolchild should know, their mission was to bring back the Golden Fleece. The fleece—a ram's fleece might be taken as the constellation Aries the ram or, possibly, the first sign of the Zodiac and thus, conceivably, the "guide." Then again, who was to say that the Golden Fleece was not the Fiery Cross of Goa itself?

Cruise-Wilkins's enthusiasm proved contagious and, by late 1949, a syndicate had been formed at Nairobi to finance his efforts. Its principal backers were Colonel D. N. Hennessy and an attorney, Mr. Mervyn Morgan, whose task it was to sort out the legal implications of the Napoleonic Code (under which Mahé operated) vis-à-vis treasure-trove. Meanwhile, the pair of benefactors supplemented Cruise-Wilkins' modest initial investment and he was on his way!

> My first study of the documents convinced me that the plan for burying the treasure had been based on stories from Greek mythology and on the position of the stars.
>
> It was a game devised by le Vasseur for his own amusement and for the befuddlement of those he intended to seek the treasure. With my first £200 I discovered a carving representing Andromeda, chained to the Ethiopian coast to be devoured by the monster.[9]

This was certainly true. Back at the Beau Vallon site, Cruise-Wilkins initially employed two dozen laborers to clear Mme. Savy's rocks of their accretions of sea grass and barnacles. It was also true that, like many a "scientific" treasure hunter before him, Cruise-Wilkinson proved vulnerable to heterodoxy.

F. D. Ommanney, who visited Mahé in the early 1950s, seems to have taken a dim view of this aspect of the man's quest:

> He [Cruise-Wilkins] imported a mineral diviner who divined, with rods and something that looked like a ping-pong ball on the end of a string, that the treasure was indeed there in a cave beneath twenty feet of solid granite, and all that remained to do was blast away rock and dig, and there would be revealed gold and silver and precious stones and Heaven knew what else worth millions.[10]

But Cruise-Wilkins was far more cautious and thorough than F. D. Ommanney supposed. At this stage, however, he achieved a breakthrough early on. Sparked by discovery of a pair of letters cut an inch deep in the now-exposed rock at Beau Vallon, he matched them with what he believed were two letters of seminal importance from the cryptograms.

> High on the slopes of Mount Simpson, Wilkins came on a perfectly flat stone with compass directions accurately drawn on it. From here, he guessed, the maps and diagrams had been charted. Guided by several apparent clues, he extended a long rope from the stone to pass over the cutting of the two letters from the cryptogram. He then measured off 630 feet, a figure he had also made out at the start of the cryptogram. After days of fruitless excavation he remembered that the pirate was not using the modern measurement for feet (30.48 cm.) but the old French measurement (32.4 cm.).
>
> Revised calculations brought him past his bungalow, over the road and on to the beach, to a point 12 feet back from high-water mark. In order to keep back the sand while digging it was necessary to build a retaining wall. In a later excavation Wilkins was to discover that his retaining wall, which is still there, was built directly over a wall constructed by the pirate for the same purpose.[11]

Since the discovery of the three skeletons in 1923, investigators had had to satisfy themselves with clues either etched into rock or lifted from the documents, copies of which reposed in the Bibliotheque Nationale in

Paris. Now, however, Cruise-Wilkins was on the threshold of excavating the first real buried proof of a method to the contradictory writings first brought to light by the notary of Victoria.

Digging down through the increasingly moist sand, the laborers struck granite at a depth of ten feet. Once cleared away, hard evidence was revealed, evidence that even cynics would find difficult to explain. For there, on its back lay the eight-foot armless statue of a woman worked in stone! Curiously, while its left leg was set in a normal position, its right was severed in two and "propped up with stones to appear bent at the knee."[12]

The line from the cryptogram galvanized Cruise-Wilkins. "Provoke a certain woman waterlogged." He likewise was puzzled by the line that immediately followed: "Release her in the vagina in order to sleep with the man who is hers." After carefully removing "Andromeda" from the pit, Cruise-Wilkins set his men to digging at the juncture where her legs had met. Lamentably, the pit began filling with water the further down he went and the small pump he had earlier purchased in Nairobi failed to keep pace with the flooding. Thus, he was forced to fall back upon random excavations around the point where the statue had lain. These, nevertheless, resulted in a number of curious finds, including rock layers packed in lime and several stone pieces, among them one that looked to him like a scimitar blade (possibly the weapon Perseus had used to rescue Andromeda from the mythical sea-dragon guarding her), and a smaller rock that he took to be carved in the shape of a ship—Jason's famous *Argo!*

Cruise-Wilkins once again tackled the elusive bearings. After a series of hit-or-miss gambits, his calculations drew him up a hill inland from Beau Vallon beach. There he stumbled upon the skeleton of a horse—a find that would puzzle him to the end. "Its leg bones had been broken and pushed up into the chest cavity and filled in with lime cement. It was as if the horse's skeleton had been buried and not its body. To Wilkins it was the symbol of Pegasus, Perseus's winged horse."[13]

Be that as it may, it seemed also to have been a red herring. Excavating around the skeleton, Cruise-Wilkins's men came upon a flat stone. Large enough to be a trap door, it proved too large to shift with the block and tackle at hand. So he despatched it with an explosive charge. Revealed was a natural cavern beneath, its walls lined with clay studded, for some unknown reason, with bits of winking quartz. There was nothing within.

The *raison d'etre* of a *sealed* chamber evidently worked by man, but empty, was indeed puzzling. The precedent of Oak Island made it hardly less so. Certainly, the synchronicity of the two treasure hunts was something extraordinary—each in the 1950s pitted against antagonists of singular ability and guile.[14]

As the facts unfolded in both cases, the conventional wisdom regarding buried treasure—that the secreting of it might safely be regarded as a frequently hasty, generally crude and always temporary expedient resorted to by desperate men in short, as *a means to an end*—was effectively turned on its head.

A man might be expected to bury his riches with an express view toward their future removal. What then to make of an individual, or individuals, to whom the means might be an end in itself, to judge by the evidence of monumental complexity, ingenuity and even wit?

Certainly, Reginald Cruise-Wilkins would come to look upon his own solitary search less as a hunt for the Fiery Cross of Goa than as a duel with a respected foe. Not to put too fine a point on it, wealth was, for him, not the compelling factor. Reginald Cruise-Wilkins would freely admit that the pursuit of Mahé's alleged treasure had changed his life. His son John, who followed in his footsteps, would go so far as to announce in 1988 that what *drove* him was neither more nor less than a hunger to prove his father right. "It is not," he emphasized, "for the money."[15]

Was such talk simply good, cheap public relations? Perhaps. But it is true that, over the years, Cruise-Wilkins came to forge a powerful bond with his quarry.

As the trail lengthened and the mystery deepened, so too did Cruise-Wilkins's resolve. "He had, he said, grown to understand the mind of the pirate. He believed he could even describe him. He had been a small man with a limp."[16]

Cruise-Wilkins carried on with his excavations around the site of the empty cavern and, subsequently, cleared a boulder upon which had been carved a dozen identical V-shaped symbols. To his hunter's eye, they reportedly resembled the tracks of an antelope or a deer.

Consulting his well-thumbed tract on Greek mythology, ever mindful of the line of the cryptogram advising that Jason be his "guide," he was reminded that Hercules figured prominently among the Argonauts. Moreover, it was this greatest of Greek heroes, the strongest man on earth and son of Zeus, who had been ordered by King Eurystheus of Mycenae[17] to perform a series of superhuman tasks. Of the Twelve Labors of Hercules, as they came to be known, the third was the capture of the Cerynitian Stag.

Returning to the V-shaped etchings, Cruise-Wilkins gave his imagination full rein. Might these not represent the hoof prints of the mythical stag and, if so, was it preposterous to speculate that le Vasseur, in his inimitable fashion, had devised his own sophisticated trial through which anyone seriously coveting his treasure would be obliged painstakingly to pass?

Mistaken or not, Cruise-Wilkins judged le Vasseur to be a man after his own heart. He, himself, born to the English love of competition, the keen enjoyment of games and sport—the thrill of the hunt—could hardly see it otherwise. He would take up le Vasseur's implied challenge, which he proceeded to act upon with a singleness of purpose bordering on the perverse, and re-enact the Twelve Labors of Hercules. Hardly could he have foreseen then, in a coincidence uncanny beyond belief, that he would conclude the first ten labors in eight years and one month, almost precisely the time required by Hercules himself.[18]

The emergence of an overall theme had a tonic effect on the ex-Guardsman's enterprise which took on a measure of order and clarity despite the Byzantine nature of the clues. The subsequent discovery of a carving of a dragon, for instance, tallied nicely with the second labor whereby Hercules was enjoined to slay the Hydra, a fire-breathing creature with nine heads.

Extrapolating from directions in the documents he possessed, Cruise-Wilkins next succeeded in digging up a collection of pigs' bones at an oblique angle from the stag's carved hoof-prints. These, in turn, he associated with the boar of Mount Erymanthus, the capture of which was Hercules's fourth labor.

The fifth labor led Cruise-Wilkins down to the beach below his bungalow. It had been Hercules's daunting task to muck out the Augean stables in a single day. According to the legend, Augeus had so shirked his duties that the thousands of head of cattle in his possession had been fouling their stalls unattended for years. Hercules, applying his subtle mind and imposing strength to this seemingly insoluble problem, diverted two rivers to flow through the stables and thus flooded them clean of their accumulated dung.

For his part, Cruise-Williams cast about for a geographical equivalent around Beau Vallon and seemed to find it at a point high up on the beach where two fresh water streams ran to the sea. Where they met, he discovered a stone buttressed by the stems of a pair of wine glasses which, he reckoned, could only have been placed there as a marker by the hand of the Buzzard.

> In the next five years Wilkins was to find seven complete labors, numbering two to eight, all with a recurring pattern, and each leading on to the next. Moreover, in each separate labor he found bones, cuttings on rock and artifacts which conformed with another overall pattern. They symbolized constellations; and the position of the symbols on the ground related to the constellations' position in the sky. Not so accurately, however, that he could have gone straight to the twelfth labor without following the whole sequence through.
>
> Certain characteristics were common to all the labors. In each, he found three circles cut into rock ... [and] in each he found a clue that pertained specifically to the corresponding labor of Hercules.[19]

Cruise-Wilkins's search eventually covered sixty-four acres and involved the work of forty-eight full-time workers. In fulfillment of the sixth labor, in which Hercules drove away the Stymphalian birds, he uncovered carvings representing winged creatures and, in that of the seventh, exhumed the bones of a bull, corresponding, so he felt assured, to the savage and beautiful Pasiphae, the bull presented to Minos of Crete by Poseidon.

Before he was finished, Cruise-Wilkins would turn up close to 200 separate clues. But his relentless efforts were not always gentle. The ninth labor, for example, led him south of his bungalow contiguous to the coast road. Hercules's task had been to fetch the Girdle of Hippolyte, Queen of the Amazons. Thanks to the duplicity of Hera, wife of Zeus, his mission ended in mayhem.

Cruise-Wilkins, though baffled for many months, finally congratulated himself on the discovery of a cleverly hidden porcelain statuette. Modeled upon the figure of a ram, it was taken to represent its astrological equivalent, Aries; this, in turn, brought to the Englishman's fertile mind, Ares, the Greek god of war and father of Hippolyte. However tenuous the link, Cruise-Wilkins spared no effort in getting at it, a fact that weighed against him in a forthcoming report issued by Mahé's Department of Public Works.

Citing structural damage to the coast road, the government demanded the cessation of all digging and blasting in the immediate area. This was the first indication that the prolonged treasure hunt at Beau Vallon was proving an irritant to the authorities. It seemed to Cruise-Wilkins an opportune moment to cease and desist, if only temporarily, especially as his coffers were all but empty. He had by now shifted countless tons of rock and sand, invested £10,000 and better than six years of his life, in completing the first eight labors.

Cruise-Wilkins chose this juncture to collate his bewildering mass of data, pack up the dozens of artifacts he had unearthed to date (the smaller items of which inhabited tobacco tins scattered about his rambling bungalow) and sail to Mombasa. At Nairobi, with coffee futures bullish, he encountered sympathy for his enterprise and managed to raise over £30,000. The sundry fruit of his assiduous labors—headless statuettes, bits of china, animal horns, a flintlock pistol and the like—would remain behind. Staying in Nairobi only long enough to purchase new winches, explosives, a compressor and pump, he hurried back to the Seychelles.

Ironically, despite the fact that the hunt now enjoyed momentum and a fresh infusion of cash, Cruise-Wilkins's luck soured. Over the next two years, during which time his workers had to be paid, shod, equipped and fed, the project languished. Clues simply dried up and, back in Nairobi, financial backers began to make threatening noises. At last, Cruise-Wilkins could claim a modest success by isolating the tenth labor forty feet north of where the Andromeda statue had been uncovered back in 1950. Still, the results were less than edifying.

Hercules, it may be recalled, had ventured to the western Mediterranean island of Erythia where his mission was to rustle a herd of red cattle and bring it back to Mycenae. The curious beasts were guarded by the vicious two-headed dog Orthrus whose master, Geryon, was himself a winged monster with three heads. Now here was one of the more colorful labors replete, one would have thought, with material for a clue master like La Buse. Moreover, en route to Erythia, our hero had memorialized his enterprise by erecting a pair of mammoth stones—the singular Pillars of Hercules.[20] Unfortunately, the best Cruise-Wilkins could find on this, the tenth labor, was the horn of a bull. So far as his benefactors were concerned, this idea lacked all credibility.

Once again, seemingly scorned by the Fates, the Englishman floundered for the driest of months now passed with negligible advances in the search. Then, while little is known of the details, Cruise-Wilkins reportedly solved the eleventh labor by uncovering three small, round, cut stones. These, it was held, matched the Golden Apples of the Hesperides, Hercules's prize after taking the vault of heaven off Atlas's shoulders and later hoodwinking him into taking up the mighty burden anew.

Cruise-Wilkins now had troubles of his own. Athol Thomas, who visited the Beau Vallon dig in its sixteenth year, reported that, on the day of the stones' recovery, his host had reached down to examine them and "massive boulders began to slip and threatened to crush him."[21] The fear was that it might have been a booby trap. Moreover, the twelfth and final labor, quite apart from providing what was expected to be a welcome climax to the operation, seemed fraught with overtones of danger and oppression. For unless Cruise-Wilkins had altogether misjudged the nature of the game, its circuitous trail now led to Hell.

Within sight of the discovery of the stones, a pig's jawbone was uncovered. As most ancient Greeks knew, one dared approach the god of the underworld only after performing the sacrifice of a sheep. No matter. The Buzzard might be excused for making a sacrifice of a pig, in this particular case, as a sheep would have been a rare article indeed in the south Indian Ocean of his day. Overlooking the mytho-poetic license taken, Cruise-Wilkins carried on.

> The kingdom of the dead was ruled by one of the twelve great Olympians, Hades or Pluto, and his Queen, Persephone. It is often called by his name, Hades. It lies, the Iliad says, beneath the secret places of the earth. In the Odyssey, the way to it leads over the edge of the world across the Ocean. In later poets there are various entrances to it from the earth through caverns and beside deep lakes.[22]

The twelfth labor was arguably the most challenging of all for Hercules. After rescuing Theseus from the Chair of Forgetfulness, the hero descended into the underworld where he was obliged to treat with Pluto.[23] Provided he did not resort to arms, Hercules was welcome to attempt to subdue Cerberus, the frightful three-headed watchdog who patrolled the gates of Hades. Hercules succeeded but, when he delivered up the snarling beast to Eurystheus, the King wanted no part of it and demanded that Hercules descend once more to the land of the dead and restore the creature to its former post.

One of Cruise-Wilkins's last discoveries at Beau Vallon beach was a carving of what appeared to be a dog with a "lashing tail" set into a granite boulder within a stone's throw of the swine's jawbone.

Having completed the twelve labors—all, that is, but for the first—Cruise-Wilkins was now at a loss as to how best to proceed. He could only assume that his documents had been mined of all the gold they were likely to yield.

Following a hunch, Cruise-Wilkins returned full circle to where the search had begun. It may be recalled that only after he had constructed a retaining wall near the site of the Andromeda statue, did a subsequent excavation reveal the existence of a similar structure erected much earlier beneath his own. It was from this point, approximately twelve feet above high-water mark, that Cruise-Wilkins began to probe his painstaking way down the beach. This time, his efforts achieved a swift and spectacular find:

> Just to the south of Andromeda, underwater caverns were discovered. Explorations here became dangerous and skin-diving equipment was sent for. Sea urchin shells, rare to the Seychelles, were exposed, and a cut rock, that appeared to represent a sarcophagus with a mummy lying in it, symbol of the dead in the underworld which Cerberus guarded.
>
> In the pirate's scheme, Cerberus might well be guarding something more tangible. Hundreds of rocks were blown up around the area. Feelings were high that at any time an entrance into the "treasure" cavern would be exposed, when four cuttings were found which corresponded exactly to the markings on one of the parchments. Wilkins grew certain that the treasure cave lay right below the boulders on which these cuttings were found.[24]

Restricted by periodic cash flow crises and the exigencies of the monsoon, Cruise-Wilkins had toiled for nearly seventeen seasons, from May to November. (The rest of the year much of the sixty-four-acre site is subject to flooding and high tides.) He came to believe that le Vasseur had lowered his treasures into a natural cavern running below sea level and then had skillfully covered up the vertical entrance with a stone slab.

This new development was exciting indeed. Nevertheless, the carving of the dog and the alleged sarcophagus only came to light after a great deal of pick and shovel work. To add to the difficulties and the spiraling expense of the operation, Cruise-Wilkins's excavations around the cavern in search of a possible opening meant the construction and maintenance of an extensive cofferdam. Nor did his problems end here.

Even as he homed in upon what he was certain would prove to be le Vasseur's treasure chamber, his backers lost heart. The excavation work their man had accomplished thus far, though admirable, was reckoned to be as nothing compared with that required to finish the job—if, in fact, the treasure did lie where Cruise-Wilkins claimed. The feat to bring it out would necessitate boring equipment, pumps of far greater capacity than the venture now possessed, a dredger and, possibly, a bulldozer.

The other option was to use dynamite. This suggestion was dismissed by Cruise-Wilkins with horror. He felt that it would, almost inevitably, bring the ceiling of the cavern thundering down upon the treasures. Met with the Englishman's steadfast refusal to permit blasting, investors in Nairobi kept him on such short rations that he was compelled to reduce his work force and husband what few resources remained.

Cruise-Wilkins's health deteriorated and, by the 1970s, his operation was all but moribund. Nevertheless, he was by now a celebrity, regularly visited by camera crews, reporters from European papers and the Russian news agency Tass.

> Mind you, the Russians obviously thought I was on to something. They sent ten blokes out here and they hung around offering me money for a share in the search. I sent them packing.
>
> And Ian Fleming flew out to interview me. Cheeky blighter used the situation as part of the plot for his book Live and Let Die.[25]

The Richard Costain Company was then in the process of constructing Mahé's new airport less than ten miles away and Cruise-Wilkins's great hope was that, once finished, the firm might be disposed to lease him its giant earth-moving equipment—the very thing he needed to get his own job done. It was only when protracted negotiations broke down that the embittered treasure hunter sensed that he had reached the end: "Can you imagine what it feels like to get this far? A quarter of a century's work come to a full stop. All for the sake of a bit more cash which would be the key to a fortune. Yes, old man, a fortune."[26]

Cruise-Wilkins had once, with the aid of a guy rope and pulleys, lowered a small boy through the interstice between a man-sized boulder and what he believed was part of the treasure cavern's superstructure. It was customary for him to walk visitors out across the beach south of his bungalow and, while wading in one or another shallow tidal pool, announce that they were standing on the ceiling of the treasure chamber itself. Nothing resembling an opening has ever been discovered there. But when the youngster squeezed back past the rectangular boulder at the head of the beach, he reportedly came up *covered in rust*.

Reginald Herbert Cruise-Wilkins was buried on May 3, 1977 at the age of sixty-six. His had been "a scientific work," he had said, "and a battle of wits against a pirate who built himself a memorial." That memorial still stands, as does the family's commitment to redeem it. After a German restaurateur applied for a prospecting license in 1985, son Godfrey left medical school in Cuba and his brother John gave up his career in communications in order to head off the competition.

By July 1988 the two had signed an agreement with the Seychelles Government concerning shares in the jointly financed venture, protection of the environment, security arrangements and so forth. Christie's of London agreed to evaluate any treasure discovered on the site while the government secured the rights over any relics of historical value with a view toward establishing a museum and tourist center at Beau Vallon.

John Cruise-Wilkins, along with his brother and three sisters, grew up on an island paradise in a beach house where the talk at mealtimes naturally turned to treasure. Their palm-shaded bungalow was a veritable museum of clues collected by their father during his twenty-eight years on Mahé. Some of them wound up in Kenya with investors; some remain. Of them all, there is one that John Cruise-Wilkins believes holds the single most important key to the mystery of the Buzzard's alleged treasure.

> In the last excavations my father did before he died, he discovered a domino with the number 62 on it. This is a crucial angle that is mentioned in the documents and, with others that we've worked out, points to the spot where we believe the treasure is.[27]

A proton magnetometer seemed to concur. Set to work over the site, the sensitive instrument picked up indications of iron—thirty-five pounds of it—lying at a depth of eighteen feet.

Just as thousands of hours of study had left him with an uncanny profile of his slight, limping adversary, so too had Cruise-Wilkins taken the visionary measure of the prize he had stalked. It was contained, he had the firm impression, in three chests, each roughly seven feet long by three feet wide. It is now up to his sons to determine whether the thirty-five pounds of iron might be that of the hasps, hinges, metal bindings or chests holding together a treasure estimated to be worth £100,000,000.

Trindade Island

A very different sort of place
—Edward F. Knight
The Cruise of the *Alerte*

Edward Knight was the Victorian "gentleman-adventurer" par excellence. Son of a career officer who had fought in the first Carlist War (1833–9), he passed a rumbustious youth at Westminster and Cambridge, later read law and was called to the bar. While still at university he purchased his first yacht and in her explored the coastal waters of France and the English Channel.

Published before the age of twenty, Knight was once challenged to a duel over an editorial dispute connected with his first travel book, *Albania & Montenegro*. His adversary balking at pistols, Knight, ever a stickler for punctilio, next proposed, in a spirit of compromise, that the two of them square off with scythes.

In 1880, aged thirty-two, he took his 28-ton yawl *Falcon* on a two-year South American voyage to Patagonia. Blown off course in an 1881 winter storm while bound homeward from Montevideo, Knight wound up 700 nautical miles east of Bahia, Brazil, facing the forbidding cliffs of Trindade island. His explorer's instinct piqued, Knight hove to off her leeward shore for a week in December, at once fascinated and repelled by Trindade's blunt-edged beauty. Ignorant of the treasure rumored to have been buried near South-West Bay, Knight suffered sufficient hardship while tramping across the precipitous isle to convince himself that it would be a cold day in Hell before he would ever again repeat such a harrowing performance.[1]

While Tom Sinnet was no gentleman-adventurer—not by a very long shot—the Newcastle ship's captain did, however, share with Knight a love of the sea and a long-standing interest in Trindade Island. But though his calling took him to the proverbial ends of the earth, his acquaintance with Trindade remained strictly second hand. A licensed merchant captain in the sometime employ of the East India Company, Sinnet's later duties bound him to the legal trade in opium which took him (1848–50) between a string of far-flung outposts to India and the South China Sea.

Only recently driven from the western seas, pirates of Sinnet's day continued to harry the shipping lanes of the East. In consequence, it was customary to muster additional hands on the Indian Ocean crossing and among the four quartermasters of Captain Sinnet's *Louisa* in 1850 was a reticent but highly competent foreigner thought to be a Russian-Finn.

This officer was long in the tooth and his habitually stern mien, further enhanced by a deep jagged scar running the length of one cheek, made for the ineluctable stuff of inspiration. Known by fellow sailors simply as "the Pirate," it was not, at first, known whether he had really earned this title.

Sinnet, in any case, found the stranger's company congenial and was pleased to show this man, kindred in years and temperament, a number of kindnesses. A spell of shore leave happened to occasion the last of these. It was in one or another noisome port of call in the Arabian Sea that the quartermaster took ill and, despite Sinnet's skillful ministrations aboard ship, he so worsened that, by the time the *Louisa* made Bombay, the emaciated officer lay dying of the "bloody flux."

Making what proved to be a final visit to see his quartermaster in the hospital, the captain was surprised that the man seemed oddly insistent that his captain secure the door behind him. Stowed beneath the patient's bed was a battered sea locker of the common sort which Sinnet was bade slide out. Unlocking and inspecting its interior, as instructed, Sinnet unearthed a roll of sail cloth within which lay hidden a cut of tarpaulin inscribed with the rough contours of an island.

> The quartermaster gave him this plan, and told him that at the place indicated on it—that is, under the mountain known as the Sugarloaf—there was an immense treasure buried, consisting principally of gold and silver plate and ornaments, the plunder of Peruvian churches which certain pirates had concealed there in the year 1821. Much of this plate, he said, came from the cathedral of Lima, having been carried away from there during the war of independence, when the Spaniards were escaping the country, and that among other riches there were several massive gold candlesticks.
>
> He further stated that he was the only survivor of the pirates, as all the others had been captured by the Spaniards and executed in Cuba some years before, and

consequently it was probable that no one but himself knew of this secret. He then gave Captain Sinnet instructions as to the exact position of the treasure in the bay under the Sugarloaf, and enjoined him to go there and search for it, as it was almost certain that it had not been removed. The quartermaster died shortly afterwards.[2]

If the stricken sailor was to be taken at his word, nineteen of his shipmates had swung one after the other from the Admiralty's gibbet at Havana in Cuba. Only he himself, cheating the gallows by a miracle, managed to escape to the anonymity of the Indian Ocean.

Clearly, this sort of deathbed melodrama has become a well-played staple of the treasure hunting genre—a too familiar (and thereby unjustly debased) *mise en scene*. In any event, such episodes recur in the parallel histories of Cocos and Trindade Islands. Both islands have over the years, enjoyed strong support as the resting place of the Treasure of Lima. Each may boast of its own peculiar heritage of treasure expeditions. Knight, for one—no stranger to the history of Cocos Island—put his money squarely on Trindade.

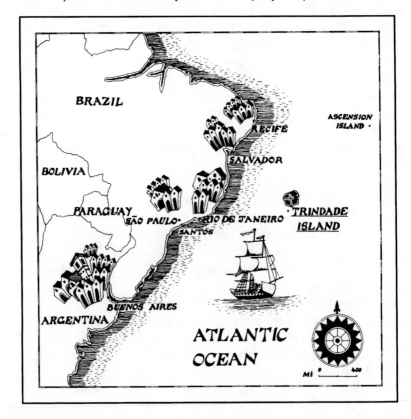

One curious detail surrounding the controversy, and well worth clarification, is an apparent muddle over patronymics. Benito Bonito, possibly of Spanish nationality and long associated with Cocos Island, was almost certainly apprehended off the Central American coast around 1822. Sometimes confused with him is his contemporary and namesake, Bonito de Soto, who operated in an entirely different theater.

This Portuguese brigand, leader of a mutiny aboard the slaver, *Defensor de Pedro,* outbound from Santos, Brazil, captured the British merchantman *Morning Star* on or about February 21, 1828. After scuttling her off the Ascension Islands, de Soto is alleged to have secreted the best of her cargo on Trindade Island before being hanged some years later by the Governor of Gibraltar.

By the by, two further brigands are linked to Trindade Island. One is an English slave captain (turned outlaw) who went under the theatrical sobriquet of "Zulmiro"; the other, a Portuguese cutthroat named Jose Santos. George Finlay Simmons, curator of Cleveland, Ohio's National History Museum, who anchored off the island while cruising aboard the *Blossom* in 1927, let slip to New York City reporters upon his return that he was of the opinion that it was most likely Santos who was responsible for secreting at the island of Trindade Lima's lost treasure whose worth he estimated to be in the range of $40,000,000.

Captain Sinnet would have been a rare seaman indeed to have forsaken such a legacy. Unfortunately, fate appears to have conspired against his direct involvement in the mystery. Incapacitated at the time of the intriguing bequest by a broken arm and struggling to cope with his unruly crew, Sinnet was chary of prosecuting a treasure hunt. Moreover, as he was captain rather than owner of the *Louisa,* how then to explain to his employers the deviation off course and unavoidable delay such an enterprise would necessitate? Looking forward to an unblemished retirement, Sinnet determined to put his quartermaster's startling revelation out of mind—at least temporarily—and so he made directly for Southampton.

Once pensioned off at Newcastle and anxious to mount his own venture to Trindade Island, Sinnet proved importunate in his assaults upon the credulity of financial backers. Possessor of a map and privy to its reasonably convincing history, the ingenuous captain nevertheless found the art of promotion well beyond his ken and could only watch with vexation as the quartermaster's increasingly open secret fast became the stuff of good-natured chaff around the public houses of South Shields. With the years, familiarity bred its inevitable contempt and the captain grew old.

Finally, Sinnet managed to enlist the support of the wealthy owner of a Newcastle shipping firm. His barquentine *John,* trading out of Santos, Brazil, could, the gentleman agreed, stop briefly at Trindade on her return voyage. It would then be up to Sinnet's son to conduct a brief survey of the

Sugarloaf. Should proof of the alleged treasure arise, so much the better; a subsequent expedition might then be considered and, such being the best that Sinnet might hope for, he gratefully consented to the arrangement.

In early 1880 the *John* anchored off Trindade as agreed. Buffeted as she was by strong winds and high seas, her captain waited impatiently for an opportunity to make a small-boat landing, for Trindade lacked the blessings of a natural harbor. With a steadily falling glass and unwilling to risk any of his crew, the captain allowed that Sinnet's son might take a stab at reaching the beach—but that he must go it alone.

Put off in the whaleboat forthwith, the poor fellow was forced to make for shore under his own steam. Tossed up upon the beach at South-West Bay, young Sinnet managed to keep his wits about him sufficiently to follow the quartermaster's directions which led him unerringly to a ravine. But after following it to the first bend as indicated, he found, to his great disappointment, that the site was buried beneath what he judged to be tons of "reddish debris."

At nightfall, he stayed on the beach and did not sleep well. Driven to distraction by hordes of marauding land crabs, Sinnet was delighted next morning to be trawled back shipward through pounding surf at the end of a lifeline.

Knight would suffer similar travails on his own visit to Trindade Island a year later. Qualifying it as "one of the most uncanny and dispiriting spots on earth," he assured readers of *The Cruise of the "Falcon"*[3] that he would on no account "set foot on its barren shores again." However inhospitable, reports two years later in the London papers that Trindade was about to host a full-blown treasure hunt soon put an end to such talk.

Before his death, Captain Sinnet finally managed to interest a group from South Shields in his notorious map. With sufficient funds duly subscribed and a vessel—the 600-ton *Aurea*—chartered and provisioned, the expedition departed England in late winter 1885. It was led by an individual mysteriously referred to as Mr. "Aem."

The unnamed gentleman might have saved himself the effort. Within a very short time of his sighting the island on March 23, matters began to go hopelessly awry. Holding out ashore for a brutal fortnight, fever-ridden and ill served by tools inadequate to the scope of the landslip, eight men finally made it back to the *Aurea* on April 17, more dead than alive. Slipping anchor the following day, they managed to leave behind them a four-foot-deep trench at the ravine beneath the Sugarloaf, the exploded remains of a possibly vital landmark and two of their deceased colleagues.

According to a report signed by Danish sailing master H. N. Ankersen, which appeared on May 11, 1885 in a Kiel newspaper, an American and four Portuguese had charted his ship out of Rio de Janeiro the previous January.

Their stated intention, he was surprised to learn, was to collect guano on Trindade Island.

> Ankersen believed that these men, either by telegram from England or other means, had heard of the existence of a treasure on this island and that they meant to anticipate the English expedition. However, they found nothing. I noticed very well that the American captain, as well as his men, were highly disappointed. Let me take this opportunity to dissuade all masters of vessels to search in this uninhabited island for fresh water. It is a matter of great difficulty and danger to put boats on shore.[4]

Knight, now indulging a true change of heart, quickly struck up an acquaintance with Mr. "Aem" in 1886. That the alleged treasure site at the ravine had been covered over by a landslip since the quartermaster's visit struck him as eminently plausible. Comparing the astronomer Halley's description of a lusher, heavily wooded Trindade in 1700 to his own experience in the *Falcon* when he had found Trindade's soil to be "a loose powder," her rock "broken up and rotten" and her forest denuded, Knight fully appreciated the volcanic isle's geologic mutability.

Equally heartening, a search of Spanish records confirmed that a ship's crew of brigands captured around 1822 and suspected of plundering churches near Lima had, true to the quartermaster's tale, been hanged at Havana. Finally, details of the island made available to Captain Sinnet by his benefactor, and later passed along to Mr. "Aem," dovetailed nicely with Knight's own first-hand knowledge of Trindade, proving beyond a reasonable doubt that the quartermaster had, at the very least, landed upon its shores.

This, in itself, struck Knight as highly propitious. As Trindade was, arguably, as little visited as any island on earth, thanks to her reefs and heavy surf, navigators avoided the island as if cursed. And though captains rounding Cape Horn from the Pacific frequently fixed her in their sights for the express purpose of correcting their chronometers, reports of actual landings were rare in the extreme.

Knight's secret intent was to return. In 1888 he closed a deal with Mr. "Aem" for the treasure ravine's bearings, then straightway purchased the cutter yacht *Alerte*. Her new skipper had just turned thirty-six.

If Edward Knight was a comparatively young man to mount a complex expedition to a treacherous isle some 5,000 nautical miles distant, the *Alerte* was a comparatively ancient vessel in which to undertake it. Built in 1864, Knight nonetheless reckoned her highly suitable. Amply beamed at fourteen feet, she measured sixty-four-feet long, boasted well-seasoned teak without a hint of rot and had once made the Southampton-Sidney run in just over 100 days.

Knight's call for volunteers, wafer thin on specifics, appeared during 1888 in the *St. James's Gazette* and generated an avalanche of responses. But out of the initial 150 applicants and the final three score Knight saw fit to interview, a good many turned out either to be the idly curious or out-and-out cranks.

All in all he found it a most tedious business. A gentleman-adventurer to the core and thoroughgoing Tory, Knight aimed to muster a crew in the grand manner of the treasure hunts of his era, heavily weighted as they tended to be toward privilege. Held in reserve were places for eight gentlemen like himself, against only four for paid hands. Knight wished, first, and, second, to assure the subscription of adequate funds—he had no intention of outfitting the *Alerte* on the cheap:

> Mr. E. F. Knight undertakes to provide a vessel, stores, etc., suitable for the expedition, end to provide at least sufficient provisions for the voyage out and home and six months beside.
>
> Each member of the expedition will pay an advance to Mr. Knight the sum of £100, and undertake to work both on board and on shore under Mr. Knight's directions. This £100 will be the extent of each member's liability.
>
> During the first six months from the time of landing on the island, the enterprise can only be abandoned with the consent of Mr. Knight, and on decision by vote of three-quarters of the members. After six months have elapsed a majority of three-quarters of the members will determine whether the enterprise is to be continued or abandoned.
>
> Each member, or, if he die in the course of the expedition, his legal representative, will receive one-twentieth of the gross proceeds of the venture.
>
> If any member of the expedition mutiny or incite to mutiny, he shall be tried by court-martial of the other members of the expedition, and, if it be decided by a majority of three-quarters that the offense be sufficiently grave, he shall forfeit all share in the proceeds of the expedition, subject to an appeal to the English Courts on his return.
>
> None of these rules apply to the paid hands on the vessel.[5]

Accorded a flat fee, paid hands were thus contractually removed from a financial stake in the hunt. Tipping, nevertheless, was optional.

In the end, Knight came up with what he judged to be eight solid gentlemen; a medical man, several barristers and a divine among them. Of the paid hands, two were able-bodied seamen, one a boatswain and the fourth a cook, John Wright, who had served Knight on two previous voyages. Intrigued by Trindade's reputation as a principal breeding ground for South Atlantic sea birds, one of the volunteers took it upon himself to enroll in an introductory course in taxidermy, only to fall ill at the eleventh hour and miss the expedition. Likewise lost to the mission was a second colleague lately initiated into the mysteries of photography, thus depriving Knight, to his lasting regret, of a visual record of his mission.

Having engaged a sound crew, Knight invested his energies in providing them with healthful victuals and suitable tools against their coming labors. Water, as always being the prime necessity, a condensing apparatus was specially constructed for the mission in Southampton; it consisted of a twenty-gallon boiler and a forty-gallon tank. At sea, these might be disconnected and utilized as drinking tanks so that, all told, the *Alerte* carried some 600 gallons of water.

For a small boat owner, Knight must have endeared himself to his delighted ship's chandler. Figuring among the *Alerte's* staples were 600 pounds of the finest salted beef and pork, barrels of top-of-the-line cabin biscuits, oats, stores of jam, vegetables and tinned meats, tobacco, plenty of rum (to Knight's way of thinking "certainly the most wholesome spirit for sea use") plus a goodly stock of lime juice, the mariner's time-honored hedge against scurvy.

If "X" truly marked the spot on the quartermaster's map (and the volunteers aimed to proceed under that assumption) the treasure site lay at the first discernible bend along a ravine near South-West Bay. Now buried under untold tons of rubble, getting at it, as all conceded, might simply prove beyond their powers. Clearly, the attempt would require certain specialized hardware. Thus, while Knight did not stint on the requisite picks, shovels, axes, crowbars, wheelbarrows and sundry carpenters' tools—he actually went one step further.

Since a great deal of excavation was certain to await them, Knight included in his inventory boring apparatus which would enable him to "explore through earth and rock to a depth of fifty feet" as well as a "Tangye's hydraulic jack capable of lifting twelve tons."[6] In the event of timbering a shaft, his budget provided for the purchase of dogs[7] and similar materials, as well as for a complete portable forge—heavy, costly and crucial to the proper maintenance of the mission's equipment. As to the camp itself, Knight's shopping list seemed endless: roomy "emigrant" tents, gardening tools, quick-growing seeds, fishing gear, hurricane lamps, books, surgical supplies and heaps of wire mesh which, it was hoped, would thwart Trindade's loathsome and prodigious land-crab population.

Entrusted to convey the party's vital stores shoreward at South-West Bay was a specially designed and constructed double-ended whale boat crafted of choice mahogany. She was both light and very sturdy and was fitted with watertight compartments against Trindade's raging seas. Great care was taken that she meet Knight's strict specifications for, should she fail to stay the course, the expedition was most probably doomed.

Finally, there were the expedition's armaments. Who knew but that the publicity generated by the *Alerte's* voyage might attract a criminal element? Thus each gentleman volunteer was issued with a Colt repeating rifle. Knight further assembled a community chest of hand guns and carbines of varying calibers, backed by a crate of ammunition. The arsenal's crowning glory (and one which might have suited a naval engagement) was nothing less than a rapid firing double-barreled whaling gun courtesy of the Duke of Sutherland, designed to discharge "steel shot, grape, shell and harpoons."

Having toasted their way to the end of a grueling round of formal send-offs, the gentlemen-adventurers bade farewell to their loved ones on the evening of August 29, 1889. At eleven o'clock the following morning they eased away from the slip at Southampton docks. According to her bill of health with which, for secrecy's sake, Knight had taken a degree of license, the *Alerte* was embarking upon a cruise to Sydney and, to judge from her lading of picks, shovels and dynamite, she might well have been making for the gold fields down under.

In fact, Knight had kept his counsel as to the *raison d'etre* of the voyage and, by all accounts, succeeded in concealing its particulars throughout his public call for volunteers. Nonetheless, if the chosen few happened to know more than the readership of the *St. James's Gazette,* they did not know all. For, unbeknownst to his crew, a visitor who presented himself at the captain's cabin, practically on the eve of the *Alerte's* departure, persuaded Knight to amend his otherwise spurious course.

The unannounced guest introduced himself as a retired Royal Navy officer from Exeter. Quick to come to his point, he assured Knight that he guessed the mission's true destination; he went on to beg leave to submit, for his host's judgement, a second destination, one that was almost certain to lie along the *Alerte's* probable course. Intrigued, Knight set out whiskey and smoking materials and then sat back to hear the officer out.

It was a matter of Admiralty record, so the officer informed Knight, that in December of 1812 a foreign seaman by the name of Christian Cruise had met at length, behind closed doors, the Commander-in-Chief at Portsmouth, Sir Richard Bickerton. The astonishing outcome of their conversation was a letter posted to Bickerton little more than a fortnight later. Signed "J. W. Crocker, Esq. Secretary of the Admiralty," it effectively empowered the Commander-in-Chief to mount a treasure hunt at the earliest possible date, in His Majesty's first available vessel, to the Salvages Islands, a small group of uninhabited islands off the coast of Madeira in the North Atlantic.

It seems that while serving aboard a Danish ship out of Africa, Cruise was stricken with typhoid fever. While in hospital in Santa Cruz, Madeira, he made the acquaintance of a dying Spanish sailor who, across the gulf of language and near delirium, nevertheless painted a clear enough picture. In the spring of 1803 he had sailed from Vera Cruz, Mexico, for Spain with a cargo whose worth he reckoned at roughly $2,000,000. En route, his vessel became separated in a squall from four companion merchantmen. A few days' sail from Cadiz her captain boarded what proved to be a neutral ship outbound, only to learn that, earlier in May, war had once again broken out between England and Spain. As proof, the British Navy had lately intercepted a flotilla of Spanish merchantmen close by. To be certain, a cordon of King George's frigates had reportedly engineered a blockade running all the way from Trafalgar to Cape Finisterre.

Loath to gamble with the Royal Navy and, at the same time, prevented by waning stocks of food and water from returning to Mexico, the Spanish captain resolved to beat to southward of Madeira and there pick up the trades before making a desperate run for the Spanish Caribbean. Successful in avoiding the enemy, his luck held true until some 150 nautical miles beyond Madeira when his disgruntled crew mutinied. Dead ahead lay a verdant, round-topped island of the Salvages group, reckoned to be uninhabited. Here they dropped anchor in a small bay on its south shore and, with their erstwhile captain held under armed guard below decks, despatched a team ashore to reconnoiter.

Cruise's narrator and his duplicitous companions located a flat stretch of dry sand above high-water mark, between the beach and a cliff; this they deemed to be a fitting site at which to bury the hijacked ship's cargo of Spanish dollars until better days. Working hurriedly in shifts, the men dug out a deep trench and therein set the bulk of the purloined fortune. In the meantime, their hapless captain was put to death and his mortal remains nailed up inside a makeshift coffin which the mutineers then placed a scrupulous six feet below ground, well above the treasure, as a sort of decoy. After filling in the trench and taking care to efface any hint of their presence at the beach, the Spanish mutineers returned to their ship and shaped a course for New Spain.

As to the yarn they intended to spin for the benefit of the Spanish authorities—and considering the ship's bizarre trajectory it would have had to have been ingenious—such went undelivered. Blown off course in the vicinity of Port-of-Spain, Trinidad, the vessel apparently foundered on a reef near an uninhabited bay at Tobago. All hands were lost but for two sailors. One perished of exposure shortly after reaching St. Thomas while the other lived to unburden himself of his confession by the bedside of Christian Cruise on Madeira.

Whatever the tale's virtues, Lords Liverpool and Bexley proved instrumental in influencing the Admiralty's go-ahead and, in 1813, H.M.S.

Prometheus, under the command of Captain Hercules Robinson, sailed under orders from Portsmouth with Cruise as its distinguished guest. In late May Robinson put in at Grand Salvage Island, anchoring the *Prometheus* in a bay off its eastern shore before divulging Cruise's secret to his officers. That done, he mustered a landing party numbering fully sixty hands and ordered a supply of picks, shovels and the like broken out of stores.

Robinson's unsuspecting tars were led to believe that they would be searching for a coffin—which was certainly the truth by half—and a £50 reward posted by the Admiralty for its discovery served to speed them on their labors. But finding the extent of the beach beyond the scope of even so large a force, Robinson cut short the excavation and despatched a report of failure from Funchal, Madeira, to Lord Amelias Beauclerk of the British Admiralty, Whitehall, where the matter of the lost Salvages fortune was officially laid to rest.

> The two millions of dollars of silver would weigh one hundred and twenty tons, and would have been contained in twelve hundred boxes, and have occupied a pit twenty feet long, ten feet wide and ten feet deep, with an interval between the boxes and the murdered Captain. In smooth water a crew of twenty men with a long-boat each carrying two tons would take sixty trips of one hour each, or three days, to bury the treasure. Hercules Robinson was confident of Christian Cruise, but thought the dying Spaniard picturesquely exaggerated the amount of treasure buried; which was probably $500,000 or $600,000, the usual "go" for a rich trader.[8]

After two days at sea, Knight called a council of his gentlemen-adventurers. After briefing them on the particulars of the retired naval officer's information, he submitted for consideration the matter of reopening the Christian Cruise case. Brought to a vote, the motion to follow in the wake of H.M.S. *Prometheus* was carried. On September 14, 1889 the *Alerte's* crew made landfall at Grand Salvage Island. But after three days of desultory excavation—working without benefit of maps or bearings—Knight and his men thought better of the detour and weighed anchor for Santa Cruz de Tenerife.

The following morning the bosun spotted the Peak of Tenerife from his perch in the *Alerte's* "cross trees." Her crew were eager for fresh fruits, vegetables and meat—the vessel's meat lockers were entirely empty. Too hastily salted at Southampton, the mission's excellent beef and pork—over 400 pounds of it—had been discovered crawling with maggots and, to the cook's despair, had to be tossed overboard. Knight himself owned to fancying a bottle or two of madeira, into the bargain, and so he eased the *Alerte* with a certain anticipation into her slip at Santa Cruz on September 18.

As it turned out he had plenty of time to enjoy his madeira for, between losing one crewman to illness and another to a failure of nerve, a week passed before the *Alerte* was ready again to put to sea.

Now she hauled for the Cape Verde Islands—this being the last watering place before the southwest crossing to Brazil. Having landed at Porto Grande Bay, St. Vincent on October 2, after a cruise of almost 600 miles, Knight suffered a further attrition of his crew. This time it was the *Alerte's* ailing purser.

Having good luck, he managed to top up his diminished following and departed St. Vincent on October 9 under full sail. After four days of steady trades, however, the *Alerte* languished as she approached the equator and did not see land until Brazil's Day of the Dead on October 31. After running down the Pernambuco coast south of Recife—two days and nights of uninterrupted sand beach and swaying palms to starboard—the *Alerte's* gentlemen-volunteers were finally greeted by the spectacular sweep of All Saint's Bay, Salvador (Bahia), on November 2, 1889.

Here once again Knight tarried. This time there were old friendships to renew (from his earlier voyage in the *Falcon*), letters to be written home and last-minute stores to be laid in; among them were two more barrels of beef, a cask of wine and a cornucopia of fresh produce: yams, guavas, papayas, pumpkins, oranges, bananas and tamarinds. To round out his purchases, which proved unaccountably dear, Knight also secured some additional tools, a supply of blasting powder and bamboo toward the future construction of a raft.

Salvador had altered little during his nine years' absence. All too familiar was the omnipresent corruption; the rank and pungent smells; the city's palpable air of sensuality and the incessant pealing of her bells—for Salvador could boast of 365 churches, one for every saint's day of the year. All, in fact, was as before but for a signal proclamation. So unexpected had been Don Pedro II's recent abolition of slavery that Knight found his bewildered subjects positively reeling from the monumental transformation.

After the color and bustle of Salvador, the bleak visage offered them by Trindade Island chilled Knight's crew to a man. After a voyage of 600 nautical miles, the *Alerte* approached Trindade on November 20, six days out of port. She would be home for the gentlemen-adventurers for the next three months.

> As we neared it, the features of this extraordinary place could gradually be distinguished. The north side, that which faced us, is the most barren and desolate portion of the island, and appears to be utterly inaccessible. Here the mountains

rise sheer from the boiling surf—fantastically shaped of
volcanic rock; cloven by frightful ravines; lowering in perpendicular precipices; in places overhanging threateningly,
and where the mountains have been shaken to pieces by
the fires and earthquakes of volcanic action, huge landslips
slope steeply into the yawning ravines—landslips of black
and red volcanic debris, and loose rocks large as houses,
ready on the slightest disturbance to roll down, crashing
into the abysses below ... The scenery was indescribably
savage and grand ... It would be impossible to convey in
words a just idea of the mystery of Trinidad.[9]

The *Alerte* could approach the island no nearer than a half mile, but
Knight knew of a viable anchorage off Trindade's leeward shore from which,
weather permitting, a small-boat landing might be accomplished. Below West
Point there ran a narrow beach strewn with boulders blown down a tortuous ravine from the summit above. Slightly to the left of a thirty-foot cas-
cade a rocky ledge, which formed a natural pier, jutted out from the beach
into deep water. By no means ideal, Knight hoped that this improvised jetty
might answer his purpose. On the morning of November 21, however, he
and his first mate, Dr. Cloete Smith, were so battered in their dinghy by
rising seas that, rather than risk being swamped, they were forced to bail
out at the last instant and swim the final yards to shore.

Trindade measured slightly more than five miles long; this meant that,
from where the two men now stood drenched to their skins, the alleged
treasure site lay roughly two-and-a-half miles to the southeast over a ridge
of mountains. South-West Bay, obscured by a series of rocky promontories
from the *Alerte's* line of vision, was the obvious choice for a camp, though it
could not be relied upon as a safe anchorage.

Charts of the island having proved unreliable, even Knight had thought
it wise to have a look from above South-West Bay for the likeliest channel
through which later to navigate the whale boat, for upon her would ultimately depend the safe landing of the men, tools and provisions.

Having previously traversed the island, Knight was painfully aware of its
perils. Between them, he and the doctor carried only dried figs, a small bundle
of beef jerky, two water bottles, a compass and some matches and tobacco rolled
up for safe-keeping in a waterproof. In addition they each carried the requisite
ration of "wholesome spirit." Lamentably, their trusty ship's biscuit had been
soaked through in the landing and they reckoned it would take them the better
part of three days to make South-West Bay and back.

All in all, the best approach to Trindade's summit was up the ravine.
Having accomplished the difficult ascent, by noon the two men could make

out the Sugarloaf fronting South-West Bay, as they pondered the likeliest route down the summit's windward face. Once below, they might enjoy a relatively straightforward trek through foothills inside East Point before cutting back south near the lava banks at Noah's Ark, so-called, and rounding South-West Bay.

> In the course of my first exploration we made so many false descents of these (windward) ravines and slopes, all terminating in precipices and driving us back again, that at last, finding no water, we were completely worn out and nearly perished of thirst.[10]

To Knight's horror, he found himself reliving the nightmare. Certain, after his former travail, of recognizing the true ravine among a labyrinth of pretenders, Knight had set off confidently in the lead, only to be frustrated at every turn.

Time and time again he led the doctor into narrow defiles, some ending nowhere in particular, others trailing off before gaping chasms hundreds of feet deep. Prodding his memory as he did, parched and bone-weary as he was, the penny simply refused to drop and Cloete Smith thought his partner quite mad. Finally, out of sheer desperation, the two men succeeded in negotiating an enormous landslip running down some 1500 feet and at so vertiginous an angle that it seemed a miracle that its component rocks and boulders had held firm beneath their sliding steps. Safely at the bottom and having caught his breath, Knight suddenly realized they had, in fact, descended his old route after all. As he stared back up to the summit, it was now clear to him that an avalanche occurring in the previous decade had completely filled his erstwhile ravine.

Over pipes that evening around a fire at their makeshift camp, Cloete Smith, ever the pragmatist, took to musing upon this disturbing phenomenon. What further indignities, he gravely wondered, might the Spaniard's treasure ravine at South-West Bay have lately suffered? Knight could only hope for the best.

Upon rising next morning, they sought water. Wary of tempting fate by doing without, Knight chose to postpone their rendezvous with the treasure ravine long enough to backtrack three-quarters of a mile north, assuring the doctor that, dead ahead, lay the ruins of a Portuguese penal colony through which coursed—or at least used to course—the most delightful of streams. In this, at least, Captain Knight proved himself unerring and the two men fell greedily upon it, drinking long and deeply. Lifting their heads between draughts, their gaze took in, as if for the first time, innumerable clusters of gannets' eggs nestled among the greenery of what they came to regard as the "down of beans" for the profusion of legumes carpeting it. Having first slaked their thirst, the hungry men feasted upon eggs, though Knight later recalled that they savored rankly of rotting fish.

By far the worst well behind them, the two covered the final stretch of their 5000 mile odyssey much like a pair of beachcombers. Moving parallel to the treasure site, they had only to follow a sandy dogleg inside South Point, then thread their way up and across Sugarloaf. Finally, below them ringed by a ragged band of coral reef and crowned in the center with a rocky islet, lay the waters of South-West Bay.

> The Pirate in his confession had spoken of a certain channel he had discovered through this reef, situated under the Sugarloaf, at the eastern extremity of the Bay. We now saw that it existed there exactly as he had described it—a broad opening in the line of the rocks, through which a boat could be pulled, and beached on the sands.[11]

Not, however, on such a morning as this, November 22nd. Knight could safely judge for himself that the kind of heavy sea presently running would make short work of just about any small, heavily laden craft attempting to negotiate a landing. Still, he was pleased to record the channel's bearings, and now felt better prepared to take the logistical measure of the treasure site beyond.

Descending to the shore, Knight and Cloete Smith searched out, and soon discovered, a ravine running down to the middle of the Bay, north of the rocky islet. At its foot, the Spaniard and his shipmates had erected three cairns of the local stone, which landmark Mr. "Aem" and the *Aurea's* crew had admitted leveling with black powder in 1885. Whatever their motive, the deed was done and the proof of it sadly evident by a jumble of stone remains strewn across the extreme upper beach.

Moving up the ravine, Knight followed what he presumed to be its initial bend. There he saw "what appeared to be a landslip of red earth, filling up the corner of it, blocking up the mouth of any cave that might exist, even as Mr. 'Aem' had described." What immediately struck Knight was that the site was different from what he had expected:

> There were no really sharp bends in the ravine, and there were several landslips. It was impossible to be quite certain of what was meant by "the first bend"; for there were bends of so insignificant a character that they might easily be overlooked; and we had no knowledge of the number of paces from the cairns to the cavern. Therefore, should we fail to find the treasure at the spot where Mr. "Aem" commenced to

dig, it would be necessary for us to clear the landslip off the
face of the cliff for some considerable distance. [12]

It was plain, in any event, that, for Mr. "Aem's" money, "X" here marked the
spot, judging at least by the evidence of an unfinished trench, an abandoned
wheelbarrow and a broken earthenware jug lying nearby. Well up from the
beach, alongside the mouth of the ravine, Knight came upon a number of old
tent poles and empty meat tins as evidence of the *Aurea's* former camp.

Back safely aboard the *Alerte,* Knight and his men, prisoners of a steadily
falling glass and rising seas, now helplessly rode out five days and nights of
unremitting gale-force winds.

At last, November 28 dawned propitious. Blessed with a clear sky and
relatively calm sea, the chastened second mate and a companion were dispatched ashore in the whale boat to retrieve Knight's boat. Meanwhile, the
Alerte's impatient crew moved tools and provisions up to the foredeck and
put the finishing touches to their recently constructed bamboo raft.

Upon her successful return, the crew stowed roughly a ton of primary
necessities aboard the boat that morning. Two miles of open sea lay between
the *Alerte* and the channel; Knight succeeded in crossing this without incident. But, no sooner did he enter the bay itself, than the South Atlantic surf
surged beneath him and his small craft with deceptive vigor and, just as the
boat's nose touched ashore, a single great wave swept across her stern. Thanks
to the watertight compartments, fitted fore and aft, the stores weathered the
debacle. Subsequent missions, however, would prove less successful and
occasioned the loss of critical foodstuffs.

After Knight's helter-skelter landing on November 28 and a lucky return trip on a moderate sea the following day, close to three weeks would
pass before he, himself, found it favourable to join his men at the ravine.
When he did so, he was delighted to learn that his gentlemen-adventurers
had put together an admirably appointed camp which was equably administered and governed by sound principles.

> Two ridge tents had been placed side by side to be occupied
> by the gentlemen volunteers, two in each; whilst a short way
> off was a larger tent, constructed of our racing spinnaker and
> the quarter-deck awning, supported by bamboos. This was
> dining room and kitchen, and also served as sleeping quar-
> ters for the paid hands. At one end of it was an elegant dining
> table—planks from the deck of some old wreck supported by
> one of Mr. Aem's wheelbarrows which had been found in the
> ravine—a few camp stools and barrels served as chairs, and
> the arrangements generally were almost luxurious. [13]

The cook enjoyed an amply equipped work place. Driftwood and dead timber, suitable for fuel, lay reasonably close to hand. Water, of course, presented a challenge. Here, Knight was thankful to have brought along the condensing apparatus as, in addition to his responsibilities for the men's nourishment, the cook served as the mission's water-bearer. Toiling in a climate particularly oppressive to Englishmen, the excavating teams soaked up the otherwise indifferent island water like so many sponges and were always prey to heat exposure and dehydration.

Indeed, it was Trindade's soaring temperatures that defined the mission's work schedule. Up at dawn, after cocoa and ship's biscuit, the men worked at the site from 5:30 until nine. Following a refreshing sea bathe, they breakfasted more leisurely on oatmeal, discovered by trial and error to be a most nourishing and digestible staple perfectly suited to their taste. Later they rested in their tents, more often than not fitfully, through the worst of the heat of the day.

By 3:30 the crew was back at the ravine, working three hours or so before sunset at which time they once again cooled off in the sea. After a coveted tot of rum, they all dined together in the mess, discussing the day's progress and preparing for that to follow. Pipes and perhaps a read followed and then they turned in, exhausted. Wednesday was a half-day and Sundays free.

To the credit of the trusty whale boat, whose sundry leaks, occasioned by a run of bumpy landings at South-West Bay, the *Alerte's* stand-by crew had stopped with tar and the defaulting taxidermist's stores of plaster of paris—the camp eventually took in eight tons of supplies.

> I need not say that the cook was well provided with culinary apparatus, and that such articles as paraffin lamps for the tents, a library of books, fishing lines and hooks, and carpenter's tools had not been forgotten. Our camp, in short, was fully furnished with everything that could be required.[14]

It is worth adding that the men erected a perimeter wire mesh fence against the maddening incursions of Trindade's land crabs and laid coconut fiber mats from Salvador over the exposed floors of their tents for greater comfort and as an imperfect buffer against the miseries of the sand flea.

By mid-December, Knight's men had made a substantial dent in the landslip. Their ultimate goal was to dig through it until they arrived at the floor of the ravine. Assuming theirs was, in fact, the bend in question, they expected, sooner or later, to come upon evidence of a cave of some sort, perhaps carved into the ravine's steep slope and subsequently covered over.

Several weeks into their labors, a trench approximately twenty feet broad and eventually as many feet deep spoke for the team's perseverance. Although bearing up remarkably well, the gentlemen-volunteers were primed for a breakthrough and Knight greatly hoped, for the good of the mission, that it might be soon.

So the men dug on. Sometimes for days their sole medium was the loose debris. This they easily enough loaded into wheelbarrows, carted down and tipped into a series of chasms skirting the ravine. Not infrequently, however, the work proved more arduous. The removal of large rocks and boulders blown down from the uppermost cliff face required the concerted efforts of the full team. Fortunately, Knight had shipped an abundance of sturdy hemp, blocks and "watch tackles" with which, on at least one occasion, he claimed "to have obtained a purchase ... equivalent ... to the power of five hundred men" over a certain gigantic specimen.

Just before Christmas, excitement swept the camp. By now deep in the trench and straining after any hopeful sign, one of the volunteers appeared at last to have found it. As his pick bit into the loose debris, he was suddenly treated to a jolt that took him in the upper arms and fairly wrested the implement from his grasp. Such *contretemps* were by no means uncommon and Knight's volunteers often saw in them cause for light jest against the rigors of their enterprise.

This time, though, their reaction was quite different for the blow had given back a hollow sound, much as if the point of the pick had made contact with the "roof of a cavern." Occasionally "little holes would open out and from time to time the earth would slip down into some chasm underneath." Digging deeper, the crew was eventually thwarted by a rocky formation impervious to even the purchase of Knight's much-vaunted watch tackles.

> The rocks were jammed together, and evidently formed the roof of a cavern, for, wherever we could clear away the earth that lay between any two of these rocks, we looked down through the opening into a black, empty space, the bottom of which we could not touch by thrusting through our longest crowbar. [15]

This singular discovery held much promise as it was just such a cavern that Knight had been led to believe lay buried beneath the rubble at the first bend in the South-West Bay ravine.

> We found that the rocks were too close together to allow of our effecting an entrance from above, so we dug down along the side of the last and largest of these until we came to its foot; and there, indeed, was a sort of cavern, partly filled up with loose earth, which we cleared out. [16]

The volunteers had spent thirty days with barely a rest from their labors to reach this point. Now their hopes, kindled to fever pitch that morning, were, by the guttering half-light of an equatorial dusk, cruelly dampened. The cavern was empty! There was absolutely nothing within. And unless most thoroughly swept clean, it left the distinct impression upon the crest-fallen volunteers of never having been disturbed by man.

For the first time, the gentlemen-volunteers entertained the possibility that they had been duped into shifting tons of debris to no gainful purpose. The directions had, after all, been frightfully vague. Then, of course, the fact could not be overlooked that, even as they labored, expeditions were being mounted to search for evidence of the self-same Treasure of Lima at Cocos Island in the Pacific. With Christmas just around the corner and his men in black spirits, a prudent Knight wasted no time in declaring a holiday.

On Boxing Day 1889, the expedition's members—all together for the first time since the dig began—pondered their options. There was no question of a mutiny; the gentlemen-volunteers squarely closed ranks behind their leader. Still, the question did arise as to whether he might have overlooked a vital clue to the treasure's precise whereabouts. Nonetheless, a unanimous vote was taken to return to South-West Bay and to carry on with the mission.

Knight, on the other hand, had equally pressing business elsewhere. What rice is to the Chinese and pasta to the Italians, so to the gentlemen-volunteers of Trindade Island, it would appear, was porridge. Hearty appetites and a recent debacle in landing the whale boat had severely diminished the supplies of this indispensable nutrient. Knight therefore deemed it an appropriate time to nip out to the nearest market—Salvador— "a voyage," he recorded in his diary, "of 1,400 miles in order to purchase a little oatmeal."

Outbound, he accomplished the journey before a steady northeaster under mainsail, mizzen foresail and second jib. Slipping anchor on December 30, Knight made landfall at Sao Antonio Point on January 4, 1890. The following morning he proceeded to confound the Salvadorian authorities.

When questioned as to his most recent port of entry, Knight could only respond, Salvador, since he had in truth passed the last five weeks exclusively off the coast of Trindade. Stirring from what Knight later described as an "Oriental" torpor, the Brazilian officials then begged him to explain his fascination with that "God-forsaken isle," whereupon Knight disingenuously betrayed a lifelong interest in birds.

Now it was Knight's turn to be surprised. Since his last visit, so the bemused officials informed him, Don Pedro's empire had faded like an overnight mist only to reappear, in the morning, in the guise of a full-fledged republic. "And a very shabby sort of revolution it had been," snorted the *Alerte's* patrician skipper, "for there had been no slaughter to give an air of dignity and respectability to it!"

Six days later, the stores replenished with plenty of fresh produce, molasses, oats and a barrel of white rum, Knight put the incipient republic behind him for what he deemed would be a lifetime. His prediction, however, soon proved precipitate.

Three hundred and fifty miles out to sea, one of the *Alerte's* less reliable paid hands, Arthur Cotton by name, ran amok. Fuddled by a surfeit of the newly shipped spirits, the rampaging sailor so menaced his shipmates that Knight found it necessary to subdue him by force and then lash him for good measure by an ankle to the forward bulwarks. Loath to inflict the man's ill temper upon his hardworking crew at Trindade, Knight thought it preferable to tack about and turn the fellow over to the British Consulate at Salvador. Thus it was not until January 29 that he made his anchorage at Trindade Island and, thanks to high seas, not until February 5 that he landed once again at South-West Bay.

No spectacular news awaited him. The landslip looked to be a dry well and the gentlemen-volunteers were understandably desolate. Failed probes at a number of contiguous bends in the ravine had, in Knight's absence, done little to boost morale. Finally, after an all-out, hell-for-leather last-ditch effort, Knight called off their quest on February 12th.

> The weather became so unsettled and the surf was so invariably high that … we came to the conclusion that the sooner we left the Island the better, and we decided to take the first favourable opportunity for bringing off our property from the shore.[17]

Colder weather was fast approaching and the men, Knight himself excluded, had faithfully served three months on a former penal island at hard labor.

Such impedimenta as might reasonably be salvaged—the condenser and hydraulic jack, for example, some tools, the odd wheelbarrow, plus rifles, tents, cooking utensils, lamps and books, were ferried back to the *Alerte* throughout the morning and afternoon of February 13. On Friday the 14th she was gone. Two thousand nine hundred nautical miles and twenty-nine days later, the *Alerte* dropped anchor at Port-of-Spain, Trinidad in the West Indies, "a very different sort of place."

No sooner had he returned to London than Knight signed on as a *Times* correspondent and headed straightway for the Himalayas where his first assignment was to cover the Hunza-Nagar War. Reassigned to Matabeleland, he hobnobbed with Cecil Rhodes in South Africa and kept *The Times* abreast of developments in the Sudan Campaign of 1896.

Less than a year later, Knight's readers found him dodging bullets on the front lines of the Turko-Greek War. In 1898 he managed to get himself arrested for spying in Cuba after his dinghy capsized off Havana shortly before the landing of Teddy Roosevelt's Rough Riders. Back once again in Matabeleland, this time for the *Morning Post,* Knight lost his right arm at the Battle of Belmont.

Taking a year off to recuperate, he next accompanied the Duke and Duchess of York (future King George V and Queen Mary) on a round-the-world cruise. Always keen for a challenge, Knight punted "single-handed" across the Everglades and took the helm of an Egyptian dhow in a run along the Nile, before reappearing in Manchuria at the side of General Kuroki during the climax of the Russo-Japanese War.[18]

Knight lived long enough to follow in the London papers the much publicized 1923–4 expedition to Cocos Island of another celebrated Briton—Sir Malcolm Campbell—in his own celebrated quest for the elusive Treasure of Lima.

Knight's reactions, if any, went unrecorded. He died in 1925.

Postscript

Baron James Harden-Hickey, characterized as "editor, Beau Brummel of the Paris boulevards and duellist," happened to first cruise past Trindade as Edward Knight was negotiating for the purchase of the *Alerte* in 1888. A true Victorian romantic and confirmed eccentric, upon satisfying himself that not a single power (great or small) held title to the lonely isle, Harden-Hickey determined to have her for his own. Moreover, it was his mad desire to establish a "kingdom" there and, by virtue of his marriage to the daughter of one of America's richest men—Standard Oil magnate John H. Flagler—the Baron was well positioned to wed his bizarre *idée fixe* to a fortune.

Harden-Hickey henceforth cut a droll figure in Paris and New York society. Fashioning himself "King James I," he appointed a royal cabinet, a minister of Foreign Affairs, a Chancellery, and personally designed court costumes, uniforms and regalia. There was a certain method, however, to the Baron's apparent madness. Sincere in his hope of attracting settlers, he published a well-reasoned prospectus outlining Trindade's virtues as a possible treasure site and extended to his potential "subjects" free land and easy credit. Once established, they might pick up where Knight left off and, if discovered, the Lima riches would, he pledged, be equitably divided among all.

Astonishingly, his offer drew a positive response and, eventually, a boatload of sanguine colonists landed on the island with considerable hardware in tow. But shortly thereafter, to the Baron's chagrin, Great Britain decided she was in need of a proper site for a cable landing and relay station in the South Atlantic and, without undue ceremony, proceeded to lay claim to his cherished realm.

Shocked into action, Brazil immediately followed suit. Finding his short-lived reign falling hopelessly between two stools, Harden-Hickey "'bequeathed the rights, privileges and even succession, together with all interest in the Trindade treasure to his Minister of Foreign Affairs. Then he blew out his brains."[19]

Balambangan Island

Honour is like an island, rugged and without a beach;
once we have left it, we can never return.
—Nicholas Boileau-Despreaux
Satires X

European commerce on the eastern seas came alive in the seventeenth century. Guided halfway round the world, often by the least precise of charts, immemorial hunger for trade drove the Great Powers not infrequently to extremes of cupidity. Immensely valuable cargoes of silk, gemstones, spices, gold, amber, exotic drugs and ivory lay in the balance. Satisfied with little short of iron-clad monopolies over their respective spheres of influence, rival trading societies, in thrall to the *sine qua non* of "protection," proved cutthroat in their dealings with client and competitor alike.

At the time China ranked high on every European trader's list; indeed, it was the commercial lifeblood of economies as far distant as North Borneo. Thanks to Holland's stranglehold on the South Pacific basin, Cathay became a cynosure of many eyes. Exporters wishing to trade with her might do so but only after first passing their goods through Dutch depots at which time goods were taxed and then trans-shipped in Dutch vessels. The result of such measures was effectively to eliminate direct trade and so add to freight costs that a good many Asian traders were forced out of business.

With access to China blocked, immigration to South Asia evaporated and Chinese settlers, already in residence, abandoned its shores in droves. The results were devastating. Agricultural land in the backcountry simply went to seed, while junk traffic in ports and harbors all but disappeared. So it is said that Malay coast tribesmen, uncommonly bellicose by nature, turned to piracy as a ready solution to their economic woes.[1]

Meanwhile, their country brethren languished. Fallen on hard times, they were pressed for tribute regardless, not only by the Sultan of Brunei but by hosts of His Highness's thieving local administrators. Joined by such Chinese as had remained, they rebelled around 1650 and it was all the Sultan could do to put down the uprising. He would probably have been unsuccessful but for the timely assistance of the Sultan of Sulu who, in appreciation of his solidarity, was awarded territory in North Borneo, including the island of Balambangan.

In 1763 at the end of the Seven Years' War, a British fleet under Sir William Draper captured Manila. Among the flotsam rotting in her dungeons was His Royal Highness Sultan Alimudin of Sulu. Set free and returned to the throne he, in his turn, was persuaded to cede the North Borneo lands to the East India Company. The agent who effected the transfer was Alexander Dalrymple, an ex-clerk from the Madras office who, by a hair, missed an appointment with history.

It had been 100 years since England, driven out by the Dutch, last enjoyed an outpost in the Far East. Dalrymple thought it high time to take up the gauntlet. Balambangan, after all, lay in reasonably close proximity to the annual passage of Chinese junks to Brunei; it was no more than 1,000 miles from Canton and well positioned between Japan, Bengal, Borneo and Java. Moreover, it was sufficiently far distant from diminishing Dutch interests in Southeast Asia, boasted two good harbors and a wealth of fresh water and timber.

> Dalrymple's proposals found favor with the Court of Directors of the East India Company for they wished to extend their trade, and it was the policy of the time to establish distant trading outposts on small islands that lay close to a populous mainland. An island settlement was considered more healthy than one on the mainland, and more secure from aggression. It was calculated to attract trade from all quarters and (in theory) could be economically maintained.[2]

At about this time a phenomenon swept England. No flash in the pan, her countrymen discovered the pleasures of tea! Little short of a sensation, the East India Company found that, if it hoped to fill the spiraling demand for this signal beverage, more ships of the line would surely have to be commissioned.

The problem, however, was that the Chinese proved uncooperative. They fairly sniffed at the niggling offers of the English. Whatever England hoped to offer, China already possessed it or disdained to do so. Silver and tin were all she coveted; the one from the Philippines, the other from the mines of the Malay Peninsula.

Dalrymple, the Company's expert on Southeast Asia, had already proved his worth by mapping a year-round trade route to Canton that defied the monsoon. Now he argued persuasively for exploiting the Balambangan concession.

Hardworking and brilliant, though of corrosive temperament, Dalrymple had produced charts and writings, published in *An Account of Discoveries in the South Pacific before 1764* (1767); these brought him to the attention of the Royal Society. The year following the *Account's* publication, he was invited to sail to the South Pacific and, under the limpid skies of Tahiti, observe and record the transit of Venus. Incredibly, Dalrymple made such uncompromising demands on his benefactors, including the stipulation that he command the Royal Navy vessel entrusted to the mission, that he cheated himself out of possible greatness. Pleased to sail in his stead was a forty-year-old hydrographer who knew practically nothing of the South Pacific—Captain James Cook.

Three years later, it would seem that Dalrymple's peculiar demon had impelled him to renewed folly. Without question the most qualified man for the job, thanks to his intimate knowledge of the region and his amicable relations with the Sultan, Dalrymple was next offered the post of Chief of the Balambangan station.

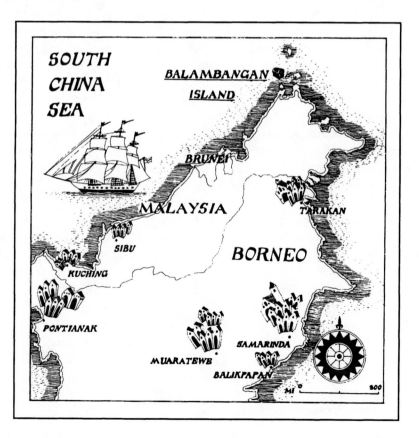

Between driving impossibly hard bargains over his commission and salary and splitting hairs over the makeup of his crew, Dalrymple so exasperated East India Company directors that his name was withdrawn from consideration. Called upon to replace him was a man cut from an entirely different cloth. Tractable, winning and pleased to take up his post at £600 per annum—a fraction of his predecessor's demand—John Herbert proved himself a thoroughgoing rogue practically from the moment he set sail.

If Alexander Dalrymple's surrogate was about to play fast and loose with his immensely powerful superiors, they themselves had already set a precedent for highhandedness in their own dealings with the Crown. Balambangan had been initially taken on the sly, "in the name of the King of Great Britain and the East India Company." It was only in 1768, however, that a Company directive despatched from Bombay to the Secretary of State for Foreign Affairs let George III in on the secret. It was apparent to all that His Majesty's most Obedient and Humble servants had, in effect, delivered him a *fait accompli.*

John Herbert received his marching orders in London on June 12, 1771 and embarked shortly thereafter in the *Britannia.* Under the command of Captain James Swithin, she was to put in at the Cape of Good Hope and there take on sheep with a view toward breeding them on Balambangan. Herbert was further enjoined to secure such plants and seeds in Southern Africa as he might deem useful. At Bombay, the *Britannia* would rendezvous with the *Success,* carrying Bengal piece goods and stores, and the *Devonshire,* entrusted with trading supplies from Canton and treasure.[4] To be parceled out among the three vessels at Bombay, for their protection, were some 400 British and Indian sepoy troops.

Herbert succeeded in carrying out his charge, though not with despatch. Expected to conclude the entire voyage within eight months, he landed in Bombay very much behind schedule and when the *Britannia* and her escort finally dropped anchor at Balambangan Island on December 12, 1773 John Herbert had, in fact, been at sea well over two years.

No wool-gatherer, Herbert had simply indulged himself in a spate of determined, if leisurely, wildcat trading to the tune of some £200,000 in Company funds. This is the equivalent of his aggregate salary as Chief of the Balambangan station for 333 years. As it was his tenure, which dovetailed precisely with the life span of the mission itself, lasted no more than fifteen months.

> To do Herbert justice, it appears that once he had reached the island, he set about the building of the settlement with energy. A low hill (the only rising ground on the island) was selected as the center of the establishment: here were the Magazine, Secretary's offices, the Brracks and the military officers' houses, fortified towards the sea by a stockade and enclosed in the rear

by a belt of thick shrub and jungle. A battery of nine guns, mounted about sixty yards from the beach, defended the stockade ... Herbert and his military advisers concentrated their defenses towards the sea, thinking doubtless that, if the land side required protection, the wall of jungle was enough.[5]

Balambangan lies on the eastern extreme of the South China Sea in what is today Indonesia. Set a few miles above that tip of North Borneo once known as Simpang Mengaran—"The Parting of the Pirate Ways"—the island is twelve miles long and rests low in the Balabac Strait—so low in fact that its contours, barely discernible among the surrounding coral reefs, have been likened to those of a sleeping crocodile. The derivation of its name from the Malay *belum bangan,* meaning "not yet risen," apparently refers to the wind; the unmistakable implication is that Balambangan was an ill-advised place for the Company to establish its premier Asian headquarters.

Such an inference may be justified in that Herbert failed to attract significant numbers of immigrants to Balambangan despite its obvious allure as a "free port"; nor did significant numbers of Chinese junks deign to land en route to Brunei. Disturbing, too, was the alarmingly high mortality rate among its sepoy garrison which, by 1775, left Balambangan vulnerable to an enemy attack.

An enterprising though unscrupulous trader, Herbert was put on his mettle, saddled as he was with an unsatisfactory commercial station. In direct contravention of Company directives, he set about dealing illicitly in opium. Buying it on the cheap from the Company's Bengal stores, Herbert sold the drug at a handsome profit in Java and the Sulu Archipelago.

His one legitimate success came in the spice trade—but at a cost. Since the founding of the Company station at Balambangan, Sultan Israel had succeeded to the throne of his predecessor, Sultan Alimudin of Sulu. Israel distrusted the English and viewed the apparent resurgence of the East India Company with distaste. Meanwhile, intent upon cornering Brunei's valuable pepper market, Herbert committed the Company to protecting its Sultan against the depredations of Illunan and Sulu pirates. However unofficial, such an alliance could only have antagonized Israel, jealous as he no doubt was of Herbert's treasury and incensed by the Englishman's peremptory treatment of his subjects.

Herbert, it turns out, had no time for grassroots diplomacy, scant regard for hierarchy and a weakness for corporal punishment. Treating all the natives with equal disdain, he came to have increasing recourse to flogging and the stocks. One Sulu chief, ignobly used, was a first cousin of the Sultan.

Datu Tating had earlier won himself a construction contract at the mission. It was later thought that he had been sent there by the Sultan to spy and had merely exploited his Sulu carpenters as a cover. Whether true or not, Tating's knowledge of the station was apparently complete for, in the company of his cousin Dacula and 300 Sulus and Illunans, he knew just how, where and when to strike.

The trap had been set to coincide with John Herbert's birthday revels, the night of March 4, 1775. A world away, British redcoats prepared to do battle with General Washington's irregulars in a field outside Concord, Massachusetts. Here, in North Borneo, bands of raiders, themselves sporting traditional scarlet coats, had been infiltrated on to Balambangan with the greatest care over several nights. Now they lay scattered about the jungle floor to the station's rear—each fighting man with his dagger and two-handed sword—silent and unstirring as so many fallen leaves.

Sprung at dawn on March 5, the furious assault caught the Company's Bugis Guards and virtually the entire sepoy garrison—many of whose officers were fuddled by drink—totally unawares. It began with a curl of smoke lifting into the morning air from a beached Sulu launch beneath the stockade and ended in a full-scale conflagration.

Tating and approximately 100 followers swept in from the jungle and caught the sepoy garrison napping, while Dacula's men overwhelmed the Bugis and, soon in command of the stockade's guns, sent the hapless defenders flying in disarray toward the harbor.

Remarkably, given the magnitude of such a rout, the station suffered a mere thirteen casualties. Mad flight may have saved the Company's troops from a foredoomed hand-to-hand battle against an enemy eager, in any event, to get on with the more pressing business of rapine. Nevertheless, the question arises as to why Herbert's officers failed to rally the retreating forces for a counterattack and, likewise, why the triumphant marauders waited fully seven hours to sack Herbert's waterfront dwelling.

> Herbert, who always kept a small boat in readiness at the landing-stage by his house, seems to have wasted no time in escaping to the brig *Endeavour.* She and the *Phoenix* opened fire on the fort. Dacula returned it with the English guns and by a chance shot cut away the cable of the Phoenix. As luck would have it, a stiff breeze was blowing off the sea, and she was driven ashore and seized by the pirates; and those who were not drowned were taken up by the *Endeavour.*
>
> By this time the Chinese huts and the large storehouse on the point were blazing, and towards ten o'clock the establishment of Mr. Cole (Herbert's second-in-command) and the other storehouses were plundered and set on fire. But it was not until past midday that the Sulus turned their attention to the Chief's house, by which time Herbert and those with him were heading for the open sea.[6]

Forfeit that morning were the East India Company's pretensions to Southeast Asian trade along with a wealth of armaments: forty-five cannon, 40,000 pounds of black powder, over 20,000 rounds of ammunition and 250 muskets. As to articles of barter, Tating's rampaging pirates inherited the station's entire stock of India piece goods, the Sultan of Brunei's pepper and what remained of Herbert's opium.

Doubtless consumed on the pyre of what had briefly been the Company's East Asia clearing house were the records of its administration—bills of lading, receipts and account ledgers—all embroidered, all spurious, all irretrievably lost. This could only have cheered John Herbert. Indeed, the convenience of Tating's liquidation later gave rise to unsubstantiated accusations of collusion against him. Nevertheless, it is a matter of record that he died penniless.

Herbert's subsequent poverty gave rise to the mystery surrounding the Balambangan treasure. Besides his considerable personal wealth, fruit of both his two-and-a-half years at sea en route to North Borneo and his extra trade in Company opium, there was the mission's store of gold ingots plus 14,000 Spanish silver dollars. It has been widely speculated that not all of it fell into the Sulus' hands. None of the treasure has ever been recovered.

To those convinced that a fortune remains buried on Balambangan Island, the scenario seems clear enough: either Herbert secreted his illicit personal wealth somewhere in the vicinity of the harbor long before the Sulu attack or he and a few chosen officers, during the confusion at the onset of the attack, dumped as much of the gold and silver as time permitted down a certain well (or wells) inside the mission's stockade.

The latter theory persisted long after Company agents caught up with Herbert at Brunei on November 9, 1775. Since it was never clarified to anyone's satisfaction,[7] the fate of the East India Company's treasury persisted as a subject of intense speculation fully a century later when the British North Borneo Company finally reclaimed the territory. By then, however, the jungle itself had largely reclaimed the Balambangan mission.

Author Owen Rutter, who returned to North Borneo after the Second World War, reported that an expedition had preceded him to the island hard on the heels of its liberation from the Japanese; it apparently failed to uncover any new clues as to the possible whereabouts of the Company's treasury. Rutter himself, working from an eighteenth-century diagram of the mission, managed to isolate the ruins of a dozen old wells all of which, unfortunately, were thoroughly choked up with sand.

If any of the East India Company's treasure does remain buried on the island of Balambangan, the secret of its location may well have gone to an obscure Indian grave with the larcenous Chief-of-Station, John Herbert.

⚓

Notes

Cocos Island

1 Hans Roden, *Treasure Seekers,* p. 134.
2 R. Charroux, *Treasures of the World,* p. 73.
3 ibid., p. 73.
4 Rupert Furneaux, *Great Treasure Hunts,* p. 103.
5 Charroux, op. cit., pp. 69–70.
6 Arthur eventually counted himself lucky to draw a suspended eighteen-month sentence after being convicted of conspiring to extort $720,000 from the hapless Maharaja whom he surprised one evening bedded down in a Paris hotel with a certain highborn "white" socialite.
7 R. Hancock and J. Weston, *The Lost Treasure of Cocos Island,* pp. 215–16.
8 ibid., pp. 238–9.
9 ibid., p. 273.
10 ibid., pp. 290–91.
11 Janusz Piekalkiewicz, *Da liegt Gold, Millionenschatze die noch zufinden sind,* p. 62.
12 ibid., p. 68.
13 ibid., p. 73.
14 In the early 1950s, while summarizing the voluminous personal writings of his ancestor Admiral Cochrane of the Chilean Navy, Bristol had come upon what he believed to be documents pinpointing the Treasure of Lima at Cocos Island.

Oak Island

1 Rupert Furneaux, *The Money Pit Mystery,* p. 14.
2 R. V. Harris, *The Oak Island Mystery,* p. 15.
3 Furneaux, op. cit., pp. 19–20.
4 ibid., pp. 23–4.
5 D'Arcy O'Connor, *The Big Dig,* p. 29.
6 Furneaux, op. cit., pp. 37–8.
7 With the death of John Smith in 1857 ownership of the Money Pit had duly passed, once or twice removed, to Mr. Graves.
8 O'Connor, op. cit., pp. 51–2.
9 Thanks to the sorry state of Lot 18 by 1933, no one was certain as to where this new "Chappell Shaft" had been sunk in relation to the original, i.e., whether slightly east or west of it. Nonetheless, the hope was that somewhere before the "treasure chamber" it would merge into the approximate center of the Money Pit.

10 Furneaux, op. cit., pp. 76–7.
11 Furneaux, op. cit., pp. 97–8.
12 O'Connor, op. cit., p. 6.
13 E. Rudolph Faribault, *Summary of Geological Survey Branch of the Department of Mines.*
14 Furneaux, op. cit., p. 110.
15 O'Connor, op. cit., p. 165.
16 ibid., p. 167.
17 Virginia Morell, 'The Pit and the Perplexities', *Canada Journal,* May–June 1983, p. 119.
18 ibid., p. 118.
19 *Halifax Herald-Chronicle,* September 17, 1976.
20 Morell, op. cit., p. 109.
21 Mildred Restall to reporter Virginia Morell, op. cit., p. 113.
22 O'Connor, op. cit., p. 202.
23 Furneaux, op. cit., pp. 112–13.
24 O'Connor, op. cit., p. 109.
25 In fairness to Rupert Furneaux, a strong proponent of the British connection, we refer the interested reader to the author's fascinating and detailed outline of this particular theory, set forth in *The Money Pit Mystery,* ch. 16.
26 O'Connor, op. cit., p. 221.
27 ibid., pp. 221–2.

Agrihan Island

1 Tim Haycock, *Treasure Trove,* p. 33.
2 Edgar K. Thompson, "The Lost Treasure of Agrihan."
3 ibid., p. 208.

Lord Howe Island

1 Sydney daily newspaper, "Travel Extra."
2 Edward Knight, *The Cruise of the* Alerte, pp. 89–90.
3 *Tasmanian Courier,* February 26, 1831.
4 Alan Villiers, *Vanished Fleets,* p. 200.
5 Maximilian Nicholls, *A History of Lord Howe Island,* p. 44.
6 1831 George IV gold sovereigns in present-day terms, depending upon their condition, are valued at between £78 and £100 each according to *The Coin Year Book 1990.*

Gardiners Island

1 William Bonner, *Pirate Laureate,* p. 5.
2 The Whig Junto comprised three earls and a duke, among other high-ranking luminaries, whose government portfolios included those of Chancellor of the Exchequer, Secretary of State, Treasurer of the Navy and Lord Keeper of the Great Seal. "The Whig leaders were a disparate group. Dissolute and hard-working by turn,

they embodied the best and worst of the age." See Robert C. Ritchie, *Captain Kidd and the War against the Pirates*, p. 445.

3 James Jameson, *Privateering and Piracy in the Colonial Period*, p. 209.

4 *The Narrative of John Gardiner*, quoted in Jameson, op. cit., pp. 224–25.

5 ibid., p. 220.

6 ibid., pp. 220–21.

7 The Narrative of John Gardiner, quoted in Harold Wilkins, *Captain Kidd and His Skeleton Island*, p. 260.

8 The "cradle blanket" or cloth of gold, given by Captain Kidd to Mrs. Gardiner, is said to have come from the *Quedagh Merchant* and was "a part of the marriage furniture of the Grand Mogul's daughter which Avery, the pirate, took with him to Madagascar. It may be that Kidd had acquired it on that Island where the Indian lady had been forcibly married to the bloody pirate chieftain." (Wilkins, op. cit., p. 260.)

9 *East Hampton: A History and Guide*, p. 178.

10 Dinitia Smith, "Wasp Nest, The Blue-Blood Feud over Gardiners Island." *New York* (Magazine), June 5, 1989, p. 34.

11 Jameson, op. cit., pp. 213–18.

12 Wilkins, op. cit., pp. 242–4.

13 The true outcome of Bellomont's mission remains a matter of some dispute. One discredited notion is that a considerable quantity of gold *was* taken from Hispaniola and that among the beneficiaries figured the Astors of New York city. A second legend holds that, shortly before his hanging, Kidd passed his wife Sarah a card on which was written the number 44106818. Taken as coordinates, this is roughly north and west of Deer Island, Maine, lying not far from the Isles of Shoals.

14 "Being committed on the high seas, piracy fell outside the jurisdiction of Englishshire courts. Admiralty courts were governed by civil law, however, which permitted conviction only by confession, or by the testimony of two eyewitnesses. Inability to produce either of these before the court allowed so many accused pirates to escape that a 1536 act of Henry VIII put these trials under common law, as though committed on land, and necessitated therefore that the trial be held within an English county. Since at that date no colonies of England existed, the law did not provide for trials overseas. The inconvenience of the procedure led to ignoring the law in many cases, but the King could call any case home, as he did with Kidd. Almost at the hour that Kidd boarded the *Advice*, King William signed an act enabling special commissions to try pirates on colonial soil." (Alexander Winston, *No Purchase, No Pay*, p. 139.)

15 Winston, op. cit., p. 157.

16 Bonner, op. cit., pp. 71–2.

17 Dubois and Manquinam, French pirates, were convicted in a separate case from that of Kidd.

18 Ritchie, op. cit., p. 223.

19 Wilkins, op. cit., p. 194.

20 ibid., p. 225.

21 ibid., p. 221.

22 Paul Lorraine, *The Only True Account of the Dying Speeches of the Condemn'd Pirates.* See Bonner, op. cit., p. 65.

23 "In between high-water and low-water mark." See Jameson, op. cit.

24 Ritchie, op. cit., p. 232.

25 ibid., p. 233.

Gasparilla Island

[1] Florence Fritz, *Unknown Florida*, pp. 31, 39.

[2] Calabozo: prison.

[3] Florence Fritz, author of *Unknown Florida*, identified the officer as Kearney's superior, Commodore David Porter, U.S. Navy Commander of the "West Indian Squadron," established in Key West, Florida, "after the United States took formal possession of The Floridas in 1818–1822." Fritz does not name the vessel in question, referring to her merely as a "ship-of-war, disguised as a merchantman," she dates the incident at 1824 (pp. 51–2).

[4] Note similarity to Robertson's alleged demise at Agrihan a few years later.

[5] Black Caesar (son of a half-Scottish father and a Negro mother) was later captured on Sanibel Island and burned to death at Key West according to David O. True, *Pirates and Treasure Trove of South Florida;* the fire was lit by the widow of a preacher whose eyes he had burned out.

Galveston Island

[1] Charles Hayes, *History of the Island and the City of Galveston*, p. 60.

[2] *De Bow's Review*, September 1851, p. 374.

[3] "Historical Sketch of Pierre and Jean Lafitte," *Magazine of American History,* vol. 10, 1883, p. 285.

[4] ibid., p. 285

[5] *World Book Encyclopedia*, vol. 12, pp. 432 e-f.

[6] *Century Magazine*, vol. 25, April 1883, pp. 859–60.

[7] "Historical Sketch of Pierre and Jean Lafitte," op. cit., pp. 289–90.

[8] Hayes, op. cit., p. 47.

[9] "Historical Sketch of Pierre and Jean Lafitte," op. cit., p. 286.

[10] ibid., p. 286.

[11] Don Seitz, *Under the Black Flag*, p. 268.

[12] "Historical Sketch of Pierre and Jean Lafitte," op. cit., p. 292.

[13] Seitz, op. cit., p. 271.

[14] ibid., p. 271.

[15] Charles Driscoll, *Doubloons*, p. 71.

[16] *De Bow's Review*, September 1851, p. 377.

[17] *Magazine of American History*, vol. 10, pp. 392–93.

[18] Driscoll, op. cit., p. 74.

[19] Lyle Saxon, *Lafitte the Pirate*, p. 163.

[20] ibid., p. 166.

[21] Carroll Lewis, *The Treasures of Galveston Bay*, p. 10.

[22] Saxon, op. cit., p. 171.

[23] ibid., p. 168.

[24] ibid., pp. 217–18.

[25] ibid., p. 229.

[26] Lewis, op. cit., p. 22.

[27] J. Frank Dobie, *The Yale Review*, vol. 18, 1928, pp. 127–30.

Isles of Shoals

1 Robert Carse, *The Age of Piracy*, p. 148.
2 The name formerly given to the Spanish silver dollar, otherwise known as a "piece of eight."
3 Charles Johnson, *Lives of the Most Notorious Pirates*, p. 48.
4 Prudence Lutrelle, only daughter of Marie Lutrelle, widow of a small planter. Even the most sober accounts of Teach's life place her as either his thirteenth, or even fourteenth, wife. See C. Driscoll, *Doubloons*, p. 196.
5 Johnson, op. cit., p. 45.
6 E.R. Snow, *True Tales of Buried Treasure*, pp. 118–19.
7 Duck, Malaga, Appledore, Smuttynose, Cedar, Star, Londoner, White and Seaver.
8 Bill Caldwell, *Islands of Maine*, p. 72.
9 Ralph Paine, *The Book of Buried Treasure*, p. 162.
10 Paine, op. cit., p. 164.
11 ibid., p. 165.
12 Alpheus Verrill, *Lost Treasure*, p. 97.
13 Paine, op. cit., p. 169–70.
14 ibid., p. 182.
15 ibid., p. 170.
16 James Jameson, *Privateering and Piracy in the Colonial Period*, p. 283.
17 ibid., p. 280.
18 Charles Cooper, *Treasure Trove, Pirates' Gold*, p. 76.

Mahé Island

1 William H. Tillinghast, *Ploetz' Epitome of Universal History*, p. 17.
2 India.
3 J. F. G. Lionnet, *The Seychelles*, pp. 51–2.
4 Robert Charroux, *Treasures of the World*, pp. 229–30.
5 In the French revolutionary calendar beginning in the year one, September 22, 1792, the month of Floreal relates to August and the VIII to the year 1800.
6 Charroux, op. cit., p. 231.
7 ibid., pp. 231–2.
8 ibid., p. 233.
9 Athol Thomas, *Forgotten Eden*, p. 137.
10 Francis Ommanney, *The Shoals of Capricorn*, p. 153.
11 Lawrence Belling, "£100 Million at His Feet?" *Sunday Telegraph*, August 7, 1970.
12 ibid., p. 14.
13 ibid., p. 14.
14 It is not known if Cruise-Wilkins was aware of the Oak Island treasure.
15 *Seychelles Nation*, July 27, 1988.
16 Thomas, op. cit., p. 139.
17 In some versions Eurystheus is known as King of Tiryus. See Edith Hamilton, *Mythology*.
18 Belling, op. cit., p. 15.
19 ibid., p. 15.
20 Present-day Gibraltar and Ceuta.

21 Thomas, op. cit., p. 138.
22 Edith Hamilton, *Mythology*, p. 39.
23 "Hades has dominion ... over all else that is within the earth, namely precious stones and metals. As such he is also termed PLOUTOS, 'wealth ... '" *The Concise Mythological Dictionary*, p. 72.
24 Belling, op. cit., p. 17.
25 *Seychelles Nation*, August 27, 1976, National Archives, Mahé, Seychelles.
26 ibid.
27 ibid.

Trindade Island

1 Edward Knight, *The Cruise of the* Alerte (Introduction by Arthur Ransome).
2 ibid., p. 45.
3 Edward Knight, *The Cruise of the "Falcon,"* 1886.
4 Knight, *The Cruise of the Alerte*, p. 12.
5 ibid., p. 24.
6 ibid., p. 20.
7 Mechanical devices for holding or grappling.
8 Harold Wilkins, *Modern Buried Treasure Hunters*, p. 269.
9 Knight, *The Cruise of the* Alerte, pp. 84–6.
10 ibid., p. 103.
11 ibid., p. 113.
12 ibid., p. 115.
13 ibid., p. 39.
14 ibid., p. 139.
15 ibid., p. 157.
16 ibid., p. 163.
17 ibid., p. 194.
18 ibid., Introduction by Arthur Ransome.
19 Alpheus Verrill, *Lost Treasure*, pp. 128–30.

Balambangan Island

1 Owen Rutter, *British North Borneo*, p. 93.
2 Owen Rutter, *The Pirate Wind*, p. 57.
3 Kennedy Tregonning, *North Borneo*, pp. 182–3.
4 Rutter, *Pirate Wind*, p. 65.
5 ibid., p. 65.
6 ibid., p. 70.
7 Mysteriously, though disgraced, Herbert was never charged with a single crime for his central role in the Balambangan fiasco.

⚓ Bibliography

Austen, H. C. M. *Sea Fights and Corsairs of the Indian Ocean*. Port Louis, Mauritius: R.W. Brooks, 1934.

Baarslar, Karl. *Islands of Adventure*. New York: Farrar & Rinehart, 1940.
Beard, Charles R. *The Romance of Treasure Trove*. London: Sampson Low & Co., 1933.
Bonner, William H. *Pirate Laureate. The Life and Legends of Captain Kidd*. California: Rutgers University Press, 1947.
Bradlee, Francis B. C. *The Suppression of Piracy in the West Indies*. London, 1923.
Burney, James. *History of the Buccaneers of America*. London: George Allen & Unwin, 1949.

Caldwell, Bill. *Islands of Maine*. Portland, Maine: Guy Gannett Publishing Co., 1981.
Campbell, Sir Malcolm. *My Greatest Adventure*. London: 1931.
Carse, Robert. *The Age of Piracy*. London: Robert Hale, 1957.
Charnley, M. V. *Jean Lafitte*. New York: Viking Press, 1934.
Charroux, Robert. *Treasures of the World*. London: Frederick Muller, 1966.
Chatterton, Edward K. *The Romance of Piracy*. London: Seeley, Service & Co., 1914.
Cooper, Charles G. T. *Treasure Trove, Pirates' Gold*. London: Lutterworth Press, 1951.
Crooker, W. S. *The Oak Island Quest*. Windsor, Nova Scotia: Lancelot Press, 1978.

Dalton, Sir Cornelius N. *The Real Captain Kidd. A Vindication*. London: William Heinemann, 1911.
De Costa, Benjamin F. *Sketches of the Coast of Maine and the Isles of Shoals*. New York: 1869.
De Leeuw, Hendrik. *Crossroads of the Buccaneers*. Philadelphia: J. B. Lippincott Co., 1937.
de Montmorency, Hervey. *On the Track of a Treasure*. London: Hurst & Blackett, 1904.
———. *Sword and Stirrup, Memoirs of an Adventurous Life*. London: G. Bell & Sons, 1936.
Dow, George F. & Edmonds, John H. *The Pirates of the New England Coast (1630–1730)*. Salem, Mass.: 1923.
Driscoll, Charles. *Doubloons: The Story of Buried Treasure*. London: Chapman & Hall, 1931.

Exquemelin, Alexander O. *The History of the Buccaneers of America*. London: Penguin, 1969.

Faribault, E. Rudolph. *Summary of Geological Survey Branch of the Department of Mines*. Nova Scotia: 1911.
Fritz, Florence. *Unknown Florida*. Coral Gables: University of Miami Press, 1963.

Fuller, Basil & Melville, Alexander. *Pirate Harbours and Their Secrets*. London: Stanley Paul & Co., 1935.
Furneaux, Rupert. *The Money Pit Mystery*. New York: Dodd, Mead & Co., 1972.

Gosse, Philip. *The History of Piracy*. London: Longmans, 1932.
———. *The Pirates' Who's Who*. London: Dulau & Co., 1924.
Groushko, Michael. *Lost Treasures of the World*. London: Admiral Books, 1986.

Hamilton, Edith. *Mythology. Timeless Tales of Gods and Heroes*. Boston: Little, Brown & Co., 1940.
Hancock, Ralph & Weston, Julian A. *The Lost Treasure of Cocos Island*. New York: Thomas Nelson & Sons, 1960.
Harris, R. V. *The Oak Island Mystery*. Toronto: McGraw Hill Ryerson, 1958.
Haycock, Tim. *Treasure Trove*. London: Fourth Estate, 1986.
Hayes, Charles W. *History of the Island and the City of Galveston*. Cincinnati: 1879.
Hormer, Elinore M. *The Sea Shell Islands. A History of Sanibel and Captiva*.

Jameson, James F. (ed.). *Privateering and Piracy in the Colonial Period*. New York: Macmillan Co., 1923.
Johnson, Charles A. *Lives of the Most Notorious Pirates* (1st ed. 1724). London: The Folio Society, 1962.

Karraker, Cyrus H. *The Hispaniola Treasure*. Philadelphia: University of Pennsylvania Press, 1934.
Kaster, Joseph (ed.). *Concise Mythological Dictionary*. London: Peerage Books, 1989.
Keel, J. R. *Florida's Trails to History's Treasure,* vol. I.
Kerdéland, Jean de. *La Course Aux Tresor*. Paris, 1944.
Knight, Edward F. *The Cruise of the "Alerte."* London: Rupert Hart-Davis, 1952.
———. *The Cruise of the "Falcon."* London: Nelson, 1920.

Lafond, Gabriel de Lurcy. *Quinze ans de Voyages autour du Monde*. Paris, 1974.
Leary, T. P. *The Oak Island Enigma*. Omaha, Nebraska: published by the author, 1953.
Lewis, Carroll. *The Treasures of Galveston Bay*. Waco, Texas: Texian Press, 1977.
Lionnet, J. F. G. *The Vallée de Mai*. Government of the Seychelles, 1969.
———. *The Seychelles*. Devon: David & Charles, 1972.

Milligan, Clarence. *Captain William Kidd. Gentleman or Buccaneer?* Philadelphia: Dorrance & Co., 1932.

Nesmith, R. I. & Potter, J. F. *Pirates of the Spanish Main*. Greenwich, Connecticut: Fawcett Publications, 1961.
Nicholls, Maximilian. *A History of Lord Howe Island*. Hobart: Mercury Press, 1952.
Norvill, Roy. *The Treasure Seekers' Treasury*. London: Hutchinson, 1978.

O'Connor, D'Arcy. *The Big Dig. The $10 Million Search for Oak Island's Legendary Treasure*. New York: Ballantine Books, 1988.
Ommanney, Francis D. *The Shoals of Capricorn*. London: Longman, Green & Co., 1952.

Paine, Ralph D. *The Book of Buried Treasure*. London: William Heinemann, 1911.

Piekalkiewicz, Janusz. *Da liegt Gold. Millionenschätze die noch zu finden sind.* Munich: Sudwest Verlag, 1971.

Quarrel, Charles. *Buried Treasure.* London: MacDonald & Evans, 1955.

Ritchie, Robert C. *Captain Kidd and the War Against the Pirates.* Cambridge, Mass., and London: Harvard University Press, 1986.

Roberts, Glenys. *Richard Knight's Treasure! The True Story of His Extraordinary Quest for Captain Kidd's Cache.* Viking: 1986.

Roden, Hans. *Treasure Seekers.* London: Harrap, 1966.

Rutter, Owen. *British North Borneo.* London: Constable & Co., 1922.

———. *The Pirate Wind.* Hutchinson & Co., 1930.

Saxon, Lyle. *Lafitte the Pirate.* London: Century Co., 1930.

Scheller, William G. "On the Treasure Trail." *Islands* (August 1994): 72–91.

Seitz, Don Carlos. *The Buccaneers.* New York: Harper Bros., 1912.

———. *Under the Black Flag.* London: Stanley Paul & Co., 1927.

Snow, Edward R. *Tales of the Atlantic Coast.* Boston: Yankee Publishing Co., 1944.

———. *True Tales of Buried Treasure.* London: Alvin Redman, 1963.

———. *True Tales of Pirates and Their Gold.* London: Alvin Redman, 1958.

Stockton, Frank R. *Buccaneers and Pirates of Our Coasts.* New York: Collier-Macmillan & Co., 1963.

Thaxton, Celia. *Among the Isles of Shoals.* New York: 1898.

Thomas, Athol. *Forgotten Eden. A View of the Seychelles Islands in the Indian Ocean.* London: Longmans, 1973.

Thompson, Commander Edgar K. "The Lost Treasure of Agrihan," U.S. Naval Proceedings, Feb. 1945.

Tillinghast, William H. *Ploetz' Epitome of Universal History.* Houghton Mifflin & Co., 1883.

Tregonning, Kennedy G.P. *North Borneo.* London: 1960.

Verrill, Alpheus H. *Lost Treasure: True Tales of Hidden Hoards.* New York: D. Appleton & Co., 1930.

———. *They Found Gold. The Story of Successful Treasure Hunts.* New York: G. P. Putnam's Sons, 1936.

Villiers, Alan. *Vanished Fleets. Sea Stones from Old Van Dieman's Land.* Cambridge: Patrick Stephens, 1974.

Wilkins, Harold T. *Captain Kidd and His Skeleton Island.* London: Cassell & Co., 1935.

———. *Modern Buried Treasure Hunters.* London: Philip Allan, 1934.

Wilson, Derek. *The World Atlas of Treasure.* London: William Collins, 1981.

Winston, Alexander. *No Purchase, No Pay. Sir Henry Morgan, Captain William Kidd and Captain Woodes Rogers in the Great Age of Privateers and Pirates, 1665–1715.* London: Eyre & Spottiswoode, 1970.

World Book Encyclopedia. Chicago: World Book Inc., 1985.

Wright, John D. *Lost Treasures.* London: Wayland Publishers, 1981.

Index

Admiral Islands, 157
Aem, Mr., 182, 183, 192, 193
Agrihan Island, vi, 85–94
    location of, 89
Anguilla, 104
Anjouan Island,159
Ankersen, H.N., 183
Arthur, Captain Charles
    Augustus, 28
Australia,eastern,discovery of, 95

Baarslar, Karl, 6
Babba, Coji, 103, 119
Bacon, Francis, 82, 83
Balambangan Island, 199–205
    location of, 203
    name, derivation of, 205
Ball, Ligberg, 95
Barataria Island, 130, 131–137
    activities, proclamation
        condemning, 133
    geography of, 131
Bartells, 16–17
Bates, George, 64
Beauclerk, Lord Amerlias, 188
Becker Drilling, 70
Beebe, Admiral William, 23
Bellmont, Earl of, 101, 103–106,
    108–113, 115, 119
Bennet, Edward, 5
Bergmans, Petrus A., 26–30
Bethune, Walter A., 95, 98
Bexley, Lord, 187
Bickerton, Sir Richard, 186, 187
Blackbeard, vi, 147–151, 156
    skull of, 151
Black Caesar, vi, 126
Blair, Frederick Leander, 55–61
Blair, William, 82
Blankenship, Dan, 68–79
Blankenship, David, 78
Blixen, Bror, 119
Boag, 10–13, 36
Bolivar, Simon, 6

Bonaparte, Napoleon, 126, 129, 130
Bonito, Benito, 5, 16
Bonnet, Major Stede, 145–149, 152
Bosley, George, 32
Boucard, Jacques, 34–35
Boulting, Henry, 104, 112
Bowie, Jim, 133, 134
Bowie, Rezin, 133, 134
Bradenham, Robert, 112–113
Bradlee, Francis, 126
Bradley, Samuel, 101
Brubaker, King John, 122
Buzzard, The, 160–165, 177

Cabral, Manoel, 16
Caloosa Indians, 120, 121
Campbell, Sir Malcolm, vi, 23–25
Cape Verge Islands, 189
Captiva Island, 125
Carrol, Sylvester, 62
Cathay, 199
Chappell, Claude, 62
Chappell, Mel, 62, 65, 73
Chappell, William, 60–62
Charroux, Robert, 6
Claiborne, Governor William C. C.,
    129, 131, 134, 135
Clarke, Thomas "Whisking", 107
Cochrane, Lord, Earl of Dundonald,
    6, 85
Cocos Island, vi, 1–39, 196, 198
    Britons, exploration by, 23
    Cerro Iglesias, 2
    Chatham Bay, 3–4
    Forbes Expeditions, 32–34
    location of, 1
    Observation Hill, 24
    Wafer Bay, 15
Cook, Captain James, 95, 201
Cook, Captain John, 2
Cotton, Arthur, 197
Creelman, Robert, 43, 48, 51, 57
Creighton, A. O., 46, 54
Cruise, Christian, 186–188

Cruise-Wilkins, Godfrey, 177
Cruise-Wilkins, John, vi, 168, 171,
    177
Cruise-Wilkins, Reginald, 166–177
Curzon-Howe, Commodore, 13, 15

d'Aury, Louis-Michel, 138
Dalrymple, Alexander, 200–202
Dampier, William, 2, 4
Davenport, Hugh M., 32
Davis, Captain Edward, 103
Davis, Edward, 2, 4–5, 15
da Gama, Vasco, 158
de l'Estang, Bernadin Nageon, 164,
    165
de l'Estang, Etienne, 165
de la Porta, Jao, 139
de Leon, Ponce, 120
de Lurcy, Captain Gabriel, 85
de Mayorga, Josefa, 125
DeMont, Andy, 66
Dempster, Jim, 18–19
Derwent Whaling Club, 96
Desliens, Nicholas, 1
de Soto, Bonito, 181
de Veuvolliers, Joseph, 162
Dobie, J. Frank, 130
Draper, Sir William, 200
Drexel, Arthur, 27
Dudley, Governor, 153–155
Dunfield, Bob, 67–69, 76

Eaton, John, 2
Eden, Governor Charles, 150
Eldorado Company, 54–56
Emmott, James, 104
England, Edward, 159, 161

Fiery Cross of Goa, 162, 163, 168,
    171
Fitzgerald, Nicholas, 12–13, 14
Fitzwilliam, Lord, 21, 22
Flagler, John H., 198
Fleming, Ian, 176

Fletcher, Benjamin, 100
Flowers, Bob, 21
Flynn, Errol, vi
Forbes Expeditions, 32–34
Forbes, James Alexander, 8, 9, 30, 31
Forbes, James Alexander II, 31, 32
Forbes, James Alexander III, 32
Forbes, James Alexander IV, 32–34
Forhan, Thomas, 47
Fraser, S. C., 55–57

Galveston Island, vi, 128–144
    Jacob's Staff, 144
    Lafitte, headquarters of, 137
    Little Campeche, 137, 138
    location of, 130
    Maison Rouge, 138–141
    renaming, 137
    Yankee Boardinghouse, 138
Gammell, John, 48, 50
Gardiner, Colonel, H. A., 65
Gardiner, John, 106–108
Gardiner, Lion, 108
Gardiners Island, vi, 100–119
    burial of treasure on, 107, 108
    claims for treasure, 119
    location of, 102
    ownership, 119
Gaspar, José, vi, 121–127
Gasparilla Island, 120–127
    location of, 123, 124
    outlaws, base for, vi, 124
Gentlemen-adventurers, 184, 185
Gissler, August, 15–22, 34, 38
Gomez, Juan, 127
Graeser, Karl, 66
Grand Salvage Island, 188
Graves, Anthony, 56
Greene, George, 68
Grymes, John R., 134
Guam, 90
Guinness, K. Lee, 23
Guise, Captain, 86

Hackett, Fred, 12, 13
Hackett, Thomas, 12
Haffner, George, 18, 19
Halifax Company, 54
Halifax, Lord, 113
Halley, Samuel, 156
Hands, Israel, 150, 151
Harden-Hickey, James, 198
Head, Nicholas, 38
Hedden, Gilbert D., 62–65, 73, 76

Hemingway, Ernest, 119
Henksee, Dan, 77, 78
Hennessy, Colonel D. N., 168
Herbert, John, 202–205
Hervey, Admiral Victor, 37
Hiltz, Cyril, 66
Hornigold, Captain, 148

Indian Ocean, 157
Isles of Shoals, vi, 145–156
    location of, 148

Jackson, Andrew, 129, 136
Jason and the Argonauts, v, 168, 170
John, Panther Key, 127

Karankawa Indians, 137
Kearney, Lieutenant Lawrence, 127, 142–143
Keating, John, 9–13, 14, 18
Kennedy, Parker, 77
Kidd Diamond, 107, 108
Kidd, Captain William, v, vi, 42, 59, 60, 63, 100–119, 134, 153
    capture, 112, 113
    execution, 116–118
    treasure, inventory of, 110–112
    trial, 113–115
Knight, Captain Edward, 97, 178, 182–186, 188–198
Knight, Tobias, 150

Lafitte, Jean, v, 128–144
Lafitte, Pierre, 129–131
Lafond, Gabriel, 85–87, 90, 91, 94
Lane, George, 28
Latour, Major A. Lacarriere, 132
Leichti, James, 46
le Vasseur, Olivier, 158, 161–165, 168
Lewis, Fred, 33
Lister, Moira, 37, 38
Liverpool, Lord, 187
Livingston, Robert, 100, 101, 131
Livingston, Edward, 134
Lockyer, Captain, 134
Londoner Island, 159
Lord Howe Island, 95–99
    location of, 96
    lost treasure, background to, 96
    Mount Gower, 97
Lorraine, Paul, 115, 116
Louisiana Territory, 126, 129, 131, 133

Lund, Lars Peter, 21
Lynds, Daniel B., 48, 51
Lynds, Simeon, 45, 46, 48
Lyon, John, 108

Mahé Island, 157–177
    airport, construction of, 176
    location of, vi, 159
    Mount Simpson, 169
    Twelve Labors of Hercules, 172–175
    Victoria Harbor, 158
Malaga Island, 156
Mangel, Captain Tony, 26, 27
Mangel, Pierre, 15
Marianas Islands, 89, 90, 92, 93
Marshall, Harry W., 46
Martin, François, 102
Mary Dyer, hijacking of, 7–9
Mather, Rev. Cotton, 155
Maynard, Lieutenant Robert, 150, 151
McCully, Jotham, 49, 51, 57
McGinnis, Daniel, 40–44, 48, 72
McIntosh, Lieutenant, 141
McNutt, James, 46
McRae, Commander James, 160, 161
Medinilla, Governor, 93, 94
Mendez, Teresa, 87
Montmorency, Hervey de, 21, 22
Moore, William, 102, 114
Morgan, Mervyn, 168
Muele Island, 26

Nance, Amos, 64
Narron, Douglas, 32
Newgate Prison, 113, 115
New Hebrides, 97
New Orleans, 131
Nicholls, Colonel, 135
Nicholls, Max, 99
Nolan, Frederick G., 72–75, 79, 80

Oak Island, 40–84
    Borehole 10-X, 75–79
    Cave-in Pit, 56, 57, 69
    Chappell Shaft, 62, 63
    Cold War, 73
    Crandall's Point, 72
    Dunfield Causeway, 68
    Eldorado Company, 54, 55, 57
    Hedden Shaft, 63
    location of, 49

lots, 41
Mahone Bay, 41
Mastermind, 53
Money Pit, vi, 40–84
Nolan Museum, 73, 74
plan of, 60
sink-holes, 68, 69
Smith's Cove, 44, 45, 50, 52
Smuggler's Cove, 40, 41, 43
South Shore Cove, 61, 67, 79
television camera, use of, 77
Treasure Company, 56–61
Triton Alliance, 69–80
Triton Museum, 75
Triton Pit, 79
Truro Company, 48–53
Windsor Rock Formation, 68
O'Connor, D'Arcy, 68, 82, 83
Odell, Samuel, 151
Old Bailey, 115, 116
Ommanney, F. D., 169
Onslow Syndicate, 45–48
Oort, Sarah Bradley Cox, 100, 113
Our Lady of Lima, 6, 7, 11, 15

Palliser, Admiral Henry, 19–22
Palmer, Joseph, 112
Patterson, Commodore, 135–137
Percy, Captain, 134
Peruvian Treasure, 87–94
Peterson, Captain H., 28, 29
Peterson, Mendel, 71
Pitblado, John, 48, 50
Plowman, Captain David, 153
Polkinghorne, Captain, 28
Porter, Dr. Andrew, 59
Povey, Lieutenant-Governor
Thomas, 154
Putnam, T. Perley, 61

Quedagh Merchant, 102–104, 112
Quelch, Lieutenant John, 153–156

Randall, Mrs. Prudence, 151

Randall, Rev. Frank B., 151
Rattenbury, Captain, 95–99
Restall, Bobbie, 66
Restall, Mildred, 65, 67
Restall, Ricky, 66, 67
Restall, Robert, 66, 67, 76
Rhett, Colonel William, 146, 147
Roberts, A. Boake, 59, 68
Robertson, Captain Andrew
Gordon, 85–94
Robinson, Captain Hercules, 188
Roosevelt, Franklin D., vi
Ross, Colonel, 135, 136
Rutter, Owen, 205

Saipan, 93
Salvador, 189
Salvage Islands, 23
San Martin, General, 6
Sanibel Island, 126
Santos, Jose, 181
Savy, Madame Charles, 163–167
Sellers, Sophia, 56
Sewall, Judge Stephen, 156
Sewall, Major Samuel, 154, 155
Sharpeigh, Alexander, 158
Simmons, George Finlay, 187
Sink-holes, 68, 69
Sinnet, Tom, 178–182
Smith, Dr. Cloete, 190, 192
Smith, John, 42–44, 48, 50
Smuttynose Island, 150, 152, 153,
156
Snow, E. R., 151
Spotswood, Alexander, 150
Stevenson, Robert Louis, vi, 39, 152
Studdert, Richard, 29, 30
Sulu, HRH Sultan Alimudin of, 200,
201, 203
Sulu, HRH Sultan Israel of, 203
Swan, Captain Charles, 2, 4
Swithin, Captain James, 202

Tating, Datu, 203, 204

Taylor, John, 159, 161–163
Teach, Edward, 148–152, 156
skull, ownership of, 152
Thomas, Atholl, 174
Thompson, Edgar K., 90
Thompson, William, 7–13
Tinian, 92
Tobias, David, 70, 71, 73, 76, 79, 81
Treasure of Lima, 6–8, 13, 15, 26,
32–35, 39, 180, 196, 198
Treasure Recovery Ltd., 27–30
Treaty of Ryswick, 103
Treaty of Utrecht, 159
Tregurtha, Edward Primrose, 98, 99
Trindade Island, 178–198
features of, 191, 192
location of, 180
temperature, 194
Triton Alliance, 69–80
Truro Company, 48–53
Twelve Labors of Hercules, vi, 172–
175

Useppa Island, 125

Vaughan, Anthony, 41, 43
Voss, Captain John Claus, 19

Wafer, Lionel, 2, 4, 9
Walking the plank, 146
War of the Spanish Succession, 145
Welch, Mary, 5, 6, 16
White, Ed, 66
William III, 101
Welling, Captain John W., 61
Wollenhaupt, Casper, 44
Worsley, Commodore Frank, 27–30
Wright, John, 185

You, Dominique, 136
Young, Richard, 12

Zulmiro, 181

Printed in the United States
115647LV00003B/259-261/A